2/04

Exit to Freedom

Exit to Freedom

Calvin C. Johnson Jr.

with Greg Hampikian

The University of Georgia Press | Athens and London

Published by the University of Georgia Press

Athens, Georgia 30602

Printed and bound by Maple-Vail

The paper in this book meets the guidelines for

permanence and durability of the Committee on

Production Guidelines for Book Longevity of the

Council on Library Resources.

Printed in the United States of America

07 06 05 04 03 C 5 4 3 2 1

Library of Congress Cataloging-in-Publication Data

Johnson, Calvin C., 1957–

Exit to freedom / Calvin C. Johnson Jr. with Greg Hampikian.

    p. cm.

ISBN 0-8203-2559-7 (alk. paper)

1. Johnson, Calvin C., 1957– —Pardon. 2. Prisoners—Georgia—

Biography. 3. False imprisonment—Georgia. 4. Trials (Rape)—

Georgia. 5. Judicial error—Georgia. 6. DNA fingerprinting—Georgia.

I. Hampikian, Greg, 1961– II. Title.

HV9468.J3A3 2003

346.03'34—dc21   2003007698

British Library Cataloging-in-Publication Data available

Frontispiece: Calvin Johnson standing in front of the "justice"
doors of an Atlanta courthouse. Gilles Peress, Magnum Photos.

This book is dedicated to my beautiful mother

Jo Ann Johnson

whose strength and spirit inspired me to believe in myself.

Unconditionally she loved me, spiritually she prayed for me,

and motherly she taught me.

—C.C.J.

To **George Whitman** for entertaining angels unawares.

—G.H.

"With God as my witness, I have been falsely

accused of these crimes.

"I did not commit them. I'm an innocent man,

and I just pray in the name of Jesus Christ

that all this truth will be brought out.

The truth will eventually be brought out."

—Calvin C. Johnson Jr.

at his sentencing hearing in 1983.

He was given a life term.

Contents

Acknowledgments   xi

A Note on the Text   xiii

Chronology   xv

The Swamp   1

The Years of Innocence   18

Innocence Lost   37

Paying the Price   50

Trapped   65

Jury of My Peers   80

Trial by Ordeal: The Verdict   103

A Last Chance for Justice   129

Care of the Body   134

River State Rebellion   145

The Board of Pardons and Paroles   163

Prison Industry   166

Sex Offenders Program   183

Anger   189

Joy   195

DNA, the Key to Freedom   205

The Innocence Project   220

Spiritual Growth   227

The Last Judgment   234

Free World   245

Epilogue   262

Afterword   269

   by Barry Scheck

DNA and the Science of Justice   275

   by Greg Hampikian

Coauthor's Notes and Acknowledgments   283

   by Greg Hampikian

Acknowledgments

This book would never have been written if not for the people who made my freedom possible. My father, Calvin C. Johnson Sr., whose advice is invaluable; my sister, Judith Johnson, who stood by me in every way; my sister, Tara Burkett, who believed in me; my beloved mom, Jo Ann Johnson, who has gone on to her eternal reward; and to all my family and friends whose prayers were heard and answered.

Thanks to my childhood friend Kim and her mother, whom I affectionately call Aunt Marti, who first told me about the Innocence Project.

Thanks to all the parties of the legal profession who made my release possible: Barry Scheck and Peter Neufeld of the Innocence Project; the students at Benjamin N. Cardozo School of Law; James C. Bonner Jr. of the Prisoner Legal Counseling Project; Bruce Maloy, Jim Jenkins, and Rebecca Guinn from the law offices of

Maloy & Jenkins; scientist Ed Blake; and all the assistants and staff who worked diligently on my behalf to make my release possible.

Thanks to my wife, Sabrina Johnson, whom I met after my release one Sunday morning in church. Her patience and understanding allowed me the freedom to pursue this project.

Thanks to Dr. Greg Hampikian and his family, whose tireless efforts and belief in me made *Exit to Freedom* a reality.

A Note on the Text

This is a true story. The names of public figures, officials, and officers of the court have been retained, but the names of many individuals, including victims of sexual assault, have been changed to protect their privacy.

Chronology

July 8, 1957 Born, Cincinnati, Ohio

1970 Johnson family moves to Atlanta

Summer 1971 Work with mentally challenged children at camp in Helen, Georgia

Summer 1972 Work with mentally challenged children at camp in Winder, Georgia

Summer 1973 Work at Early Learning Center as children's coach

1974–75 Work as shoeshine at Hartsfield Airport after school and weekends

Spring 1975 Get job at radio station WRAZ

June 1975 Graduate high school

Fall 1975 Enter Clark Atlanta College

Fall 1976 Work at WSB radio

Summer 1979 Begin work at Delta Air Lines warehouse

Spring 1980 Graduate from Clark Atlanta College with B.A. in Communications

1981	Travel extensively; get engaged; continue work at Delta
April 1981	Arrested for marijuana possession and then burglary; brought first to College Park Jail, then to Fulton County Jail; plead guilty; sent to Buford Prison
November 20, 1981	Begin serving sentence for burglary at Buford Prison
December 30, 1982	Paroled
January 1983	Begin work at courier service
March 7, 1983	Fulton County victim is raped
March 9, 1983	Clayton County victim is raped
March 14, 1983	Arrested and taken to College Park jail, then to Clayton County jail
August 19, 1983	Indicted for rape of Clayton County woman
November 3–7, 1983	Tried in Clayton County court; convicted of rape
November 14, 1983	Sentenced to life for rape (plus concurrent sentences: fifteen years for aggravated sodomy and fifteen years for burglary); sent to Wayne Correctional Institution
August 7, 1984	Indicted for rape of Fulton County woman; spend brief period in Fulton County jail
September 1984	Fulton County trial results in acquittal on all charges
1985	Injured, transferred to Men's Correctional Institute (Handicapped)
1986	Transferred to Mt. Vernon Correctional Institute

1987	Transferred to Rivers Correctional Institute
Winter 1989	Riot at Rivers
1992	Contact attorney James Bonner at Prisoner Legal Counseling Project about sex offenders course; ask about DNA evidence
1993	End Prison Industry work
April 18, 1994	Provisional extraordinary motion for a new trial filed; evidence not yet found, motion not granted until 1999 release
June 9, 1994	Unsuccessful parole report recommends sex offenders program
December 1996	Prisoner Legal Counseling Project loses funding; make first contact with Innocence Project
June 16, 1997	Last unsuccessful parole hearing report; next hearing scheduled for March 2003
1997	Transferred to Hancock prison; active in Kairos ministry and choir; work in isolation department
1998	Ordained
June 15, 1999	Exonerated by DNA evidence and released from prison
June 16, 1999	Appear on *Today Show*
June 17, 1999	Appear on *Good Morning America*
October 11, 1999	Speak at Clayton State College, meet coauthor
Late October 1999	Take ministry trip to Africa; begin working for MARTA
July 8, 2000	Marry Sabrina Middleton

July 28, 2000   Mother, Jo Ann Johnson, dies

October 18, 2000   Daughter, Brianna Jo Ann Johnson, born

November 2002   Selected as founding board member of Georgia Innocence Project

February 2003   Appear before Georgia state legislature along with D.A. Robert Keller to endorse new rules for evidence preservation

May 28, 2003   Calvin and members of the Innocence Project were invited by Georgia governor Sonny Perdue to witness the signing of the new Genetic Evidence Preservation law, which requires evidence to be saved for at least ten years. D.A. Robert Keller happened to be at the capitol and spotted Calvin, who invited him to join the ceremony. According to the *Atlanta Journal-Constitution,* the district attorney said that only a miracle had saved Mr. Johnson's evidence. The governor told Johnson he hoped the new law "will allow us to do justice better."

Exit to Freedom

The Swamp

I had never even heard of an armadillo before I saw one

in the swamp. The snakes that occasionally swim past my
thighs don't scare me as much as those armor-plated rats.
Even though I carry a bush axe with a blade sharp enough
to saw a man in half, the armadillos seem to have no fear
of prisoners. Maybe it's our ill-fitting prison whites with
the broad blue stripe, or the fact that our every move is
rhythmic and predictable.

We work as a ten-man crew, swinging our blades in
a monotonous arc from the first light of dawn until just
before sunset. The lead man starts the line, and the rest
of us maintain his pace. We keep the team staggered so
that the blades will not collide. Each man in succession is
two paces right, and two paces back, from the one in front.
We move like a ten-blade human lawn mower, and we are
as reliable as a John Deere.

In order to keep us working, the Boss Man barks out

encouragement like, "Move it on, move it on. . . . Come on now, keep it going!" His authority rests on his shoulder in a loaded shotgun and on his hip in the ever-present service revolver. On several occasions he has used those guns, firing over our heads to stop fights or as a warning against straying too far from the line.

The work-detail guards are uniformly large, tough-faced Caucasians. Long days in the sun qualify them as rednecks both literally and figuratively. Although we always call them "Boss" to their faces, among ourselves we refer to them as SSOB (sorry son of a bitch). We spend nine to ten hours a day together, but we have nothing in common; even the animals know the difference between the Boss Man and the convicts. We are like two different species—opposites in many ways. Convicts don't carry guns, don't shout, and never make sudden moves.

In South Georgia the sun beats down without mercy, and prison clothes, while practical to clean, are not designed for swinging a sickle in knee-deep mud. As I work I realize that I am less than five hours from Atlanta: from the air-conditioned car that was sold to pay for my trial, from the woman I was sure would have married me, from the college that graduated me, and from my parents, who know that I am innocent because they were with me at the time the crime was committed.

In the swamps you work, and obey, and get mad. No one talks, and—contrary to movie depictions—absolutely no one sings. When the lead man gets to the end of the row, he walks twenty paces over, turns around, and begins again. If the Boss Man is pleased with his pace, we continue on unmolested, but if we haven't kept up with the Boss's expectation, the lead man is treated to a few choice words of "encouragement." It is the lead's responsibility to see that the job is completed in one day.

We are not supposed to work if the temperature goes above 98 degrees or if it starts to rain. But in prison there are more exceptions than there are rules. In summer it's generally a given that two out of ten men on a detail will "fall out." Usually it is heat exhaustion, but fire ants can eat the skin off your legs before you realize that you are knee-deep in a nest, and hornets have a nasty habit of hiding in stumps and flying into a man's pants. Even when these events occur, there is no break in the line beyond what is medically necessary. When we lose a man, the line just shrinks and the Boss man's bark gives more encouragement than usual. A smaller mower needs to move faster.

It is not easy to get off the swamp detail. Some men have literally died trying. Their tales of "escape" are passed down by the older prisoners. I heard of only one case in which they didn't find the body, but no one believes that he actually survived.

Of course, a man can just decide not to work; it's called bucking. But such a man is punished and then reassigned to even more difficult labor. Injury is another method of escape: a slight turn of the blade is enough to cut to the bone and produces a sure infection. Most of us, however, will not stoop to self-mutilation. After considering all these methods for several months, I decide that there is only one sure way to get out of the swamp, but it requires teamwork.

I had heard about a detail that lay down their sickles together and bucked. Bucking is usually a solo act of defiance and is easily dealt with by the guards. But when an entire detail bucks, that gets the warden's attention. And anything that gets the warden's attention is likely to get you reassigned to Reidsville, the most notorious prison in the state. Reidsville houses the inmates who are shackled and bound all day, men who are the unredeemable psychopaths of horror novels. The only advantage of that institution is that work details are rare and voluntary. The disadvantages, besides the company, are that transfers are impossible, and the parole board rarely stops by. Still, after a summer in the swamps I feel ready to buck.

The word spreads through our crew that we are going to buck and take our chances at Reidsville. It will probably add several years to each of our sentences, but the swamp is hell and we want out. I organize the men and devise a signal: a simple whistle will stop the line. I tell everyone that we will do it as soon as I return from my court date in Atlanta. In a few days we will all say *adios* to armadillos.

When I return from the court trip it is late at night, and the men are already in bed. I don't notice at first, but the place seems roomier; in fact, there are several empty beds: ten of them.

"Where's Too-Sweet?" I ask, waking a sleeping man. "Hey, where's Too-Sweet, and where's Cowboy and the rest of my crew?"

"Ah, man, you didn't know? Your crew bucked."

I had organized them so well that they figured they no longer needed a leader. My crew was already in lockdown awaiting transfer to Reidsville.

Some men can take the swamps better than others. They develop strange mechanisms to cope with the constant attack of insects, thorns, and reptiles. The snakes take on a mystical quality for a lot of swampers. There are prisoners who catch them and sneak them back to the camp in their clothes. Snake meat can be cooked when access to the kitchen is available, or dried in strips and chewed like jerky. Men make wallets and key chains from the skin, or just hang the carcass on a fence post in the belief that it will bring rain. Rain means no swamp work. But rain in the South Georgia summer is rare no matter how many serpents are split and hung to dry.

It is at least 100 degrees in the swamp today, and even the armadillos stay in the shade. The Boss seems unaffected by the heat, and for some reason he is pushing us harder than usual. He has even stopped the water boy from bringing us drinks between breaks, and I know that we will lose more than the usual two men today; it's early, and we have already lost one. We are in a deep gulch, swinging through weeds up to our necks. Based on the sun, I guess it's about 10:00 A.M. Suddenly, the man ahead of me slumps over and falls face down into the mud. The lead man notices and calls up to the guard, "Got one monkeyed, Boss!"

To monkey: a verb of unknown origins. It accurately conveys the inhumanity of the swamp. When a prisoner falls out and drops from exhaustion, he is hardly considered a man. He is a bad spark plug on the lawn mower. He must be removed and replaced quickly. There is a certain comic indignity to exhaustion, and the lighthearted term allows us to ignore the more somber consequences of being worked to unconsciousness.

The Boss offers his usual encouragement: "Hollings, get up!" But there is no response. When the heat gets this bad, I know that a man can be seriously hurt, and Hollings is unresponsive. The line stops for a moment, and no one moves. For me, it is a moment of epiphany. I realize the truth of the situation, and the force of injustice just incapacitates me. In my controlled anger I hoist poor Hollings across my shoulders and follow the fresh mowed trail back to the prison bus.

The Boss remains belligerent; he tells the other men to get back to work. He says the same to me before he radios for a car. I walk back to the line and begin swinging in rhythm behind the new man in front of me. But after three or four arcs of the bush axe, I cannot continue. It is not fatigue or the sun, it isn't snakes or wasps; it is a simple act of will. I plant the axe head firmly in the ground and rest my elbow on its handle. The line continues on, and it is like a dream to hear the slicing recede as I stand still.

I enjoy a moment of something like freedom. I say without words, I am resting. When the lead finally notices my inaction, the line halts. After a few moments the guard is shouting in tones reserved for the rebellious and insolent. The others begin mowing again, but I do not budge. Finally, the Boss calls my name directly. "Johnson! Get off that bush axe! Get back to work!"

I stare straight into his eyes and see the sweat bead on his forehead. I watch as a drop rolls down his temple. We are both getting madder but with opposite effects. His voice gets louder and his movements quicker. For me, everything slows down, and for the first time all day I feel my shoulders relax.

"Johnson, get off that bush axe and get back to work."

I am as still as a golfer waiting to putt.

"Johnson, I'm gonna tell you one more time. Get off that bush axe and get back to work!"

It is a particularly hot day, and I have become too angry to continue. In prison there are many names for the shutdown, and it has a thousand faces. Some men quietly sink into madness, others suicide; some flare like bonfires out of control. I must admit to a certain amount of pride in the way that I stopped working.

"All right, Johnson. Do I have to lock you down?" His smile is pure rage.

There are certain expected responses among prisoners – anger and swearing are common signs of the shutdown. Threats and even violence are all accounted for in the prison code. But I do the unexpected, the forbidden. I look him straight in the eye and smile back.

I have never seen a red neck get redder. His throat strains tighter than a rooster in midcrow and for a moment I think, He's gonna fire that shotgun.

"Hold up!" he shouts to the lead man. Then I hear the metal rustle of handcuffs jostling toward my wrists.

Being handcuffed while in prison is like being blindfolded in the dark. It is one of those formal redundancies designed to drive home the absurdity of the situation. I have done nothing sinister today. I am serving a life sentence for a brutal rape I did not commit, and the only rule being broken is one concerning swamp work in 100-degree heat. All the same, the Boss Man looks as if he is about to wet his pants he is so mad, mostly because I smiled at him. I know that I am going in the hole for at least a few days, and I could soften the punishment by being contrite, but an apology would take away my last hold on dignity.

"The hole" is an all-metal cell with no windows and only a slot for receiving meals. Men in solitary are without privileges: no phone calls, no visitors, and no reading materials except the Bible and, supposedly, your legal documents (though usually they allow just the Bible).

I read the Bible every day, but it doesn't ease my angst. In the hole I read Hebrews, chapter eleven, over and over again. It begins, "Now faith is the substance of things hoped for, the evidence of things not seen." Evidence not seen, that is my only hope. Somewhere there is evidence that will free me. The Bible chapter continues with a list of men who waited patiently on God. Some of them, like Abraham, lived long enough to see their dreams come true; others, like Abel, were murdered or, like Joseph, were imprisoned unjustly. I take a special interest in Joseph: falsely accused of attempting to rape Potiphar's wife, he had been thrown into prison. I secretly hope that I will end up redeemed like Joseph.

It is hard to keep track of time in solitary, but generally after a few days the guard comes around and asks, "You okay now?" In other words, are you ready to play according to the rules again, even if the rules are subject to change at any moment? The correct response is, "Yes, sir, I'm okay now."

After three days I hear the guard approaching. He asks through the door, "Johnson, are you okay now?"

I answer, "Put me on a new work detail."

His response is to leave, and I know that he will not come back for a few more days. In order to hasten my rehabilitation, my meal service is reduced to the "silver bullet": an inedible mixture of scraps and rotten meat.

On his next visit he asks the same question, and I respond with the same answer. Just as he did the previous time, he walks away without another word. It is a simple game. I have plenty of time to consider my strategy. I even imagine the guard walking back to the prison office. He has some coffee, finishes his shift, then goes home to his family and has supper. I read Hebrews again.

A prisoner who is accused of wrongdoing by a guard has two options. He can take his punishment and return to the fold, or he can ask for a hearing. But the hearings are run and adjudicated by guards and staff; the convicts call it Kangaroo Court. While my bold response to the jailer costs me a few more days in the hole, I still believe I might have a better chance of justice by dealing directly with him rather than by requesting a hearing.

He comes back a third time, and I give him the same response. My voice is hoarse from disuse and malnutrition; it is just a whisper.

For the first time he responds: "Johnson, what do you want?" He is tired of our game.

"Put me on a new detail. Appling County . . . one of the city crews."

Working in town is like a vacation compared with the swamp. The loads are lighter, and we even have occasional interaction with the public. The crew spends a lot of time cleaning roadsides and doing heavy landscaping, but it isn't like the backbreaking monotony of the swamp. The one benefit of my previous work experience is that I have become quite skilled with every sort of garden implement; so when especially large trees have to be manually removed, I am usually consulted.

On this day one particular tree requires a bit of thought. The Boss shows it to us in the morning and says that it has to fall by evening. It is an ancient hardwood, about six feet around. When the men ask me how we should do it, I suggest that we put four men on it, covering about two-thirds of its circumference—any more would be too dangerous. The rest of us can clear brush and then sub-in each hour. Since the easiest and safest part of chopping is the beginning, I and some of the more experienced men start the day clearing tall weeds and picking up trash along the highway. We decide that the best workers will take the last and most important shift: we will be the ones to fell the tree.

We march into the tall grass and leave the junior woodsmen trying their best to land clean blows into the trunk. Their early attempts are comical, because the axes are too small and dull for the job—the heads get hopelessly wedged into each new cut. As we walk away from them, the juniors plead for advice, but we know they can't do any damage; as long as they keep hitting the tree, it will eventually fall.

"Just keep working, we'll be back in a couple of hours." We laugh and begin filling our orange bags with waste.

Cars often honk as they pass a prison work crew. Since that sometimes can indicate something interesting to see, a lot of us look up in response. One old guy, driving an antique Ford Fairlane, slows way down and honks like crazy. After he catches my eye, he throws something into the weeds about fifteen minutes ahead of us.

"Hey, Sonny, that old guy threw something out—up ahead."

"Yeah, I saw it—looked like a brown bag. Probably just garbage from his car."

"I don't think so. He waited till I looked at him. I think it's something for us."

Most of the old guys just throw out dirty magazines that they don't want their wives to find, but occasionally there's something more interesting.

"Maybe it's nothing, but just keep your eye out, okay?"

"Sure, man, whatever."

When we finally get close to the drop-off point, Sonny runs over to the bag, opens it, drops his jaw, and looks up to heaven. He bends down low and gulps half the bottle, then hands it carefully to me.

"Go on, man, the rest is yours."

Boone's Farm Apple Wine is not exactly my favorite beverage, and I have never been much of a drinker, but I check over my shoulder to make sure the guard is distracted and then guzzle down what's left. When I'm finished, I push the empty bottle into the soft ground and continue swinging.

Our bush shift ends about fifteen minutes after the apple wine incident. The heat, and the fact that we burned off lunch hours before, combine to make the cheap wine especially potent. These factors also cause the ill-tasting ferment to bubble in my stomach as we approach the hacked-up tree.

The men we're replacing are the third crew to go at it, and they're now exhausted. Thankfully, the trunk has been reduced to about a quarter of its original size. They hand us the warm axes and go off to get two other replacements to join us.

I look over at Sonny, who is obviously drunk, and he looks positively stupid in his dirty prison jumper. He laughs weakly at our predicament, and from his silly grin I surmise that I look just as bad.

"W-well wh-what are we gonna do? Johnson? What *shwould* we do?"

"Man, pick up the axe and swing it right there."

"Right where?" He stares intently into the space between him and the tree, working hard as a baby to keep his head level.

"Swing at the part that's left," I instruct him as best I can.

"Okay, okay." He sighs, then curses under his breath, and finally lets out a high-pitched groan as he swings the axe. The blade strikes obliquely and bounces off as if the tree were made of rubber.

"It's not gonna come down," he says, sadly.

"Ah-right, I'll do it." I pick up the axe and with all my strength swing at the tree. I miss. The blade lands deep in the ground, a few inches from Sonny's foot.

"See, I told you, man," he says, shaking his head slowly, "it's too thick for these kind of axes."

The two other men on our chopping team show up and grasp the situation immediately. They share a few choice words with us and demand that we return to the road crew before we kill somebody.

We see the sense in that advice and hobble over to the field where the others are mowing. As the numbness from the alcohol begins to wear off, fatigue hits like a mental blizzard. All I want to do is sleep – not just a nap but a nice, deep coma. My head begins to pound harder and harder until each bang carries a painful echo that makes me wince in anticipation. We join the bush axe crew, but our work is so sloppy that they have to stop the whole detail several times to get the two of us back into formation.

When we return to the camp I go straight to bed without dinner, without water, without taking my shoes off. That was the last drop of alcohol I have ever tasted.

While I prefer in-town work to the swamps, working around free people is often like a circus – with us in the center ring. Prisoners are considered by some to be entertainment, and occasionally the audience likes to get into the act, especially the women. Many women feel a great attraction for prisoners. Perhaps it is the strange combination of safety and danger that an imprisoned man represents. The convicts who exploit these women tell me that our neediness attracts them. Whatever it is that attracts the women, most ladies correctly assume that prisoners are desperate for female attention. Even the most self-disciplined man turns his head when the first pretty woman he has seen in two years walks by.

Some women who pass a prison detail are not satisfied with just being the object of strained attention. It is not uncommon to be flashed by women who probably feel that they are performing some sort of charity. A lot of men on the details openly flirt with girls, many of whom want to establish contact with the muscled and dangerous young men. These girls often throw out their phone numbers and addresses. Some of them eventually visit and send gifts.

While these relationships may sound crazy, they actually make sense. The men obviously benefit, but the women get something out of it, too. Having a prison lover offers a number of advantages over dating a free man. First of all, everyone on work detail is in terrific shape. We work all day and when we return to the prison, one of our few recreational options is to lift weights. Second, prisoners are really grateful for every small gift. To a man in prison a bag of candies or a carton of cigarettes is like a Rolex to a man on the outside. We also have a lot of time, time to write love poems or attentive letters. Who on the outside writes letters anymore? Possessive women find comfort in the fact that we are unlikely to be having an affair with another woman, and there's always a legitimate reason that we don't call or come over. Finally, if absence makes the heart grow fonder, then a life sentence is the ultimate aphrodisiac.

While such flirting may be fun, more serious relationships are problematic for the prisoner, and love is hell. My engagement lasted longer than most. Beth and I had talked of marriage before my arrest, and that promise of permanence held us together. She visited each month, making the long trek from Atlanta; my heart broke each time I watched her leave.

In the visiting room the guards watch over a strange mixture of human emotions. Children visit their fathers in the same room where young lovers try to hide more than a caress beneath the table. It is impossible to remain aloof when a few feet away a woman tells a man, "It's over," or grandparents say that they are getting too sick to visit again. There is never a completely good visit in prison, and the best that one can hope for is a type of corrupted joy that usually ends in abject loneliness. Perhaps it is for this reason that visitor requests always dwindle after a few years. It is a credit to Beth that she visited me faithfully for four years. Still, I knew it was a losing battle. But even when I could see the end coming, I told no one about my heartache.

I could have talked to my dorm mates—we have a lot of time for talking—but prisoners do not make good friends for many reasons. The men who do form close bonds behind bars often find that the friendships end in sadness. Because prison is a daily insult to one's dignity, it requires a great deal of discipline to maintain any sense of control over your destiny. Forming intimate relationships under such circumstances is difficult and sometimes dangerous. The most insidious aspect of prison friendships is that people come and go. For the lifer there is no way to visit a friend who is freed or even transferred just down the road. And guys who do get out have enough challenges without worrying about the folks left behind bars. Very few of them visit after they are released, and some wardens even forbid their return.

My sense of self-preservation, and the fact that I did not want to be hurt, kept me from forming any close relationships for the first ten years of my incarceration. While this may seem cold, the alternative was to create friendships over which I had no control. Some men feel a compulsion to establish close bonds under any circumstances, but I do not share that need. My initial strategy was to avoid all emotional attachment while in prison. The only links I had to the world of human love were my family and Beth. Even so, I encouraged her to leave me and get on with her life.

It is part of the pathetic spiral of prison life that those you love most, the ones you need in order to survive, seem much better off without you. Visiting me in prison was a great hardship for my loved ones, and their only reward was to see me locked up in a dingy place filled with other sad people. Visits from my friends and family kept me alive during the initial years of anger, but I always felt bad about the trouble that they went to. The worst part of visitations was witnessing Beth's passing youth in monthly intervals.

The other inmates spared no cruelty when describing their version of her life on the outside. I was told a thousand stories of what my girl was doing with other men.

"Hey, man, Jody got your girl and gone."

"What does that mean? Who's Jody?" I asked Old Brick.

"Don't pay them no mind. Jody is the just the name they use to tease everybody," he explained.

"Yeah, wait till I get out, then *I'll* be Jody," said Too-Tall with a sickening grin.

It is difficult to feel confident against those accusations. There is no one more impotent than a prisoner in love. He is unable to give his beloved even the mildest comfort or cheapest distraction. He is forbidden from earning money, unable to give gifts, and completely unsure of the possibility of freedom. While everyone in prison tells fantastic tales of devoted women on the outside, the truth is often sadly different. In many ways fantasy is better than the reality of love in prison. The men who get phone numbers from strange women watching the chain gang have the easier relationships.

I ponder all this as I wait for Beth. After months of punctual meetings, today she is late. Her usual morning visit is delayed, and it is near the end of visiting hours. As I watch the clock, I hardly need an explanation. When she finally arrives, she is upset and chastises me for not being grateful that she came at all. "You have no idea how hard it is to drive up here every month. You just have to walk across the yard. . . ." It is clearly a defensive move. Something has happened, something has changed, though I will never hear the whole story.

The following month there is no visit at all, and it is left for me to write the letter. How ironic. After all my encouragement that she move on, even while she loved me, in the end she is leaving me without an explanation. It is a real low point, and I feel utterly powerless.

Beth was the last link to my youth, the unbroken line to the potential I had known as a young college graduate. Now she is someone else's girl. I had almost gotten used to humiliation in prison. Each day when we return from work detail, we are strip-searched. Clothes off, arms up, mouth open, bend over: "Spread 'em." We have no privacy, no bathroom doors, nothing but a sheet between you and fifty other men at night. But still, a man with a woman on the outside can maintain a certain sense of dignity, a belief that "they can't take everything away." Now that belief is gone. I have lost the only part of me that was still living on the outside. In one way it is a relief, like the death of a beloved sick relative. But I am terribly lonely. For me, there is no one to talk to except God, and I am still angry at Him.

After a few years I hear that Beth is married and has two children. We don't stay in touch, but one day when she is having trouble in her relationship, she comes to visit me. It is great to see her, but I know that we can never be close again. I can never forget the secretive nature of her leaving. I had offered her freedom all those years, but the split came without any explanation, robbing me of what I needed most–to be able to give her something meaningful. In the end I couldn't even give her freedom. Our visit ends warmly, but it is lukewarm.

As in any human community, there are loyalty groups in prison. Many convicts hang out with other men from their hometown–the original "homies." Membership in such a group has its privileges–and responsibilities. I scrupulously avoid belonging to anything in prison, and for the most part, my autonomy is respected. Fortunately, my large size and aloof demeanor mean that I do not require protection, and since I don't seek friendship, the groups hold little appeal. My lack of interest is not seen as belligerence, and I maintain a safe relationship with several groups. For example, when a group plans to execute a vendetta, I am usually invited to participate or "just stay out of the yard." I always choose the latter.

While it is easy to see the harm of these groups, it's important to remember that their primary function is protection. I recall one prison in which there was a particularly strong white man named Hercules. Herc had a terrible habit of beating up smaller black guys. Fighting back was ludicrous, because he was easily the most massive man in the joint. After he knocked around a young guy from Fulton County, some of the homies got together and asked the victim if he wanted revenge. The injured man replied enthusiastically and became part of the group. As usual, I was offered an invitation to the "party," but I declined.

On the prescribed day several prisoners procured baseball bats, and about fifteen men jumped Herc in the yard. They had intended to do more damage than they effected, because as big as Herc was, fifteen men with bats are less likely to hit their target than one another. Fortunately, no one was too seriously hurt, and the guards broke it up with shots fired above the mob's heads. The incident curbed Hercules' mean streak and brought another homie into the fold.

You can be whoever you want to be in prison. The result is that everybody is in for dope dealing, and nobody is a sex offender. While thieves and murderers are acceptable, I know better than to confide in anyone about my conviction. I am also careful to hide my college education, which could be construed as snobbery. Prison etiquette is stricter than Emily Post, and the punishment for trespasses can be severe. Some rules of prison behavior are obvious, but others are a mystery to the novice. Fortunately, there is a sort of informal schooling that goes on in the system. The county jail, where you await trial, is the schoolhouse, where recidivists tutor the newcomers. I was an excellent student.

Never be a hero.
Don't accept gifts, especially those that just appear on your pillow, such

as, for example, some Little Debbie cakes. If you eat them, someone might come back looking for them.

Don't let anybody fight for you.

It's better to get beat up than to get away without fighting.

Never talk to the guards.

Avoid debts, and pay your debts as soon as your money comes in.

Don't sit on another man's bed without permission.

The education I receive in the county jail proves invaluable from the moment I enter the prison system. It's important to understand the rules of prison behavior, and especially prison commerce, before you're locked up. You can get just about anything you want behind bars, but it costs money. If you don't have money, you can take out a line of credit with one of the "stores." Prisoners who run the stores stockpile valued commodities and sell them on credit. For example, a Snickers bar today will cost you two or three tomorrow. If you don't pay tomorrow, then the interest compounds. Of course, there is a system for collecting on bad debts, and debt collectors are paid in goods for their services. One debt collector I recall was named Lefty.

Lefty was as strong as a moose but had fewer scruples. He could be hired for two cartons of cigarettes to beat or maim another prisoner. The storeowners often used him to intimidate debtors. Lefty earned his name because his right eye was made of glass, and he always took it out before a fight. Whenever I saw him lurking in the shower room, I knew that a "collection notice" was about to be served.

One day as I'm toweling off, I see Lefty by the sink. He has removed his eye and placed it on the soap dispenser. This is a sure sign of trouble, so I head for the door. Earlier that day I had heard that someone had run up a substantial debt. The debt wasn't the big problem, however; the real issue was that this guy hid some money he had received from home and pretended that he was broke. But he didn't even stop there. The deadbeat tried to get other prisoners to buy goods for him so that he could conceal his assets. When we heard about this deception, we all knew there would be trouble. It was clear that enforcement was imminent when Lefty showed up at the dorm with two cartons of cigarettes for his footlocker.

Just as I am leaving the bathroom, Lefty jumps the deadbeat. Unfortunately, a new guy is getting out of the shower and doesn't understand what's going on. Somehow his education has been flawed, and he violates the first rule of prison life: never be a hero. Because he is a weightlifter, the new man is able to stop the attack and alert the guards. However, the adage never to get between fighting dogs is especially true in this place, and the fact that the new guy speaks to the guards afterward only makes matters worse. The code of prison etiquette has been changing as guards and prisoners have more interaction, but in the 1980s only dead men broke up fights, and only snitches talked to guards. That night I remember learning just how seriously the code is taken.

The new man, sleeping in the bunk below me, is snoring loudly. Apparently, he has ignored the warnings to stay alert at night. There are fifty guys in the dormitory, and no matter how closely the guards watch, anyone intent on violence will succeed. I know that the new guy will be repaid for his act of bravery, but I don't know when. There are lots of ways to get a man in jail. Even cowardly violence is treated with more respect than pacifism. The most cowardly option is to "squirrel" a guy while he is sleeping. Squirreling involves wrapping metal objects, like batteries or padlocks, in a sock and swinging it repeatedly into a sleeping man's face. As I finally fall asleep, I am thinking that the new guy will probably be squirreled. I am wrong.

I awake to the horrible sounds of a man being stabbed in the bed below me. The metal frame shakes with the force of each thrust, and in a few seconds the storekeeper has carved his own revenge. The sound of snoring has been replaced by the awful sound of gasping and gurgling. Several men shout, and the commotion attracts the guards, who take the injured man away. I do not sleep the rest of the night.

The new man survives the stabbing, and after a few weeks of convalescence he is placed in "protective custody" or PC. The custody is both protection and punishment. Under PC you have no contact with fellow prisoners, no free movement in the courtyard, and the only outdoors you see is from a cage on the roof. As bad as it is, protective custody is the only refuge for men who violate the social contract. There is no second chance. Sometimes people end up in PC just because they are famous, but usually it is after a near-death experience.

The most common offense that brings on a near-death experience is being a snitch. In the old days snitches were punished severely. I can remember only a single exception to that rule. In one dorm where I lived, the men learned of a snitch and piled all his belongings at the door. He was told that he could either request protective custody or be killed. He moved out.

Most of the snitches I knew of were not so lucky. In the old days they were fortunate to escape with their lives, but times are changing, and it's hard to tell where prison society is headed. The prisons have been evolving rapidly, and us old-timers have difficulty adjusting to things like inmates talking to guards. The changing rules cause a great deal of confusion for new inmates. They are treated one way by the old men and another by the young. For example, an old guy will always beat you up for sitting on his bed, but the young ones tend to have a looser attitude about protocol. The most striking change to me over the years has been the increase in the number of snitches. Increasingly, they are used by prosecutors to testify about prison confessions. No one in prison believes their stories, but they are professionals who can often sway juries. When you live in a police state, loyalty is morality, and the snitches are out for no one but themselves. I could never understand snitches.

To those on the outside it is hard to imagine the rules that we live by in prison. But it is not fair to judge prisoners according to the norms of the free world. It may seem proper to always fight for what is right, but survival in prison requires that you choose your battles wisely. If you are innocent, it is best to remember Jesus' command to his disciples, "Behold I send you forth as sheep in the midst of wolves: be ye wise as serpents, and harmless as doves."

The Years
of Innocence

There is no quiet place in prison. Sounds of men echo along
the concrete walls twenty-four hours a day. Before lights
out, the television blasts like an endless tease from the
outside world. Some men find that a comfort, but I consider
television part of the punishment; its constant noise is a
reminder of freedom lost, of options unavailable.

I spend most of my day just thinking, but little of it is
focused or purposeful. It is hard to concentrate on anything
in prison because of the noise. Men argue, some cough
incessantly; the metal doors and electronic locks slam and
buzz all day. And it is not just the sounds I hear that form
this audio torture, it is also the sounds I miss. There are no
children, no birds, and no silences. Freedom is a symphony.
I can hardly imagine the comfort of a carpeted home, the
sound of a sleeping woman, or a patio with birds. Instead,
I am fed an empty diet of sitcoms with laugh tracks that

bounce from the concrete floor to the metal ceiling. It's best not to think about the noise.

Boredom is every prisoner's enemy. Some men smoke, others develop nervous tics like tapping their feet or endlessly biting their nails, but we all daydream. There are extended periods of anxiousness, and I often feel like a child, waiting for something to end. My mental television replays scenes from my own childhood often, as if trying to find meaning for this incarceration. I had a family once. A happy home with loving parents. A rich family history.

My mom and dad met at Fisk University, where Calvin Sr. was an Omega Psi Phi, and Jo Ann Jones was a Delta Sigma Theta. Dad finished his degree in history, and Jo Ann, like so many other college women of the time, left school to become a wife and mother. When Dad entered law school at the University of Cincinnati, Mom took a job there as an administrative assistant. After his graduation they settled in Cincinnati and had my sister Judy two years before me; Tara came six years later. From the beginning my older sister Judy was incredibly bright—and a tattletale. I was a good student, and I tagged along with Mom and Judy whenever they went to museums or the symphony. But I was also a boy, and having a tattletale sister was not always easy. No one actually got away with anything in our close-knit neighborhood anyway, because the watchful neighbors felt it their civic duty to discipline any child who strayed from propriety. Misbehavior was punished on the spot by the nearest neighborhood adult and was followed by a whipping at home, meted out by the offender's parents. Our community was an extension of our family, and we all loved living there. There were dance and music lessons during the week, and the formal rituals of Episcopal worship at St. Andrews Church on Sundays.

My lifelong fascination with cars and motors probably began with my Uncle Rich. He was so proud of his 1949 Ford Roadster that he named her Bessie. She was a baby blue two-door coupe, and Uncle Rich told me that she was "a classic." Everyone else mocked him for his devotion to old Bessie, but Uncle Rich and I adored her. I jumped at every chance for a slow drive around the neighborhood with my smiling Uncle. One day as he was turning the giant steering wheel to round a corner, he said to me, "C.C., you're the only one who appreciates old Bessie." He let the wheel spin back through the fingers of his gloved hand. "So upon my demise, I will leave her to you."

I was greatly pleased by his promise, but I had no idea when or how often a "demise" occurred. When I asked my mom about the word, she said, "It's when people die." The thought that I would survive my favorite uncle was disturbing. No one I was close to had died, and I had never considered mortality. I wanted Uncle Rich to know that it wasn't the car that I enjoyed, it was him. We never again discussed his demise, or the transfer of old Bessie, and that suited me just fine. Gifts and death were not compatible in my mind; presents were for happy times.

My parents were very active in the civil rights movement, and politics were discussed in our home with the same excitement as sports. But Mom and Dad shielded us from most of the violence and injustice of the time. Growing up, I never personally felt the sting of racism–people were just people.

In 1966 my dad was asked to run for office, and he won. He became the first black state senator from Hamilton County, Ohio. One day Mom took me to visit him in the rotunda of the capitol in Columbus. I was nine years old, and his colleagues gave me a round of applause. I still remember that echo.

When the senate was not in session, Dad worked as a lawyer with labor unions and building companies that developed housing for the elderly and those with low incomes. He loved his work and kept very busy, but he still had time for the family every evening. Because he was not a trial lawyer, the only courtroom experience he received was when he was recommended by the court to represent indigent defenders, a responsibility of all lawyers in the state. On one case he was asked to defend a man who was obviously not in his right mind. The man had killed a woman he didn't know because she walked by his window every day, and he was jealous that she walked with other men. He called her his girlfriend and had imagined they were dating. Dad filed an insane plea for this client, but the court-appointed psychiatrist denied the plea, saying the man could not be considered insane, because he had never been sane. The judge talked to the client gently and asked him if he wanted to go to the "farm" and help take care of the chickens. The client agreed and was committed for life to the state's mental facility, which did indeed include a farm where the patients learned how to care for chickens.

Dad was a popular community leader, and he was often given the place of honor at ball games. Our family usually had the best seats at parades, too. At one of those parades, my mother told me to watch and see who was in the limousine with Pops. When they drove by, I recognized Bobby Kennedy.

Some of the peace that my family and neighborhood offered was shattered on the day I came home from school and found my mother weeping, sitting on the couch in front of the television – it was April 4, 1968. On the screen were file tapes of protest marches: dogs biting protesters – dogs held by policemen. The reporter somberly repeated the news that Dr. Martin Luther King Jr. had been shot. I remember that day, because for the first time I was forced to confront racism in my protected, segregated world.

When I was thirteen, my dad accepted a job in Atlanta working for a building company that specialized in high-rise developments. Mom was able to find a good job at Clark Atlanta College (it later became Clark Atlanta University), and she looked forward to moving into a big new house. I was reluctant about the move, and my dad tried to cheer me up by promising me a minibike once we got there. As we settled in to our new home, I don't think the neighborhood kids knew anything about me except, "He's got a minibike!" But that was enough to bring them around in droves.

The new neighborhood was more secluded and spread out than I was used to. There was more privacy than we had in Cincinnati, and the trade-off was a little less "family feeling." It was a young, upwardly mobile community, and there were kids in every house.

Atlanta in the 1970s was an exciting place to grow up, and my parents moved us into the heart of the Black Renaissance. Some of the great figures of the modern era were our neighbors. Up the road from us lived my classmate, Lisa Young. One day, she invited me to her house, and I met her folks, Andy and Jean. Andrew Young was the mayor of Atlanta at the time and already a historic figure. Mayor Young had been one of Dr. King's most trusted confidants, and he would go on to become the first black United Nations ambassador under President Jimmy Carter.

Next door to us lived Frank Pitts, the Kansas City Chiefs wide receiver, and one house down was Willie Williams, the great New York Giants cornerback. Benjamin Mays, the president of Morehouse College, lived around the block, as did Maynard Jackson, a future mayor of Atlanta. The neatest thing for us kids, though, was that all of these homes were open to our roving band of hard-playing teens. The celebrities were always polite to us; they were regular people – just normal moms and dads. Of course, it didn't seem that way when we first moved there, but it didn't take long to get used to the famous neighbors.

Larry and Hanky's house was one of the neighborhood hangouts. Shortly after moving in, I was invited to a tent sleepover in their back-yard. I was happy to be considered one of the guys, and I jumped at the chance to sleep out. We had a small fire and roasted marshmallows; we told ghost stories and talked about girls.

Around midnight we were finally settling down to sleep when a car pulled into the driveway. The flashlights were doused, and the kid next to me said, "That's Hanky and Larry's dad. We'd better keep it down." A few minutes later we heard him approach our silent tent. He opened the flap and stuck in his head. "How you boys doin'?" he asked casually.

My jaw dropped, and I was in shock. When the man left, I said to the boy next to me, "That was Hank Aaron!" To which he responded, "Oh, that's just Hanky's dad."

The whole neighborhood – and all of Atlanta – was breathless in 1974 as Hanky's dad closed in on the all-time home run record. I'll never forget when he hit number 714, tying the great Babe Ruth. The stadium in Atlanta immediately sold out for the next home game on April 8. All of us who couldn't get tickets were glued to the television that evening. It was a cold night for April, and the L. A. Dodgers were leading 3–1 when Mr. Aaron got to the plate. We all held our breath for the first pitch. Ball one. The next pitch was a fastball and he swung. Contact. My heart stopped as the ball sailed in a straight line toward the outfield. It was low – almost a line drive – headed directly to the left fielder, but somehow it just cleared the wall, moving right over his head. With that swing the papers finally recognized Hanky's dad as the greatest slugger who had ever lived.

Being surrounded by such a great crowd of athletes inspired my competitive nature. I enjoyed playing basketball and football with the neighborhood boys and dads. Frank Pitts often hosted sports parties. After the team's Superbowl victory in 1970, Mr. Pitts had a bunch of his friends over to watch the videotape. The players knew the game by heart. I recall Ernie Ladd, the Chiefs' tackle, announcing every slip and false step before they occurred on the tape. He was a natural comic, and the room was filled with the howling laughter of giant men. There was one moment during the game when Frank slipped. Ernie knew exactly when it would appear on the screen, so just before it happened he called out, "Okay, Frank, I want you to go long, and slip – right on your butt." On the television a second later, Frank fell, and we all crumbled in laughter. Ernie was a natural showman, and none of us were surprised when he went on to fame in professional wrestling.

After the video the athletes wanted to come by my house and play basketball. It sounded like a great idea, and I brought the crowd of NFL players to my driveway. What I didn't realize was these giant competitors played basketball with the same robust vigor that they played football – and they played it as a full-contact sport. I was used to "playing rough," but they took it to another level. The only rule they had was, "Only sissies call fouls."

Frank Pitts was a great neighbor and a true inspiration. He encouraged me to be disciplined in body and mind. Whenever he left town, I was entrusted with the care of his house. It was a responsibility that I took very seriously.

My encounters with all the professional athletes were positive, and they inspired me to try out for several sports. I made the varsity football team and eventually attained a starting position. To keep in shape during the off-season, I joined the soccer and varsity tennis teams. I was never a great tennis player, but I won Most Valuable Player in soccer as a roving fullback. Football, however, remained my favorite sport, and I dreamed of playing in the NFL.

I'll never forget my dedicated and quirky football coaches. Coach Mac talked the whole time we were on the field, and I found it such a distraction that I tried to stay away from wherever he was posted. My other coach, Doc Thurman, was an ex-football star who never minced words. In fact, he often dispensed with words altogether and preferred the "object lesson." Once during a scrimmage, I blocked an opponent using only necessary force. After the play I was called to the sidelines and was loosening my helmet when Doc barreled into me and knocked me off my feet. As I rolled on the ground trying to recover my wind, he said, "That's the way you hit!" I was about to hit him back, until I realized that it was probably suicidal. Instead, I took that anger to the field, and on the next play hit my opponent so hard that his helmet flew off. Doc flashed me a brief smile.

I enjoyed the physical discipline of high school sports, but I resented the off-field restrictions. We were not allowed to party, and we had a firm curfew: 10:00 P.M. "or else." One Friday night we found out what the "or else" was. Several of us attended a party at a friend's house. There were all types of kids there, and we were just having some good clean fun. No one noticed that the curfew had passed — until we heard the familiar sound of Coach Mac's pickup truck. His leaky muffler seemed to mimic his incessant grumble, and its rumbling brought instant terror to the entire team. We each fled from the nearest door or window, and it was total pandemonium.

However, Coach Mac knew better than to come alone, and he instructed his squad of assistants to surround the house. They caught us fleeing into the woods like rabbits running from dogs. I was lucky to escape, but someone mentioned my name during interrogation, and on Monday I was summoned to the gym. My reduced sentence involved bending over the coach's desk and being swatted with a board from his removable wooden desktop. I clearly remember the sting and humiliation of those licks. Physical discipline was the norm back then, before the prohibition against corporal punishment. The coaches believed in licks more than laps. I can't imagine how they adapted to the new ways of school litigation. Perhaps they all just retired.

As a teenager, I also developed interests other than sports. I plunged headlong into reading some of the classics of Black consciousness and

Black power: Malcolm X, W. E. B. Du Bois, Booker T. Washington, and the speeches of Dr. Martin Luther King Jr. In the fashion of the seventies, I grew my hair into a full, round afro. I had platform marshmallow shoes and a wide-brimmed white hat, and I even wore gloves on dressy occasions.

All of this *maturing* took place in the general absence of white people. My neighborhood, my church, my school were all black. There were a few white people in each of these places, and I certainly had nothing against them, but my life in Atlanta was clearly Afrocentric. While I remember having white friends and schoolmates back in Cincinnati, the only contact I had with whites in Atlanta was when we played schools from other communities. Of course, white culture still dominated the television and newsstands (even the store mannequins were all white), but the races actually lived apart in Atlanta during the seventies. In terms of mixing, not much had changed since the day when Dr. King was stopped for driving through a white suburb in the sixties. The laws had evolved, but many of the people had not.

On Saturdays we would often gather as a group and go roller-skating. I was very good and took my choreography quite seriously. We dressed to the teeth, and in those days no one would think of wearing a helmet or knee pads. Instead of safety equipment, I wore my red three-piece, bell-bottom suit with a white fedora hat. I may not have dressed athletically, but I could skate like a pro—racing and jumping around the rink. I was so fancy that at times folks would stop skating and just watch me. Their attention fed my pride, and as they say, pride goeth before a fall. One day when everyone was staring, I slipped and fell hard. More than my pride was injured, and by the time I got home, I already knew that my leg was broken. Dad, however, thought I was exaggerating, and he advised me to sleep it off. I tried, but in the middle of the night I demanded that he take me somewhere for treatment. He never doubted my capacity for pain again. That slip cost me the starting position with the football team, and I missed an entire year on the varsity squad.

While I always made decent grades and maintained a disciplined exercise routine, I also had one addiction. In high school I began to smoke pot. My friends and I never saw it as a big deal. It didn't seem to interfere with our grades or sports, but looking back, of course it affected many aspects of our lives. Every habit, every hobby brings new friends. It's as if we join some large extended family with each practice we adopt. For drinkers there are bars, cigarette smokers have their designated places, and for me pot was intimately associated with many of my worst experiences. Back then I would have denied any connection between pot and trouble, but I speak from experience when I warn young people about marijuana.

In the ninth grade we had a wonderful young biology teacher, Mr. Lawrence, who encouraged impromptu scientific investigation. As a result, he had a room full of budding experiments. My friends and I contributed a small set of botanical studies, which yielded rather healthy plants that escaped identification for some time. When Mr. Lawrence finally became suspicious of the pointy-edged leaves, he insisted that we remove the unusual plants immediately. We complied and "discarded" them out by the creek, where they matured until they were taller than us.

Unfortunately, while we smoked all the pot we grew, we did not grow all the pot that we smoked, and that meant getting involved with buying drugs. This usually posed no problem, as pot was a ubiquitous substance in the 1970s. It was possible to go to several street corners and purchase grass at just about any hour of the day. A nickel bag ($5 worth) could get several friends high, and it hardly seemed like a crime.

When you smoke pot regularly, people know. My dad tried to warn me about it and told me to "never bring that stuff into my house," which I didn't. While I never developed an affection for alcohol, cigarettes, or other drugs, pot was a regular part of my teen years.

On the more positive side, I was an active member of the Key Club and really enjoyed our field trips. As one of the officers, I attended a memorable convention in Houston, but I found the local excursions most interesting. On one trip we visited a "boy genius" who had built his own radio station, WRAZ. It was a low-wattage community station that nonetheless attracted commercial sponsors and produced quality ads. The young black man who started it, Wayne, was held up as a model of entrepreneurship. He and I were about the same age, so I asked him how one could get started as a disc jockey.

"Well, you just go down to the Federal Bookstore on Peachtree Street and get the book to study for your third-class FCC license." He looked at me through his thick glasses: "You go and pass that test, and I'll hire you." He smiled as if he had said this a hundred times before.

Six months after the Key Club tour, the station owner seemed surprised to see me show up with my operator's license in hand. But he was true to his word and said that if I were serious, he would train me. Wayne himself was serious about everything he did. For training I was introduced to one of the great music broadcasters of the day.

Douglass Whatworth Steele lived in Atlanta and hosted a national countdown show. His house was filled with music memorabilia and awards, and I was impressed that he would take an interest in an anxious young upstart like myself. He worked patiently with me on announcing skills and taught me that most DJ's confuse volume with excitement.

"You have to remember the circus announcer," he told me. "He never shouts into the microphone, but his tone embodies excitement. He doesn't scream, 'Attention everyone,' but maybe he repeats it slowly—because it's important." He gestured toward his throat, "Tone and inflection are everything. Just remember the ringmaster: 'Hur-ree, hur-ree, hur-ree.'"

After I completed my brief training period, Wayne tested my skills and then hired me. Soon I was earning a hundred and twenty-five dollars a week (an unheard-of sum for a high school kid), and saying things like, "WRAZ, this is Calvin C. Johnson *Junior* playing the hits for you." I enjoyed every aspect of my job, and Wayne was a fascinating character to work for. His business acumen was sharp, he was technically brilliant, and he always inspired confidence, if not awe. He was also a bit cocky and was never intimidated by officials or powerful leaders. In short, he was a young black media star. Everyone in Atlanta media knew Wayne; many current DJ's and TV stars got their start working at WRAZ.

Some people in the media, and perhaps in law enforcement, were irked by Wayne's ability to get to a crime scene with almost instant speed. He used his contacts and a police scanner to race against, and often beat out, the larger media outfits. The radio station's car was similar to the sedans used by police, and its scanner was always tuned to the police band. Wayne supplemented his salary (and his ego) by scooping the major media outlets, and then selling them video footage for their stories. I lost track of him when I left the station in 1978, but everyone I met in my later media jobs had high praise for the young genius. That all changed when he was arrested several years later, accused of Georgia's crime of the century—but I am getting ahead of myself.

In addition to my paying jobs, I also enjoyed volunteer work. When I was thirteen, my friend David Randall told me about his job at a summer camp for inner-city youth.

"They have a lot of mentally handicapped kids, and it's kinda sad," he told me. "But it's also a lot of fun, and all the kids are great." David spoke with a passion uncommon to boys our age, and I was taken in by his enthusiasm. "At the end of the summer," he continued, "the kids with the most serious handicaps come. They're ten-year-olds, and some of them are in wheelchairs or are blind or deaf—but we all have a blast."

It sounded like a good time, and I always loved working with younger kids, so I called the director. The first summer that I volunteered, the camp was held in the mountains of Helen, Georgia. At first, I felt really sorry for the kids who were handicapped; they had all sorts of injuries and deficits. Some kids had prostheses, others were in pain, and one was a hermaphrodite of undecided gender. But after a day or two, we were all just friends; fun is all that counts when you're a kid. Those children helped me realize that everyone has his own talents and weaknesses, everyone including me.

In the evening we would gather by the fire and roast marshmallows. We sang campfire songs as the sun set, and the crickets joined our chorus. As soon as it was really dark, the kids wanted to hear ghost stories. I tried to make them thrilling but not too frightening, and I always ended by pointing into the woods and shouting, "Oh my goodness, here he is now!"—at which point all the children would scramble for the dorm and snuggle in the safety of their own beds.

During the day we had to come up with creative solutions for kids in wheelchairs who wanted to do things like canoe or swing from vines. There was a lot of lifting and supporting, but we were able to fulfill most requests. For many of them it was the only time that they escaped the watchful eyes of overprotective parents. All kids need to take risks and with risks come injury, but the children loved us all the more for letting them fall.

When we had no scheduled events, I would take the kids on nature walks, "hunting for snakes." While I had no knowledge of herpetology, I had watched a few *Wild Kingdom* shows, and I did a good impression of a naturalist. I instructed them with such expert advice as, "Snake hunting requires you to be quiet and to keep your eyes open."

The kids, especially the visually and mentally impaired ones, would point to objects with varying degrees of snakelike form and shout, "I found one! I found one!"

Each time they shouted I would encourage them by complimenting their skills of observation.

"Coach Johnson! I found one! I found one!"

Nakisha wore glasses thicker than Coke-bottle bottoms.

"That's very good, Nakisha, a lot of sticks look exactly like – ahh! It moved!"

All the kids ran over to see their first live snake, and that night Nakisha went to bed a celebrated hero.

By the end of camp we had formed a very close bond, and many of the children cried when it was time to go. I tried to comfort them with promises of next year, but for most of the kids that was too far away, and for some of them it would never come. I learned a lot from the kids about tenacity and finding joy in all circumstances. It was not fair that they had such incredible obstacles to overcome everyday, but they chose to enjoy the life they had. I kept my promise and volunteered again the following year. Those two summers in the country are wonderful memories. They were my first exposure to dorm life and have served as a great contrast to the prison dorms that became my home for so many years.

Although the summer work was fun, I wanted to make lots of money in the fall. In addition to the radio station, I tried to find a weekend job. When I heard how much shoe-shiners made at the airport, I begged my dad's friend, Mr. Braxton, to give me a chance. Willie Braxton owned the shoeshine concession at Hartsfield International Airport.

He rented the chairs out to men who worked hard all week but were often reluctant to come in on weekends. Saturday travelers are more casually dressed and are far less likely to want a shine than their weekday counterparts.

"I would be happy to work any weekend," I told Mr. Braxton. And so it was that I became a shoeshine.

My first day on the job, the old shiners greeted me with great skepticism. A lot of boys try their hand at shining shoes, but most of them tire of its rigors, especially under the critical eye of veterans like my mentor, Mr. Duke.

"That wasn't too bad, boy, but you can't ever sit down on the job. I'm sixty-four years old, and I ain't never sat down in this airport—ever. You got to squat and move quickly; it's like you're on the line of scrimmage. There is nothing relaxing about a shoeshine, unless you're the customer—or the shoe," he said, laughing quickly, then putting his hand on the small of his back. "If you're doin' your job right, then your back has to hurt."

I took his advice, and the next customer tipped me well, but the old-timer was still unimpressed.

"Two minutes and fifty-five seconds!" His face was a caricature of disappointment.

"What?" I asked indignantly.

"You should be able to complete a thorough job in less than two minutes—unless it's a spit shine."

Challenged by his high standards, I waited for a third chance to practice my skill. For this one I was in the squat position before the customer even sat down—and I stayed there. No more sissy strokes; I worked the leather quickly—with a powerful and smooth sawing motion, like giving a massage between rounds at a prizefight. There were no pauses, though occasionally I snapped the cloth back to tautness, the towel leaving the shoe for only a millisecond.

Total time: one minute, fifty-five seconds.

The old man smiled. "Take every job that seriously."

I was good with engines and learned to drive a car by the time I was thirteen, sometimes being allowed to drive around the neighborhood.

On a few occasions my parents had to travel and left Judy and me home alone; our younger sister, Tara, would stay overnight at a friend's house. I knew that in case of an emergency I could always take the car, but emergencies being rare, I wanted to practice, and soon I was driving whenever they left on a trip. Judy would have told on me, but I was driving her friends as well, so there was an incentive to keep our secret.

By the time I was fifteen, my minibike was too small for me. Although I liked driving the car, my heart was set on getting a motorcycle. My parents hated the idea, because I had already taken some serious spills on the minibike, but I saved all my money in the hope that someday they might change their minds. Whenever I brought it up, however, my dad would say, "C.C., we've already talked about that," and although I could never recall an actual discussion, the point was moot.

So, my bicycle remained my chief form of transport. I rode my Royce Union as fast as I could, all the while pretending it was a motorcycle. One day as I was burning down the fastest hill in the neighborhood, out of nowhere, a big old wooly dog ran into my front wheel. I went head-over-handlebars and landed in the road, but the bike continued on its way without me until it hit the curb. There was a loud "pop" as the tire exploded, and the front wheel collapsed into a semicircle.

I looked to the side of the road where the dog had sat down. At first I thought that he was injured like me, but the expression on his face looked more like laughter. He stared at me awhile, then kind of shook his head, laughed some more, and trotted off happily. I was incensed. I picked up my bike, and like a wounded warrior, followed my nemesis to his lair. My pants were badly ripped; my face, knees, elbows, and hands were all bleeding; and I was mad as hell.

A rotund man in shorts answered the door of the house where the dog finally rested.

"Son, what's wrong?"

"Look what your dog did to me!" I wailed.

"Oh, Jake!" he said to the dog, who couldn't care less. "I'm sorry, son; he always chases the bicyclers. Audrey, come look at what that beast did to this poor young man."

His wife, who was as large as he, appeared from the back room. She told me to come and sit by the sink. Then she took out her first-aid kit and tenderly patched me up. Their name was Hamilton, I learned, and they were both so nice that I soon forgot my anger. When she was finished, she told me to go out back and see her husband again.

"I'll pay for the damage to your bike, son, and I'm so sorry about what happened."

I was about to tell him not to worry about it, when I spotted the canvas-covered lump near the shed. He saw me staring and asked, "Wanna see the bike?"

It was a Suzuki 550, a beautiful blue machine with crash bars and twirling pegs.

"Man, I sure would like to have a bike like that," I told him.

"Well, I'm trying to sell it," he said, with a sigh, "for that no-good son of mine. I keep telling him to get it out of here. I was gonna keep it for myself, but I fell off the first time I took it out. I won't even get on it now." He pursed his lips and shook his head. "I still owe $500 on the thing, and I'd be happy to get just that."

When he asked me if I wanted to start it up, I forgot all about my injuries and hopped on. The bike turned over on the second kick, and he shouted, "Take it around the house."

What an incredible thrill. It was ten times faster than my old minibike—and I never even took it out of second gear.

When I returned the motorcycle to its place beside the shed, Mr. Hamilton put his arm around my shoulders and said, "Calvin, you're a natural on that thing. If your parents will sign the bill of sale, I'll let you have it—as long as you promise to pay me $50 a month, for 10 months."

"There's no way that my parents will let me have a bike, Mr. Hamilton," I said sadly.

"That's what our son used to say, but it's hard to resist when you see your child having so much fun. I'll let you take it home if you want, and I'll take responsibility until you tell your folks. There's some trails behind the school where Mike used to ride. Why don't you take it for spin, and then see if your dad will let you keep it."

I rode for the rest of the afternoon, but when the sun went down,

I thought that my motorcycle days were over. I held little hope for Mr. Hamilton's suggestion, but I figured it was at least worth a try. So I pulled into the driveway, left the engine running, and honked the horn. My whole family spilled out into the yard, and Dad was the first to speak. He was concise.

"Take it back."

While he was usually able to avoid any discussion by simply saying, "We've already discussed this," I had the peculiar advantage of actually having the bike between my legs. This introduced a novel factor in our traditionally brief treatment of the subject.

"But, Dad, you've got to try it. It's not like the minibike—it's a lot safer." My smile took up the majority of my face. "Hop on, Pops?"

My father was an experienced lawyer who knew better than to allow me this demonstration, but he was also a generous dad who loved me deeply. I was surprised when he got on the bike and put his arms around my waist. It was the slowest ride that I have ever given.

Mom was next, and then a faster ride for each of my two sisters. The wind in their faces and the joy on mine sealed the deal. I became the proud new owner of a Suzuki motorcycle. For the next ten months I made every payment to Mr. Hamilton on time, which greatly impressed him, and gave him more ammunition against his own irresponsible son. My bicycle accident had turned into a great blessing for both of us, and his dog never chased me again.

The bike was my pride and joy. I practiced my riding skills with the dedication of a racer, and I yearned for a racer's speed. The trails were fun to ride, but it seemed unnatural to inhibit the street bike's potential by keeping it in second gear. Soon, I was a regular sight on the neighborhood roads; then I started driving all over the city.

Because I had only a learner's permit and not a motorcycle license, I knew that I had to stay clear of the police. There were a couple of close calls, and once or twice I had to outrun the cops by turning onto the dirt trails near my house. One squad car finally got sick of me, raced ahead, and then turned sideways to block the road before a bridge. The officer was obviously unfamiliar with the agility of a skilled rider and the nerve of a scared teenager. I shot right through the narrow space between his bumper and the guardrail. The stunt actually required me to lift my legs beside the handlebars in order to avoid amputation (waving at the same time was unnecessary, but strangely satisfying).

I was always a bit of a daredevil, and as a teenager with a driver's license, it became a profitable personality trait. There were several places around town where drag racing on the street was popular. I got to be so good with motorcycles and cars that other people would place bets on their own cars and then ask me to drive them in a race. I was fearless and rarely lost. My childhood nickname, C.C., took on a new meaning, "Crazy Cal." I was never caught racing, but there were several close calls. I remember clocking a hundred on the empty highway early one morning, just for fun, but a second after that century mark I saw a police car on the side of the road. He didn't follow, but I took the next exit and stashed the car in a friend's garage just to be safe.

As an offshoot of my racing skills I used to give motorcycle thrill rides to intrepid friends. For the most part these were just fun tours around the neighborhood or open accelerations on the highway, but one time my pal Benny asked me to help him with "a plan." He wanted to snatch some pot from a street peddler. At first I refused, but he egged me on with dares and promises of money.

There was a guy in south Atlanta who stood on the corner all day with a big paper sack in his hand. He had a long beard and dreadlocks that he sometimes kept wrapped up in a colorful cloth. He looked like a poster child for a rehab clinic. We all knew what he had in the sack, and cars would pull up all day long to score little plastic bags of pot.

"All right, C.C., you drive up the street and then slow down like you're going to buy a bag. I'm gonna lean down real low and snatch that *do-rag-wearing freak's* sack."

I got caught up in the adrenaline of an adventure without even considering its consequences. We drove through town, laughing and talking over the wind, and as we approached the pot seller's corner, my friend egged me on once more, just in case I was having second thoughts.

"Come on, C.C., we're gonna have a whole lot of money when I sell this stuff."

I pulled up to the curb, and we put on a cool attitude, as the guy walked up to meet us. He had an easygoing swagger, and the sack swung loosely in his left hand. His right palm was already open, waiting for payment.

I kept my hand on the throttle, and my eyes on the road. When I felt a sudden jerk, I knew that Benny reached for the bag.

"Go, man, go!"

I popped the clutch—faster than I meant to—and we sailed away with my front wheel in the air. We got away with it, and I justified the act a thousand ways, but my real motivation was just for the fun of it. To me life was an adventure.

I finished the requirements for graduation early and was able to skip the final quarter of high school. I loved the independence of being a graduate, and moving out was an incredible temptation. At seventeen, I left my parents' home and took a job with an in-town radio station, WSB. It was there that I discovered my preference for off-air production, and I switched from music to news programming. I covered visiting sports teams and such dignitaries as Senator Howard Baker. It was an exciting and prestigious job.

I shared an apartment with a woman who was twelve years my senior. The relationship was comfortable, she took care of me—actually doted on me—and we always had lots of fun. She paid all the bills and wasn't very demanding. However, eventually the differences in our ages and interests began to show. The real problem was that I was a very young man, and I had no intention of settling down. When her desire for permanence became clear, I moved out.

Living on my own was tough, and I had to work hard to cover my living expenses and save for college tuition. I visited my mom regularly but didn't talk too much to dad, since I knew that he thought I was "hard-headed" and "too independent." Still, I knew they were glad I was earning my own money, because they were under some financial stress. The housing boom collapsed in the mid-seventies, and Dad was working only sporadically; with Judy in college and me getting ready to start college, they were beginning to fall behind.

In addition to the radio station, I worked as a night watchman and took on other odd jobs. A car was a luxury that I could not have afforded had it not been for an unexpected gift. My beloved Uncle Rich passed on, and although there were a number of folks who looked forward to getting behind the wheel of his classic two-door coupe, he had promised it to me. When the will was read, the family was shocked to learn that he had left old Bessie to young Calvin in Atlanta. And so it was, that upon his demise I flew to Ohio and drove back with Uncle Rich's pride and joy. Bessie was the coolest car in town: a 1949 baby blue Ford Roadster.

Innocence Lost

In the fall of 1975 I enrolled at Clark Atlanta College,

where my mother worked as an administrative assistant.
The traditionally black school attracted talented students
from all over the country and had a good reputation for its
Communication Studies department; I decided to major
in communications.

I still enjoyed hanging out with a variety of people
and made a lot of friends both at college and in the nearby
housing projects. Because of those friendships, the college
kids assumed I could tell them where to find the best pot.

Almost everyone was experimenting with marijuana
in the seventies, and even kids from the best homes were
anxious to find some good weed. The terrible thing about
acting as a go-between is that only the bad influences are
transferred. I did nothing to pull my poorer friends up, but
they certainly helped bring me down. Of course, at the time

I felt as though I still had it all under control. I knew I could just say no if things ever got out of hand.

By the end of my first year in college, I was walking the razor's edge that separated my southwest Atlanta friends from my acquaintances in the projects. The two sides of the divide were like different countries. In the southwest section of Atlanta were teenagers who drove sports cars and rode to parties in rented limousines. The projects were filled with young people who walked or rode bicycles. To be honest, the biggest attraction of the projects were the pretty girls who were easily impressed by a young man with money. These people longed for the things that we took for granted in our neighborhood.

The powerful men of the projects all possessed the allure of the underworld. They were drug dealers or ran the numbers; some of them were pimps or loan sharks. These men were the antithesis of the honest, hard-working fathers of the southwest. But ambitious men of any ilk ply their trades with the same zealous energy and firm resolve. To their own code they are true. Unfortunately, the code of the underground includes every sort of vice.

While my good and bad friends rarely mixed well, occasionally I met a college student who wanted to hang out in the projects with me. Charles was one of those hybrids. We met in an American history class, and he seemed to share my interests in both hard work and fast living. He was from up north, and his people clearly had a lot of money. His good looks and life of privilege had taken him far, and he was just as cocky as I was. But he didn't understand Atlanta.

"Charles, I'm warning you – don't go to the projects without me."

"Don't get so worried, C.C. – I'm from New York *City*." He accented the last word as if it conferred magical protection. "We have projects, too," he said, laughing. "Relax, man, I'm not afraid of some Atlanta brothers."

"I'm just saying that if they don't know you, it doesn't matter what color you are – they'll rob you."

"You are so uptight, C.C. Re-lax." He shook my hand with his own stylized grip and flashed me a bright smile. "I'll see you tomorrow."

Charles and I found the excitement of the ghetto to be a tonic for the predictable comfort of our middle-class lives. It seemed to be a sensible balance – work hard at school, blow off steam with people who really know how to party. The way we saw it, we were just taking in the best of both worlds. Charles was thrilled to meet someone at Clark who knew Atlanta's poorer side, and he was doubly pleased to learn that I knew "the Main Man" of the Carver Homes project. Carver had a serious reputation.

A week after warning Charles about the projects, I got a frantic call from him.

"Calvin, you got to call your friends!" he shouted.

"What happened?"

"They stole my car – stop laughin' – that's my daddy's car. If he finds out I was over there, he'll kill me."

"Charles, I can't do anything for you now. I told you, if they don't know you, they'll rob you. The only reason that my stuff is safe is because I know them, and they know who I know."

"So call the Main Man – get my car back, C.C!" He was either crying or about to start.

"You're crazy," I said. "I told you not to go over there without me."

The projects could be rough. There were gangs and guns, and people were jealous over the things they lacked. My friends and I would show up in our fancy cars and nice clothes, and the poorer boys would watch their girlfriends come over to chat with us. Sometimes the girls would even leave with us, which of course made the young men mad as dogs.

For the most part my time in the projects was trouble-free. Because I knew the Main Man, I could park Uncle Rich's '49 Roadster anywhere I wanted to, and no one ever bothered it. My connections assured the car's safety, and my easygoing manner ruffled few feathers. However, some of my friends were a little over the top, and they occasionally provoked trouble. We all knew that trouble with the homies is a natural consequence of rich boys hanging around poor girls. We tried to avoid arguments, but the most desirable women always attract multiple suitors.

Sharon was one of the prettiest girls in the projects. She was also the target of my friend Brad's lust. He and I would take our cars down to Carver Homes and park beside her building with our radios on. She would come out with her friends and talk to us, and on rare occasions she might go out with us for a quick bite to eat. It was all very innocent, or at least we thought so.

One spring day I was leaning against my car talking to Sharon's friends, when I heard an angry male voice.

"So this is the little rich boy that's been spendin' money on you."

I turned around ready to fight but froze when I saw who was speaking. He was so big that Brad looked like a child next to him. There was no doubt that he could have taken us both. I watched as he reached into Brad's car and slapped Sharon's face.

Brad looked stunned and scared. I was hoping that he wouldn't do anything stupid. If he struck Goliath, he probably would be killed; and if a fight started, I would be compelled to join in. What a mess, I thought to myself. Then it suddenly got worse.

Four or five other guys started walking across the dirt yard toward the parking lot. They were friends of the jealous man, and he turned to meet them, probably to coordinate our destruction.

In a quick act of good judgment Brad chickened out, turned on his engine, and gunned it.

"Get in the car!" I shouted to the girls. Old Bessie started with a single turn, and her 350 horses roared as we burned rubber.

We were long gone before the men could decide how to dispose of us. I hoped that our abject fear was enough to console them.

Cooler heads prevailed when the extent of my connections were explained to the offended brothers. I was so spoiled back then that I thought the situation was fair. I took everything for granted. A nice car, beautiful home, even the love of my family, none of it inspired me to gratitude; I was fortunate and proud. It seemed natural that pretty girls should be interested in me, and I saw nothing wrong with impressing them with my relative wealth. But the worst part of my pride was my utter lack of fear. I felt no danger in associating with people who made a living from crime. As long as I didn't participate, I felt righteous.

An old lifer whom I met in prison explained it to me this way: "Young men think that they can hang with anyone and suffer no consequences. They believe that somehow their good morals will protect them and maybe even lift up their friends. But if you're standing on a chair, and I am standing on the floor, it's much easier for me to pull you down, than for you to pull me up."

The inevitability of that lesson would soon be demonstrated in my life.

Even as I meditate on the mistakes I've made, I can't completely ignore the positive side of my college years. I worked hard at school and was a good student. I paid my own way and always had challenging jobs. At the radio station downtown I would fill in for the producers who took weekends off. I also had a reputation as a good cameraman, and the college media department gave me plenty of work. Because I was responsible for maintaining the equipment, I got to meet film students from sister schools who borrowed our cameras.

I remember one particular film student from Morehouse College who frequently borrowed equipment. He had a reputation for quality work and was always interested in learning about new devices. His talent was obvious, even in those early days. Years later, when I was imprisoned, I wasn't surprised to hear that that student, Spike Lee, had made it big. I didn't bother to tell anyone that I had known him in college, since college is not something that prisoners typically brag about; but I followed his career with interest.

During my sophomore year I received a very strange job offer. One of the big shots in a local gang heard that I was a daredevil. He was looking for a college kid who could be trusted to expand his market, and I must have sounded like a good prospect. He approached me during a visit to the projects and casually offered me a job supplying drugs to college students.

"All you have to do is sell some stuff from your dorm room," he explained as if he were an Amway salesman. "We're looking for someone to supply the *need* at the school."

I had supplied pot to friends, but I was not at all anxious to get involved with gangs or the mob. That kind of danger held no appeal. I remembered what had happened to the man we called "Mr. Jakes" at Carver Homes. Whenever I saw him, he was always nattily dressed, but

I got the feeling he was scared, like a dog with a choke collar. At first he sold reefer, then he ran the numbers, and then one day I heard someone found his body in a garbage can. I did not aspire to Jakes's vocation, and I made that clear; but the offers continued each time I visited the projects. Finally, the gang leader actually visited my dorm room.

"Look," he said, "I don't think that you realize what I am offering, or who I am." He was wearing what looked like a gold motorcycle chain over his tank top. "I'm gonna tell you a number," he continued, "and then you check tonight to see what number comes up."

That night I asked a bookie in the dorms what number had come up. When he told me, my jaw dropped.

"How much did you lose?" he asked.

I told him I didn't play.

The man with the gold chain had been right about the number. But I found his influence more frightening than tempting. I again said no – very politely. I liked money, but my freedom was everything. I didn't want anyone to own me, and I didn't want to end up in jail or a garbage can.

In my junior year I shared an apartment for a while with a student who helped me learn about still photography. Andre and I shared three passions. We loved fast cars, beautiful girls, and photography. We would spend hours in the darkroom discussing composition, lighting, and development techniques. We also had some fun times racing. When I first moved in, I had my uncle's Roadster and my motorcycle. Andre knew, though, that I had been saving my money for something really special. Finally, one day I showed up with our common dream, a brand-new yellow Trans-Am. That car took our road revelry to new heights.

When my dad saw the car he gave me a worried look and said, "Boy, you better stay out of Clayton County with that thing."

I brushed off his comments, but he added, "That place is a bedrock of segregationists. Driving around in that yellow sportster – you're a marked man."

Most of the time I drove the Trans-Am slowly, and it actually had a calming effect on my passion for speed. I didn't race it much, because I wanted that new car to last forever, just like old Bessie. Andre, however, seemed willing to take greater and greater risks in order to impress our friends. His thrill-seeking came to a head early one Sunday morning as he was tearing up an empty highway. I never found out exactly how fast he was going, but he certainly attracted some attention. His spectators eventually included a squad of Atlanta cops, a television crew, and a police helicopter. After a long chase he was apprehended and subsequently lost his license. The punishment taught him a lesson, and his experience in making the news seems to have inspired him. Last I heard, he'd become a very successful press photographer.

My constant need for money was both a blessing and a curse. Fortunately, I landed a great job in the warehouse with Delta Air Lines that summer. I liked the work, and I loved the perks. I have always had the travel bug, and as a young college student with free airline tickets, I was in seventh heaven.

At that time employees had to pay only the tax when they wanted to fly. It was company policy that we dress up for all flights and presented a professional image, but we got to fly first class (when there was room), and I loved the luxury of prestige travel. I also enjoyed asking my friends about *their* weekend plans.

"Hey, Bill, where you guys going this weekend?"

"I don't know, maybe the Variety on Saturday night. Where you goin'?"

"Vegas."

That summer I was able to keep ahead of my expenses because I was able to find some inexpensive housing. I was invited to stay with a college student who had free rent in a very nice apartment. She was the well-supported daughter of a successful preacher, and she liked me a lot. Her dad knew nothing about us, and sometimes we both felt guilty sharing her place (but not so guilty that either of us moved out). The relationship was good for me, in that I stayed away from my less savory friends. But at the end of summer, I moved back into a college dormitory and renewed my old ties.

My dorm room became a popular place, and I always had something for guests—especially lady guests. We had parties that lasted all night, but somehow I always made it to work on time, and my grades remained good. My nickname, C.C., took on yet another meaning. While I never did any drug except pot, the girls called me "Champagne and Cocaine." I always had a bottle of bubbly in the fridge, and I knew where to send people to get whatever they wanted.

I still felt as if I had everything under control; after all, I was a good student who was about to graduate. I had a steady girlfriend and a great job; life was good. It was also very fast. My work kept money flowing in, but the party life kept it flowing out. Although I made a good income, I saved nothing. I paid my bills on time, but there wasn't anything set aside for emergencies. The temptation to get involved in illegitimate deals increased with the demands of my lifestyle, but I still said no to illegal moneymaking schemes. In fact, I even stopped getting weed for my friends. I told everyone that they would have to get their own from now on; I was not going to buy pot for anyone.

I graduated from college in 1980, and stayed with Delta Air Lines, hoping to move up through the ranks. In 1981 I saw my old radio boss on the TV news. It was Wayne, the young media genius whom I hadn't seen in three years. But this time he wasn't covering a story, he *was* the story.

For two years Atlanta had been reeling from a series of child kidnappings and murders. Each month we watched the death toll rise, until it reached twenty-eight young people. The murders baffled police. There were all sorts of theories about who was killing the young men. Some rumors had the Ku Klux Klan responsible, since most of the victims were minorities. The comedian-turned-activist Dick Gregory was blaming the Atlanta-based Centers for Disease Control and Prevention, saying they harvested interferon from the bodies for a novel cancer treatment. The city was in a panic. Then in June 1981, Wayne B. Williams was arrested as a suspect in two of the murders. It was my old boss, the one with a knack for arriving at crime scenes before the police.

The Atlanta child murders, and the subsequent trial of Wayne Williams, made front-page news for almost three years. In the end Wayne was sentenced for two of the murders. The physical evidence against him was a series of fibers found on the victims' bodies that matched blankets and carpets in his home. The paper reported only one eyewitness. Someone had seen Wayne dumping something off a bridge, and the next day one of the victims washed up downstream.

It is curious that the newspapers referred to Wayne as a "self-employed talent scout and video cameraman"—a far cry from the "boy genius" that we had known. The media can create or destroy a reputation overnight, and few people have the resources to hire press agents or publicists. When the papers reported Wayne's arrest, I'm sure most people sighed, "Thank, God, they caught the guy." Never mind that the Constitution proclaims us innocent until proven guilty. If the paper prints your mug shot, or a headline with your name, the public knows you're the bad guy. Unfortunately, reporters usually get their information from the police, so for the average arrested person, the news is just another organ of the state: a wealthy adversary, who can accuse without penalty. I had no idea at the time of Wayne's arrest that I would soon face the same adversary.

When someone you know is accused of a serious crime, it is easy to be prejudiced one way or another about his guilt. There is no way that I can tell if Wayne is lying when he proclaims his innocence. That's one thing I have learned over the years; it's hard to judge people who claim they've been railroaded. I try to avoid all such judgments completely; I just treat everyone with respect and judge them according to the behavior that I observe. In the end God is the only perfect judge. Proof is nothing more than conviction. In our system you are proven guilty or innocent depending on which side convinces a jury. Conviction is its own proof.

After graduation I found myself increasingly over my head financially. I never talked about it when I visited home, because my father had been unemployed so long, and my mother's job as an administrative assistant at Clark was barely enough to make the mortgage. She had also been diagnosed with diabetes, and we were worried that she might have to cut back her hours, as well as her Mary Kay sales. In comparison, things were going pretty well for me—until the night that the trouble really began.

I had finished a tough week at Delta and was looking forward to relaxing with a couple of friends. I wanted to get a nickel bag of pot to share that evening, so I drove to Fourteenth Street. There was a small green house at the end of the road where I would occasionally buy grass. The protocol was that you would drive up slowly, pull over, and turn your lights out. Then someone would come to the car with a small bag of pot, and you would hand him five dollars. It was a simple exchange.

I had my money ready and was rubbing my tired eyes when a man in a knit cap came up to the car.

"What do you want?" he asked.

"Just a little bag," I said, and handed him the bill.

"This is some pretty good stuff," he said. I didn't recognize him, and conversation was not normally part of the exchange. I looked in his eyes, and in an instant my life changed.

He raised his arm and aimed a pistol at me: "Out of the car, hands on the ground! Hurry up! Police!" The words banged through my skull like a sixteen-pound hammer. It was a stinging, numbing, angry-at-my-self sensation.

At the station I was booked and processed like any other law-breaker. As soon as I was allowed to, I looked up a lawyer who special-ized in drug cases. I knew that I needed a good one, because the law in Georgia was very strict. In fact, rumor was that the judges were trying to send a message, and the next few months of sentencing would be especially harsh.

"I need a lawyer to represent me in a drug case," I began.

The voice on the other end of the phone calmly asked a few ques-tions and then responded, "I'll take your case, but my court rate is seven-fifty."

"What? Seven hundred and fifty dollars a week?"

"A day; and with filing and preparation time, you're looking at seven days, at least."

I was desperate. I hired him over the phone, then began to panic. I had nothing saved, and my job at Delta was in jeopardy due to the arrest. I was independent from my family and had been enjoying the high life of travel, fast cars, and late nights. Dad was trying to start up a cleaning business, and Mom was not in perfect health—they were in no shape to help me. Judy had a good job but was just getting settled in Washington, D.C., and she was already helping Mom and Dad out. The next day one of my friends reluctantly posted the bond, and I went home to my apartment. The more I thought about my situation, the more frustrated I got. I just wanted to clear this up, then start my life over, get a good job, and settle down. But how could I possibly clear this up at seven hundred and fifty dollars a day?

I tried to get help from my friends, but most of my college buddies who had partied with me every night suddenly couldn't talk on the phone. The only friends who stuck by me were the ones in the projects, and they had no money at all. Besides, to them an arrest was nothing, just an initiation, a chance to prove your manhood. They had plenty of tips about courtroom strategies and even prison life – if it came to that. But they had no money.

My friend Tony was typical. He had a brother in jail and gave me a lot of free advice.

"I can't go to prison," I told him.

"You'll be all right," he said coolly. Tony's brother had recently been represented by a public defender and had received a stiff sentence.

"I just need to get the money for this lawyer," I said. "They tell me he gets everybody off."

"Well, I know where you might get some money fast," he said, between drags on his cigarette.

"What are you talking about?"

"There's a new fence down here, and he'll give you some good money for anything."

"I don't have anything to sell."

"Well, you just have to go over to the Park," he said, pointing in the general direction of a new apartment complex. "There's plenty of nice stuff over there."

College Park was a new, upscale apartment development.

"I'm not gonna steal anything," I said, laughing nervously. "I'm trying to stay *out* of jail."

"You told me yourself," he said, and shrugged, "you need the money." He took one last puff of his cigarette – right down to the filter. "You know what happens if you get a public defender? Just think what two years in jail will do to that college diploma. If Delta doesn't want you now, who's gonna hire you when you get out of prison?"

He had given me the best advice that he could. He knew that a good lawyer was the difference between justice and mercy. The rich got mercy, and his brother got justice.

Tony continued his counsel, assuming that I could be convinced. "Find a place where no one's home, just go in, find some jewelry, and get out. I'll take it over to the fence for you; he already knows me."

I tried not to think about his suggestion, but as the court date approached I got very anxious, because the lawyer demanded payment in advance or he wouldn't represent me. Finally, one week before the trial, I decided to take Tony's advice. In my mind I thought I would do just this, just one more bad thing, and then go totally straight. *Go in, find some jewelry, and get out,* he had said. It sounded simple.

That same evening I drove into the apartment complex and pulled up to the first ground-floor unit in which it appeared that no one was home. I can't remember if I went in through an unlocked door or the window, but once inside, I found myself in the kitchen. It was surreal, and I had no idea what to take. I was as quiet as I could be, even though I was convinced that no one was around—until I heard the knock.

Then I heard a radio—*no, a walkie-talkie*—in the backyard.

I ran to the front door and threw it open.

"Hold it!"

I slammed it shut, ran out the back—another officer, his gun drawn.

"Get down on the ground! Hands behind your back! Do it! Now!"

Someone had seen me go into the apartment.

The cops were not vicious, but they were not gentle either. I still have the scars from the cuffs that were clamped too tightly on my wrists. I felt sick, but it wasn't the pain of the cuffs that made me ill, it was the shame.

I appraised my situation in a different way now. It was not a simple mistake to be cleared up by some fancy lawyering; it was a tragic mess. Yet

I felt strangely calm. Perhaps I had been numbed by the first arrest just a few weeks before; or maybe, having to face my own guilt brought me a measure of peace. One thing was clear, there was no easy way out. I was going to prison, and there was no sense fighting it. I had willfully done something against the law—against someone whom I didn't even know, and I had no excuse, not even to myself. How it all came about didn't matter; what mattered was that I should confess, serve my sentence, and start over. I would become a new man, from the inside out.

Paying the Price

Jail is a rude awakening, but it is indeed an awakening.

I discover that while individual prisoners don't fit any particular mold, the rules of life behind bars are always dictated by the strong. In order to survive, it is important to play the game wisely from the start.

The old Jefferson Street Jail in Atlanta is where men are held before trial. All sorts of guys come into these overcrowded cells. Many innocent men await trial, sometimes for months, and many violent criminals use it as a way station between the outside world and state prison. The seasoned felons are expert manipulators, bent characters who know more about the human psyche than any university professor. Their expertise in domination is learned through practice and honed through experimentation in the most controlled laboratory on earth, a jail cell.

Our cell has no window. It is a concrete-block room, built for four men, housing nine. This means that five of us have to sleep on thin mats spread over the damp floor. There is an open toilet in the middle of the cell and a leaky shower in one corner. We have no privacy, and cellmates are forced to experience one another's most private moments. I am sure that it is not an accident that the toilet sits right beneath the TV. Since all of us in the cell are being held before trial, the population changes as men are tried and sent to prisons all over the state. Many of my cellmates are recidivists; some of them have spent more time in jail than on the outside. I am convinced that most of them belong behind bars, but I am not one of them, and the contrast helps steel my goal of absolute obedience to the law. When my sentence is complete, I will never come back to jail.

The routine is always the same. In the morning our breakfast comes in through a slot under the door. Each man gets a tray—as long as he gets it before someone steals it. There is a clear plastic cover on the food (foil might be fashioned into a weapon), and most of the meal is stuck to the plastic. The grits are hard, and the bread is rubbery. Lunch and dinner arrive the same way, and the only real breaks in the routine come during visiting hours and once a week when the guards bring the phone around. For nine men we get forty-five minutes of telephone time. This means five minutes of collect-calling apiece, which includes dialing, busy signals, whatever. Like everything else in jail, phone time becomes a commodity. It is something to trade or is a way of paying off debts. It can be bought, borrowed, and stolen. I savor every minute of it.

I know that I have to be tough from the get-go. Fortunately, I am in good shape, and in the Fulton County jail it is a plus to be black. We are the majority race in most city jails. As Richard Pryor once said about his own prison experience, "I went in expecting justice, and that's what I found—just us." But black or white, you still have to prove yourself. Among prisoners, everyone is a possible subjugate.

My test starts subtly. During the first few weeks I receive a lot of mail, and to men in a cage every blessing is an instant source of envy. Two of my cellmates become particularly jealous of the volume of letters that I receive. One day, while I am showering, they take a stack of my mail, intending to read it.

"Hey, Johnson, you sure get some chubby love letters. How 'bout we share 'em with the brothers who have illiterate girlfriends?"

I am aware that my reaction at this moment will determine much about my life behind bars; subconsciously, I have been waiting for this.

"Neither you nor anybody else is gonna read my mail." I am still dripping wet, wearing just my towel, but I yank the letters from their hands. "We'll do whatever we have to, but nobody reads my mail – except me."

There are two of them, and I haven't established any support among my cellmates. It could cost me a few days in the infirmary, but I know it will establish an important precedent. I had been warned by an older prisoner, "First, they'll take your stuff, then your food, and finally your manhood. You got to fight them at every step."

The cell is silent for a moment; no one watches, but everyone is attentive. I am ready to swing my fist at any provocation, but luckily they back down. This simple challenge establishes that I am not the easiest target in the cell. They will have to find someone else to break.

In jail the only law is the law of the jungle. Its first commandment is that the strong dominate the weak (though some men live in strange commensal relationships). Domination is an obvious aspect of prison life, but I was shocked to see how deftly the bullies wield their psychological weapons.

Since the majority race in most cells is black, the most vulnerable victims are white. This has less to do with racial identity than with practical considerations. Young white men from affluent homes are soft and easily intimidated by hardened black criminals. A life of privilege and civility has its benefits, but it renders you useless against men who take sadistic pleasure in mind control. The tough young whites have no problem, and the weak blacks are victimized; but the white children of affluence are especially marked for servitude.

The domination that usually occurs is both subtle and premeditated, not the typical prison rapes depicted in films and novels. Oftentimes when a new prisoner comes in, two of the older inmates collude to establish one of them as the threat and the other as the protector. The threatener acts out a hollow con, an in-your-face intimidation that presages violence, but the protector is the true menace.

When a new man comes in, someone always asks one of the guards what he did.

"Who's the new kid?"

"Some rich little bastard, got caught with an ounce of coke."

"Is he gonna make bail soon?"

"Nah, looks like his folks are having some trouble, and the judge is a hard ass."

In the cell the young man carefully arranges his stuff in his locker, then stands near a corner. He looks away when anyone approaches him or uses the toilet. His fear is palpable. Suddenly, for no reason, a large black man bounds up to him and stares dead into his eyes—inches from his face. He freezes.

"Did you take my goddamn cigarettes? 'Cause if you did, I'm gonna cut your neck from ear to ear."

The threat is credible, and the kid is near tears.

"I-I didn't take your cigarettes." He does not even consider fighting. "Look, I'll get you some tomorrow—a whole carton."

Then suddenly, "Lay off him, man." An older inmate attempts to restore the peace. "He didn't take nothin' from you."

"You stay out of this, old man. This little punk thinks he's hot stuff. I'll show him something hot tonight—let's bring out the welcome wagon for his little punk ass."

The older man continues in a soothing voice, "I said lay off him—he's cool. He's just a kid. We'll take care of that cigarette thing tomorrow." He moves toward the two of them and says to the aggressor, "Tell you what—have the rest of my pack; it's over on my bed."

And so a friendship is established. The older man watching out for the younger, consoling him when he has legal problems or when no one shows up to visit. Sometimes, just like a big brother, he holds him when he cries—and in jail just about everyone cries. To the boy and his parents, the older man is a protector and savior, but to the savvy prisoners he is known as a "war daddy."

The parents speak to the older man when their son calls; they may even send him gifts or money, but they have no idea what is really going on. Their son has been tamed, his spirit broken, and he has become the war daddy's "boy." It doesn't happen all at once, but after a time the young man gets used to the older man's affections, and even begins to rely on his comfort. The game usually works out well for the war daddy, and eventually the young man becomes completely submissive and willing to perform sexually for his protector. The pleasure for the older man is a combination of sexual comfort and pure domination; it is to him a game of human chess. I learn the rules by quietly watching.

We are so crowded in this jail that we can almost hear one another's thoughts, but mind reading would be redundant, because a lot of guys think out loud. Some even talk about their partners on the outside by name.

"Oh, man, you should see Johnny now—over on Tenth Street, he got him a new Mercedes, and an F-10 pickup, and he is livin' high in that old blue house. He's always got five or six kilos of coke over there, and the finest ladies. . . ."

Next thing you know, Johnny is in jail with us, wondering how he got caught.

Undercover cops are more prevalent in county jails than in prisons, because they know that men so recently used to freedom love to talk about life on the outside. I never talk to anyone unless I have to.

One day as I'm sitting in my cell, some unexpected visitors approach. It is a detective, whom I recognize from my arrest, and a white lady whom I have never seen before. Her eyes look at me with an inhuman hatred. I had heard that the apartment I broke into was owned by a single man, so surely she's not here to see me.

"Hey, Johnson, there's someone here who wants to talk to you," the detective says.

This is obviously no friendly chat.

"Well, I don't want to talk to anybody."

The woman stares at me again with the same intensity, and I hear her say, "That's the guy." Her comment sounds like trouble, but I comfort myself with the thought that my dad has arranged for bond, and I'll soon be out. I turn away from them and walk to the opposite side of the cell.

"We want to talk to you about some other crimes in the neighborhood, Johnson," the detective calls through the bars, "and this lady is a victim of one of those crimes."

"Look, I don't know anything about any other crimes. I have already told you everything."

"We'd still like to talk." His voice changes slightly. "We know what you've done."

I have no idea what he is talking about, and I wonder if it is just an interrogation trick. The cops are allowed to lie. "I have nothing to say without my lawyer present."

My family hires an attorney, and on our second meeting he conveys a strange offer from the police.

"They say they might go easier on you if you keep your ears open and help them with a case they're working on."

"They want me to become a snitch?" I bristle. "There is no lower life-form, and I will never be that desperate."

"I'll tell them that you declined," he says blandly.

I never regret that decision, but I do worry about its effect on my sentence. I ask my lawyer about the strange woman and the cop's comment, but he just shrugs it off.

After borrowing money for the bond, Dad comes to get me. He is given some shocking news.

"A hold's been put on your son's release."

"What kind of a hold? The judge set bail, and I have the bond." My father, who has the money in hand, is perplexed.

"Pending other charges."

"What other charges? I was told it was breaking and entering, and carrying a concealed weapon."

"There may be more soon. Have a seat, and the detective will see you in a minute."

The weapons charge is for the Buck knife I always carry in my pocket. I bought it when I first started at the Delta warehouse; it is a standard tool of the trade. On my first day at work the old crew chief told me, "You got to get you a knife." He took out his well-worn blade to show me. "Get you a Buck knife; that's the one we all use — they make the best knife."

Since that day, the knife had been my constant companion. It often came in handy at work, but my possession of it adds a great deal to the seriousness of my crime.

While my father waits to speak to a detective, I wait in my cell, expecting to leave soon. But the detective's words echo in my mind, *We know what you've done.* I review the facts in order to calm myself. I have told the police the full story and given them a signed confession. I have agreed not to fight the breaking and entering or the weapons charge, even though the "concealed weapon" is not a weapon at all to me. There is no need for a trial, because I have admitted everything. I am not going to quibble; I broke the law and agree to be at its mercy. My dad is posting bond, and he'll be here any minute.

The detective finally meets with my dad.

"What's this about 'further charges,'" he asks.

"It's related to a sexual assault on the same night as his arrest," the detective says matter-of-factly.

Dad is heartbroken, but somehow he musters the energy to spring into action. He calls my lawyer and asks him to come to the station immediately.

After a conversation with the district attorney, my lawyer comes to see me. He does not look hopeful. He explains that there have been some assaults in the neighborhood where I was arrested and that I may become a suspect.

"Calvin, they are offering you a plea. You plead guilty and get twelve years—do eight."

"For breaking in?"

"Breaking and entering, the weapons charge—because of the knife . . . and," he lowers his voice, "sexual assault."

"I told you, I am not pleading guilty to something that I did not do. I broke into a house, and I had the knife in my pocket—they know I won't fight any of that." I look him square in the eyes. "I did not commit any other crime."

"The woman says she identified you."

"How?"

"She came down here."

I remember the crazy-eyed woman.

"Calvin," he shakes his head, "they brought that victim down here to I.D. your voice."

"But I didn't talk to her."

"You must have said something."

"I said that I didn't want to talk to anyone."

"She says it was you." He sighs and shakes his head. "It's not a proper I.D., and we could fight it because they shouldn't have brought her down here like that, but a victim—especially a young white woman—is going to be a powerful witness against you."

"I did not assault her or anyone else!" I shout, scared and angry.

"They have some other circumstantial evidence," he says. He looks down at his notes. "Do you remember what you were wearing on the night you were arrested?"

"My shorts and a T-shirt."

"And no underwear?"

"No. I often don't on summer nights, especially if we might go swimming."

"The victim said the assailant wore cut-off shorts with no underwear."

"My shorts are store-bought, they're not cut-off."

"Do they have a fringe?"

"Yes."

He looks at me and takes a deep breath.

"Calvin, I do have one last question."

"What?"

"The detective said the perpetrator was uncircumcised."

"What?"

"The woman repeated several times in her deposition that the man who attacked her was uncircumcised. She noted it during oral sex."

"I was born in a Jewish hospital in Cincinnati!" I proudly exclaim.

His face brightens for the first time. "That's a godsend." He shakes his head and laughs. "Okay, I think we can fight it. She was very clear in her deposition about the foreskin."

My feeling of relief is short lived. An hour after my lawyer's visit, one of the officers who arrested me drops by. "We'll get you next time. Your kind always repeats, and we'll be ready."

The following night my lawyer returns to tell me about the latest negotiations.

"They'll accept a plea on the two charges alone—they'll drop the assault. They cite some sort of 'problem' with the evidence, and they don't want to go to trial on the sexual assault charge."

"Thank God for circumcision!" I am relieved that the ludicrous charges have been dropped, but my lawyer looks as though he has some bad news. "What are they offering?" I ask.

"Twelve—do eight."

"What? That's the same thing they offered with the assault charge."

"They say they've got your confession on the burglary, and they're not moving. I know it's ridiculous, but the detectives still think you did the assault. They'll be happy if you get the full twelve."

"Can you do anything to change the D.A.'s mind?"

"It would probably be a big waste of your money," he says, speaking with the practical resignation of a man who knows the justice system. "I'm sorry, Calvin. I advise you to plead."

It is a depressing dilemma, but in the end I decide to spare my family the cost of a battle that we would probably lose. I need to take responsibility for my life, and pleading guilty to my crime is an important start. It is frustrating that the sentence was affected by a crime that I did not commit, but I want to pay my debt and move on. I plead guilty to burglary and possession of a weapon.

I am shackled about the waist, my hands are cuffed to my side, and my legs are chained together. This is the standard travel wardrobe of the state prisoner. First stop is the diagnostic center in Jackson. Based on my performance there I will be assigned to a more permanent prison home.

Upon arrival, my hair is shaved off, then I am stripped and sprayed all over for head and body lice. I am given a prison jumper and told that a doctor will examine me soon. The inside of Jackson looks just like the prisons you see on TV: rows of steel cages lining an open walkway.

The state of Georgia uses many classic diagnostic tools for assessing inmates. So, I demonstrate my ability to fit round objects into circular holes and correctly match cubes with square openings. I am interviewed by a counselor who asks about suicidal tendencies and drug use; then I am examined by a doctor who says less than five words to me but grunts his satisfaction that I am healthy enough to work. My fitness for prison having been established, I begin my rotation through several jobs, starting with the kitchen.

I was never much of a cook and preparing food is a bit of a novelty. The newness, however, fades as we peel and cut vegetables for a thousand men. Nonetheless, I maintain my resolve to do everything well and be a model prisoner. I also remember the advice that I had been given at the county jail, to stay independent and distant.

Mad Dog is my aptly named partner in kitchen work. I don't see him as vicious, but he has a reputation, and everyone gives him a lot of room. On our first day together, we are eventually left alone working in the kitchen. We silently prepare vegetables as the sound of machinery and motors echoes over the tile floors. It is a hypnotic sound, and I am soon lost in thought as I peel carrots.

Suddenly, I feel a chill run down my back – literally. An ice cube slips beneath my collar and down my back. I turn around, and there is Mad Dog, grinning like a teenager at his girlfriend. In the free world such a prank might be taken with good humor or shrugged off as sophomoric, but in prison every encounter is a like a move in chess. You can't afford to let even a pawn slip past your guard, because it will be followed by a rook and then a queen. I grab the nearest dangerous object, a thick plastic measuring cup the size of a man's head. In one continuous motion I push him against the wall and swing that cup across his face. Without a word spoken, I hit him as hard as I can and open a gash in his chin that requires stitches.

My cellmate hears about the incident and treats me like a dead man. At lunch the next day, the whole table says that he'll get me back real bad. Some advise me to consider protective custody. I ignore their warnings, but I watch my back every moment.

Two days later he finally returns to the kitchen. I don't know what to expect, but I am prepared to defend myself against anything that he dishes out. At first we just go to opposite corners of the room, but then he walks up to me, and he is the first to speak.

"I apologize – it was wrong, what I did. I'm sorry." He sticks out his hand to shake. "No hard feelings?"

"Nah, no hard feelings." We shake hands as if we had been opponents in a tennis match. For the next few hours, as we mix batches of gravy and powdered potatoes, I think about what has happened. Maybe he wasn't trying to dominate me with that ice cube, maybe he was just scared of the new guy and wanted to be proactive. There is no way to know, and there is no sense discussing it. We have settled on being equals: independent men thrown together for no good reason. For the next two months we work in silence.

When I finally learn which prison I have been assigned to, I ask one of the old-timers about its reputation. Smoker has been in and out of prisons since he was eighteen, and he knows first-hand about every institution in the state of Georgia. He also loves to tell stories about the old days, and he freely dispenses advice. "Buford! Boy, that's a hard-time prison," he says. His voice is scratchy from cigarettes. He coughs for half a minute then collects himself. I give him a piece of my candy bar and invite him to sit on my bed.

"You're goin' to a place where you've got to have you a shank – everyone does."

"What's a shank?"

"You are green, Johnson." He finishes the bite of candy, and I can tell he wants some more, so I oblige.

"A shank is a blade, or a knife of any sort."

"How I am supposed to sneak a blade into a prison?" I laugh.

"Don't have to. You'll get you one in there. That's the beauty of Buford, they have the best shanks in all of Georgia – they have a welding shop." He smiles and savors the nougat for a few seconds, and then adds, "Most places, you has to make your own, but over there you can buy one cheap. Some places they search you good – every day. But guys still know how to keep they shank handy. Sometimes you'll see a man sittin' in the same spot in the courtyard every day. Day after day, like he has a nest full of eggs. That man is sittin' on his buried shank," he says, pausing and pursing his lips for emphasis.

"Sometimes, them guards sweep through the yard with a metal detector, and most times they find plenty of sharp objects. But metal is not the only kind of shank. In some camps you can't get metal, so guys make shanks from broken concrete or busted windows."

Smoker is a true scholar of prison life, but this story sounds unbelievable. "In Buford, you get yourself a fine shank – right away."

Less than an hour into my stay at Buford, the old man's prophecy comes true. One of my cellmates returns from his job at the welding shop and is surprised to find a new bunkmate.

"What's your name?"

"Johnson, Calvin Johnson."

"Johnson, you need a shank?"

"Yeah, I guess so." I have no idea what to ask for. "Do you work in the welding shop?"

"Yeah. What size you want?" He speaks quickly; to him this is simply a business transaction.

I hesitate. "What size do you have?"

"No, Johnson, I don't *have* any. I'll make it up fresh for you."

I nod.

"So, you want it large or small?"

"How much is a small one?" I ask shyly.

"Five bucks."

"How about the large?"

"Five bucks."

"Then I'll take a large," I grin. I want the biggest shank I can get.

At the time it seemed like a wise choice to get more metal for the same price, but I hadn't considered how I was to carry my new possession. Hiding a seven-inch piece of sharpened metal in my sock is rather cumbersome, and occasionally painful.

While it may seem dangerous to have eight hundred convicted men walking around with sharp metal blades, Buford was actually one of the most peaceful camps in the system. I never had to take out my shank, and neither did anyone else. Everyone knew that if a man had to show you his shank, he was going to use it. What worked for the

United States and the Soviet Union with nuclear missiles also worked for the convicts at the Buford camp. It was a clear demonstration of mutual deterrence. A peaceful stand-off.

Every freedom is scarce in prison, except the time to think about your life. You can review it looking to improve yourself, or with the intent of perfecting your corruption:

"Next time, I won't leave no witnesses."

"I would have got less time if I'd killed him."

My own meditations continue to bolster my resolve to be a model citizen, but my thoughts are always silent. I keep my mouth shut.

I think about my life on the outside. How I had squandered much of it, letting others serve me, or just being lazy. In reality I probably wasn't that different from the average young man in my neighborhood, but average is a shoddy standard, and I vow never to fall to it again.

I think about my grandmother and the time I had lived with her during the summer. I ask myself over and over how I could have been so selfish. Why didn't I help her more? She was so old, and I was so young and strong. Why did I let her do everything for me? I helped out only when she asked me. *I* should have been serving *her*. Instead, she cooked for me, cleaned up after me—she did everything.

When I think about my fiancée, Beth, I vow not to repeat my self-centered ways. Beth is kind like Grandma, but young and pretty. After work each day, she used to cook a wonderful meal and then make a sandwich for my next day's lunch. She is a good woman, a help-mate; someone who has my best interests—my success—in mind. She will wait for me because she believes in me and wants to settle down, to spend our lives together—to have children.

I think about my mom and dad. After all they have done for me, look what I have done to myself. How could I have shamed them like this? They were proud parents who expected us to be high achievers. They brought us up to be good, moral people, and I have squandered their blessings by my mistakes. I promise to make it up to them as soon as I get out.

These daily meditations are my rehabilitation. In the end all reform is internal and personal. Prison programs can help a little, but renewal is from the inside out. Just as I had let my peers begin to corrupt me until they had reached my very core, renewal has to reverse that process, starting from the inner man.

One program that helps me is the voluntary religious services. The visiting fellowships are important to many of us, even those who are not too serious about God. The emphasis on rebirth and acceptance, the talk about love; these are messages universally needed by men who desire another chance at life. While prison can foster review and repentance, it can also demoralize and humiliate beyond recovery. The church ministries do much to prevent that utter destruction of character. I have watched many men break down and turn their lives over to the Lord after a service.

The most moving sermons feature ex-cons who come back to visit.

We start with singing, and then the pastor offers a prayer before introducing the speaker.

"Brother Andrew Walker is here today with a special word for you. He was incarcerated in this very prison for eleven years. Many of you know him, and he tells me that some of you knew him before his conversion. He says that he was a hard man, unreasonable and uninterested in righteousness. That has certainly changed."

The speaker takes the podium, and there are already tears in his eyes. He wears a suit, and the contrast to our uniforms is painful to us all. We know that he will go home to flannel pajamas and his wife in a nightgown. We will all go to bed without seeing loved ones — children, wives, or parents.

A hanky crosses his face and then he begins. "Brothers, friends, . . . I had written things to say to you, but I can't even speak." He takes a minute to clear his throat.

"I left here five years ago, scared as hell that I would be coming back, because I didn't know what else to do. But God knows things that we can't even imagine. . . . He has good plans for us."

He sobs briefly. "I am actually happy to see you, Brothers."

We laugh a bit uneasily.

"I have brought some folks to introduce to you. First, the good people of the prison ministry who have stuck by me," he says and nods toward the man who introduced him and toward the two guitarists at the front of the room. Then he bites his lower lip to steady it. "And then my other family. . . . Brothers, I would like you to meet my wife, Sarah, who just like the Sarah in the Bible has an old husband who everyone thought had no seed left."

We laugh.

"Well, . . ." he pauses, then just whispers as if his throat has nearly closed, "she has given me a baby." He begins to sob and cannot speak, so his wife says softly into the microphone, "This is our daughter, Emerald."

Sarah looks over at her husband, who smiles, still unable to speak, and then gently reaches for a picture beneath his Bible and holds it against her dress. "He really wanted to bring her, but that's not allowed." All the treasure in the world could not make us more envious than that green-eyed face no bigger than an apple: a miracle that we can only dream of.

The proud daddy again takes the microphone, and by now many of the men in the room are bowed over in their seats, sniffling or silently praying.

He again clears his throat and tries to hold back the crying. "I can't speak . . . but God wants me to tell you, 'Be of good courage and do not fear.' It's from . . . Joshua. . . ." The reference is never finished.

By the end of my second month in prison, I decide that I am completely rehabilitated. No more pot, no more visits to the bad part of town. No crime—not even a parking ticket. I swear not to smoke or drink ever again, not even coffee. And on the rare occasions when drink or smoke is offered in prison, I turn it down.

I am a new man. When I get out, I will start over, work hard, marry my girlfriend, and be a good daddy.

Trapped

At Buford I attempt to hide my college education, but the
disguise is not perfect. Eventually, the counselors recruit me
to help out in the prison school, and since I have no desire
to become a welder, I accept the job. For the most part the
work is routine: maintaining equipment, filing, and working
in the library. The chores actually help me pass the time, and
I befriend the librarian. He is a gray-haired man with glasses
who would look like a college professor if he were dressed
differently. Everyone calls him Mr. Books, and he commands
enough respect to keep the reading room fairly quiet.

The teachers and I have very little interaction; while I
am glad to see women like Miss Lee in the prison, I am not
especially friendly to any of the instructors.

"Watch out for those lady teachers," Books warns me one
day. "Some of them are looking for a husband." He winks,
adding, "Or at least an occasional substitute."

When I nod to indicate that I understand, he continues,

"You've got to really watch out. If they don't like the way you flirt, you'll get a disciplinary report and spend a month in lockdown." His warning sounds like the voice of experience, and I take all such warnings seriously. My record is completely free of disciplinary reports, or D.R.s, as we call them, and I am not going to let any temptation compromise my release.

Among the schoolrooms I love the library most of all. I read every chance I can, and I enjoy helping others find whatever nugget of information they need. There are many times when I am alone among the books, and I relish being surrounded by quiet knowledge. Sometimes I get so lost in the stories, that I *almost* forget where I am. Such moments of bliss are not long lived, however, since the guards make regular tours through the school and library.

One day, as I move a box of donated travel books, I catch myself daydreaming about the free world. I wonder if I will be able to travel in my next job. The squeaky cart is piled high with coverless paperbacks, department-store throwaways of outdated vacation guides and novels. The books are too heavy to ship back to the publishers, so the stores send back only the covers for credit, and we receive the coverless pages for our library. It is hard to judge a book without its cover, and I am forced to read a bit of each text before I can sort them, by subject, onto the shelves.

I notice that a peg is missing from the science fiction shelf, causing it to tilt. I wonder what use some poor prisoner has found for that missing piece of wooden dowel. I improvise a temporary repair by using a large book to stabilize the plank from below. The shelf now sits with tentative balance, but it rocks if I push down on one corner. I suddenly remember seeing pegs in the storage closet.

The closet is very large and really should have a light. It will be difficult to find the small peg in the crowded space. I make a mental note to request a lamp from maintenance as I turn the handle to open the door.

When the light from the outer rooom penetrates the closet, I don't know whether to scream or laugh. Mr. Books has his left arm up the back of Miss Lee's shirt, and his right arm is awkwardly bent, disappearing under her plaid skirt. I say nothing and close the door, which seems like the only decent thing to do. The shelf can wait.

I return to the books and consider the situation. Miss Lee is a fair bit younger than Mr. Books, forty or forty-five. She is a schoolteacher who works full-time for the prison system, and he is a librarian serving a life sentence. They certainly know the risk they're taking. If they are caught, he will be locked down for months and will never return to the library; she will be relocated or flat-out fired. This type of prisoner/staff conspiracy is one of the stranger aspects of prison life, and it's not just convicts who are afraid of being caught. There are a lot of rulebreakers in prison.

I say nothing about it to either of them. Over the next few days we have only the necessary, cordial communication that work requires. I avoid them both by spending a lot of time at the repair table in the back of the library.

Bookbinding is an ancient art, and some of the older books in the library are finely crafted. We don't have any of the proper binding tools to repair the leather-bound legal tomes, or the old schoolbooks with embossed covers, but I do my best with glue and vises. The workbench is small and crowded with audio-visual equipment that I patch together for the teachers; however, I have cleared a special area for binding repairs, and I have learned a lot by dissecting the damaged volumes. I am happy to keep busy at the bench, and Mr. Books has delegated a good bit of work to me so that he is free to pursue his new chores — especially cleaning the faculty bathroom. Whenever I notice the key gone from the desk, I can be sure that Mr. Books is scrubbing away.

As the weeks go by, I feel increasingly nervous for the lovers. Whenever I see the guards approaching, I instinctively check to make sure that Mr. Books is in plain sight, and he usually is. Although the guards intend to surprise us with their inspections, over the years Mr. Books has become an accomplished student of their habits.

One day at noon I see two guards approaching, talking casually as they look around. This is not a scheduled inspection. I glance at the librarian's desk, but there is no sign of Mr. Books or Miss Lee. As quickly as I can without attracting the guards' attention, I check the desk — no bathroom key.

I cross the room, faster than I should, and knock on the door.

"You better stop *scrubbing*, Mr. Books; the guards are coming."

A moment later Mr. Books emerges from the bathroom with a

garbage can. There is no trash in it, so I throw in a couple of damaged books. He walks past the guards as they stroll along the shelves.

I warn Mr. Books: "You've got to have someone watch out for you, otherwise you two are going to get caught."

The old man is contrite, like a kid caught with his hand in the cookie jar. "Thanks, Johnson. What do I owe you for saving me?"

"Nothin', man. Just let someone know when you're cleaning the bathroom."

A week later he again asks me what I want for helping him out. "Look, Johnson, Miss Lee insists that we get you something. If you don't tell me what you want, she'll probably get you a fruit basket or a calculator."

I laugh. "Well, I don't want a calculator, but she can get me some vitamins or weightlifting supplements if she wants. Those aren't contraband."

"Consider it done," he says.

The next day a box of vitamins and PowerBars appear on the repair bench. The gift inspires me to work out harder and longer. I am proud of the way I look, and I feel fortunate to have Miss Lee supplying my nutritional needs. Unfortunately, Mr. Books sees the potential of his relationship in a new light because of these gifts. Soon, he asks for some vitamins, too. And then shampoo, and cologne, and liquor, and pot. After a while, he's like the Avon man, selling products to the other prisoners and taking orders for more. Eventually, the money goes to his head, and his prison-store rivals become jealous.

After a couple of months the guards figured it out, or someone told them. They didn't catch them in the act, probably because they didn't want to, but it was over. Mr. Books went under lockdown (pending investigation), and we never saw Miss Lee again, though I heard that she was simply transferred to a new prison. Later, Books was released from solitary without a hearing, and he went back to being a book lender instead of a drugstore. He looked a little worse for wear, but at least he kept his job, and he never gave me advice about women again.

▓ The criminal justice system is controlled by those it employs. That obvious fact can have serious consequences for convicts. Mistakes in the record become part of the official history, and reversing those mistakes requires the cooperation of the very people who made them. In my case the sexual assault charges that I was never tried on (because unlike the perpetrator, I was circumcised) were somehow entered into my official record. The parole board wanted nothing to do with me once they read this false history. According to their documents I had pleaded guilty to burglary, possession of a weapon, *and* sexual assault. Therefore, even though I was an ideal prisoner, my parole folder was dead-docketed – not even considered.

I didn't know any of this until my family requested a meeting with the parole board. During that meeting they were told that I was considered a high risk to the public because of the sexual nature of my offenses. My family was perplexed. I had pleaded guilty only to burglary and possession of a pocketknife.

"This record's not correct," my dad tried to explain to the board, but they believed the official paperwork was accurate. It took my family months to get the true version of my conviction to the parole board. I find it hard to believe that the error was just an oversight by the district attorney's office. (That office continued to supply erroneous documents related to my case even after I was released.)

In the prison system even if the official record is flawed, it will always triumph over the truth, unless you can afford excellent legal help. Fortunately, my family was willing to spend whatever they could to get the truth out. Once the parole board heard the correct version of my sentence, they judged me according to the merits of my case. I had a stellar prison record and had never committed a violent crime. The fact that the prisons were overcrowded was also in my favor. After twenty months behind bars, the board decided that I could serve the rest of my sentence on parole.

On the day before New Year's Eve, 1982, I participate in a ritual that I had seen dozens of others enact: I give away all my possessions (only the most destitute prisoners, with no one on the outside, keep their belongings). As I stand on the border between the free world and prison, I consider the exchange rate: what would a precious transistor radio be worth on the outside? I distribute my toiletries, headphones, books, stamps, everything that has added value in prison. I keep only my notebook and the clothes my family has brought for me to wear to freedom.

If you don't have family to bring you fresh clothes, the prison issues a donated set; and if no one is coming to pick you up, they'll give you a bus ticket—one way. I am one of the fortunate ones, and today I am thankful for my loving parents. My dad is there when the last door slams behind me.

There is a superstition among prisoners: "When you leave," they told me, "don't look back—or else you'll return."

We walk together to the parking lot, beneath an overcast sky, and I do not look back. On the ride home, I cannot believe the beauty of the landscape flying by. Pops talks easily about plans and memories, but I just can't wait to scrub the prison dust from my skin. We will be going to their new, smaller home in College Park.

When the door opens, the first thing I notice is that Mom is visibly weaker. I understand now why she has dropped her lucrative Mary Kay business: she has a hard time just walking around. Somehow, she has managed to cook all my favorite foods, and they even have a bottle of champagne to celebrate my freedom. I eat everything, but I don't have any alcohol. My mistakes are behind me, and I begin a disciplined life of perfect legality and propriety. After dessert, I take the hottest bath I can stand.

By the time I get out of the tub, the sun is setting and I stroll onto the porch to enjoy the horizon. I notice some crumbs on the floor and grab a broom to sweep them off the ledge. When the job is about halfway done, I hear Beth, my fiancée, come in, but for some reason I just keep on sweeping. I am so used to the slow routine of prison that instant joy is not an available emotion. When she comes onto the porch, I say hello but continue my sweeping.

It's hard for those around me to understand my adjustment. They seem to think that freedom is made of pleasant events and special pleasures. But it wasn't food or a hot bath that I really craved for twenty months. It wasn't even the company of those I love that I missed most. It was simply freedom, and freedom takes some getting used to. When I finish sweeping, we embrace.

My parole officer is a man who projects a sense of exhaustion and overwork. After living with criminals for two years, I understand how unpleasant his job must be. I am sure that he started out as a caring, nurturing idealist. But his caseload is so heavy, and the recidivism rate so high, that he no doubt is just treading water. He seems pleased with my attitude and is genuinely surprised when I tell him that I have a job. He shakes his head happily when I give him a complete list of addresses and phone numbers of everywhere I might go.

"Who's Beth Bailey?" he asks, peering at me from over his glasses.

"That's my girlfriend, sir. I spend a lot of time over there on Friday evenings."

"You know you have a midnight curfew?" he asks. He tilts his head and raises his brow.

"Yes, sir."

He looks over my employment papers from the courier company. "And all you have is a bicycle for transportation?"

"I'm gonna get a car as soon as I can afford one. But for now my dad can take me to work, especially if it's raining."

He sort of smiles. "Looks like you're well on your way, Johnson." He leans back in his chair and seems to relax a bit for the first time. "If you're a little over the curfew at your girlfriend's, just give me a call so I know where you are, okay?"

"Thank you, sir."

"Keep your appointment with me each month, and everything should work out fine."

"Yes, sir."

My life is so organized that my parole officer never has to wonder where I am.

Dad gets me up at 4:00 A.M., and we ride to work by 5:30. After work I go to the gym and lift weights until suppertime. Every evening, except Friday and Saturday, I am at home with my family; and any evening that I am not at home, I am at my girlfriend's with her family. I do not even call my old friends. I stay busy and focused, because I have two years to make up for.

The courier company is the same one that employed me part-time when I was in college. I told them about my record, but they didn't seem perturbed, and they always need good drivers. While I am earning only a fraction of what I had been making at Delta, I know that just having a job is essential to my self-esteem. It is important for a man to earn his own money, and the little that I make saves me from having to ask others for help.

Work, gym, home, sleep. By March the pattern is firmly established, and Monday the fourteenth is just another workday. I finish my shift and head out into the warm spring afternoon. As usual, I work out at the gym and then take the bus home. There is something so peaceful about a bus ride. You can mull over your thoughts and just gaze out the window without being disturbed. The quiet, sporadic conversations going on about me are like the chatter of birds, and I like to hear other people laugh, even when the joke is unintelligible. I have no idea that I am enjoying my last day of freedom for sixteen years.

I leave from the side of the bus and begin the short walk home. This walk is usually my final unwinding before entering the bustling house. It is a time for deep breathing and inspiration. However, there is something odd about this day. The weather is perfect—spring in Georgia can start as early as December, and by March the crocuses, daffodils, and even the tulips are in bloom. Yet an unseen thing oppresses me. Although there is no one in sight, I have the strange feeling that I am being watched—not benevolently but maliciously. It is a feeling I have not had since being in prison. In fact, it is more intense than the way I felt in prison, because I am completely alone. Alone, that is, except for this dark feeling. I consider that tomorrow is the ides of March, the day Caesar was ambushed. I try to convince myself that I am just being paranoid, yet I sense it isn't so.

My steps, which should be silent, seem to scream out that I am alone and vulnerable. I slow down, but every noise is amplified.

There is a stretch of thick Georgia pines just ahead; it will happen there, I am convinced. As I get closer to the woods, I peer intently into the underbrush and let my eyes follow the gaps into darkness. A sparrow flies out between branches, and I wonder what she has seen. Something moves in my peripheral vision—a branch or falling leaf, and I can now feel my blood's ebb and flow.

I do not want to cross the small bridge over the creek, but there is no use running. I will walk to my destiny. I don't know what is looming ahead, but I am sure that some lethal malevolence awaits me. Suddenly, like a dream—a childhood miracle—my mother's car rounds the corner. She is as unexpected as lightning on a clear day, and I feel my feet begin to run toward her the way they did when I was a boy. As the car approaches, her smile materializes behind the windshield. She is happy to see me, but I am just relieved.

I say nothing about my premonition; she has been through enough on account of me. We enter the house together. Dad is there, too. I don't tell him either. I am home, and home is safe. My life is in perfect order, I have no enemies, I have broken no laws. I am a good son. Then the knocking: sharp bangs on the door. Not a pleasant request for entry, but a demand, the official weight of the state behind each knuckle.

Mom opens the door. An officer, plainclothes, now two of them, several cars parked out front.

I hear my name, and they produce the cuffs. There is no time to prepare. No one asks if I would like to pack a bag, make a call, go to the bathroom. I am the state's property, and its agents will dispense with me according to their rules. Love, family, even bodily functions must be suspended for the awesome power of the police. I am under arrest.

I review my activities—not because I think there is any hint of wrongdoing, but because I want to be sure that all of my movements are known. I have hardly had a moment alone in the ten weeks since my release, so this should be an easy matter to settle. Yes, this is a terrible mistake, and it will soon be straightened out. No one could actually build a case against an innocent man, one who has reported his every step. This is a mistake, and it will soon be straightened out. Phrases repeat in my mind. I was at work, and then the gym, and then at home. I was never alone. This is a mistake, and soon it will be straightened out.

The house is surrounded. Officers emerge from our backyard, the bushes, the neighbors' shrubs.

"Why me? This is a mistake! I haven't done anything." It must have been them in the woods; the dark feeling was real. Were they hoping I would run?

"This is a mistake! I don't know what you're talking about. . . ." I recognize the officers—they are the ones who accused me of the assaults two years ago.

"We got you this time," one of them says.

It is best for me not to say anything; they will not change their minds. It is a mistake, and it will soon be straightened out.

An echo rings in my head, words from the past. The officer beside me—it was two years ago—he said it then: "We'll get you next time. Your kind always repeats, and we'll be ready."

I calm myself. Thank God that my every minute is accounted for, because I *do* have enemies. These two officers really believe I did something. Thank God this will never go to trial.

At the Clayton County jail I am photographed, and I learn that there were two rapes during the previous week, one in Fulton County, where I live, and another a few miles over the line in Clayton County. The attacks are so similar that the police are sure it was the same perpetrator. Apparently, the two officers are convinced that I am a rapist. It is ludicrous, but they still think I committed that attack two years ago—even though the perpetrator was uncircumcised. *How can these men still think I'm the guy?* I had no idea that they were out to get me, but as soon as I was released in December they began showing my old arrest photo to rape victims.

Two days after I am booked, there is a live lineup. Me and six other black prisoners. They have us say something to the one-way glass. On the other side of the glass are the victims, the detectives, and my lawyer. I hate every second of this justice roulette. There are seven of us. What if pure chance falls on me? One out of seven.

As soon as it's over, my lawyer comes to see me. He is very confident of success.

"She picked someone else out," he says with a smile.

I am relieved. "Can I go home now?"

"The cops will probably still want to keep you overnight—until the hearing—but I'm sure that the judge will dismiss it in the morning.

One more night behind bars is not enough to shake my confidence, but it is disturbing. The Clayton County jail is an overcrowded dormitory, and everything here seems forty years out of date. Most distressing is the attitude of the guards and prisoners in terms of race. The black inmates have a slavelike mentality and don't trust anything that a fellow black man says. Several times I answer questions for other prisoners, but my answers are disregarded until verified by any white man. It is a twilight-zone experience, back to the Jim Crow days of deep southern prejudice — *white folks know stuff.* This type of nostalgia does not bode well for my chances of a fair hearing. Nonetheless, the charges are so absurd, and my alibi so airtight, that I don't fear being sent to prison.

Clayton County is predominantly white. The jail, however, like all jails, contains more than its share of black men. I am surprised, however, that there are some majority-white dormitories here; that is never the case in Georgia prisons. In prison, African Americans are the definite majority.

Before my hearing, a black prisoner arrives from Alto in North Georgia. In Alto you have to fight to survive, and this man is primed for battle. All day long he seems nervous, and some men, like wolves, are attracted to the smell of fear. During the night I am awakened by the sound of an altercation. I have no idea what they are fighting over, but it doesn't matter. I know better than to interfere with fighting inmates. It seems especially prudent to feign sleep, since it is a black-and-white fight in a cell where five black men sleep with twenty-five whites. The guy from Alto is small but scrappy, and he is fighting his heart out against a bigger opponent.

From my pillow I notice several white prisoners rising from their beds and heading toward the combatants. One white guy in particular is getting quite close to the action — suddenly he reaches over and grabs the Alto man from behind.

The adrenaline shoots into my blood; I can't just watch them jump this guy. I tumble from my bed and stop the closest bystander from interfering. There is some sense of civilization in a clean fight between two men, but mob battles bring only chaos and crazy violence.

"Hey!" I shout at him. "They'll be no double-teaming, no triple-teaming, nothing!"

Everything stops for a moment. "We'll just break it up now, or let it be clean." The authority in my voice surprises even me. I am not that big, and the racial balance is not in my favor; there is no physical reason for the men to even listen to me. But the fight stops — just like that.

The next day the man from Alto thanks me. "Man, I never thought that you'd come down off your bunk to help me out. Nobody else would do something like that."

"I surprised myself," I say honestly. "I just didn't like the odds you were facing. You were doing your best. I've never seen anyone fight so hard."

"Cowards die," he says with the solemnity of scripture.

It's decided that I will face the Clayton County charges first. My lawyer explains that there are three phases: The preliminary hearing gives the judge a chance to throw out the charges after looking at the initial evidence. If the judge upholds the charges, then a grand jury is convened to consider whether an indictment should be issued. If an indictment is issued, then we can plead or go to trial. He thinks the judge will throw out the charges at the hearing – the absurdity of the case against me is evident. The hearing is a quick, informal affair. My lawyer is present along with the officers, the judge, and the victim. I see her for the first time: she has a prominent nose, and she is white. I wonder why she is doing this.

Did the officers put her up to it? Does she have a relative who's in trouble? Maybe the cops promised her some help if she would accuse me of a crime. She looks as if she has not had an easy life; she's no goody-two-shoes. Was she actually raped? How could she believe it was me?

She is asked how she had identified the accused. She states that it was from a photographic lineup. My lawyer asks her if the pictures were black-and-white or color. She can't remember. "I think they were color," she says.

The officers testify that the photos were black-and-white; the judge asks to see the pictures, and he is handed the tiny mug shots. My lawyer asks the victim if she identified me in the live lineup. She did not; she identified someone else. The judge seems to appreciate the discrepancies and deliberates for a few minutes. I share my lawyer's confidence that he will release me immediately.

The photo that they had shown the victims was from my arrest twenty months before. At that time I was clean-shaven, just like the perpetrator. However, at the time of the attacks, I actually had a full beard and mustache. In order to prove that I was not the clean-shaven perpetrator, my lawyer shows the judge my work I.D. In that photo, taken around the time of the rapes, I have a full beard and moustache, just as I now appear before the judge.

When the victim's original description of the attacker is read, it describes a man without any facial hair. I turn to my lawyer, touching my beard, and we are both quite sure that the judge will dismiss the charges. They could never go to trial with all these contradictions. It wouldn't even make it through a grand jury.

At the end of the hearing the judge examines all the documents on his table. It is obvious to me that he is going to dismiss the charges, and I whisper to my lawyer, "Can I leave as soon as he announces his decision?" My counsel nods just as the judge begins to speak.

"The prisoner will continue to be held without bond until the grand jury convenes." The words punch my stomach like a fist.

"Don't worry," my lawyer says, "the grand jury won't indict."

I am back in jail and have recovered from the shock of the hearing. My lawyer, Kenneth Secret, is confident that it will all end very soon. He reminds me that I have been in jail for only a few days, and another week or two won't kill me. Mr. Secret is so confident that he appears cocky. He tells me that I'll have to submit to blood and hair tests, but he smiles when he says it. We both know that the more evidence they collect, the closer I am to going home.

The blood is taken by a trained phlebotomist, but the hair sampling is a true indignity.

"One more from your arm, and then we'll start with the beard and moustache. . . ." They take samples from every part of my face. "Let's take some from the back, and then a few around the nipples." They tell me to remove my pants. "Mr. Johnson, bend over, we need some hairs. . . ."

A few weeks later we hear the good news from the lab. My lawyer has such a big smile when he comes to see me that I am sure I will going home that very day.

He makes some chit-chat about my family and then says, "Well, the hair and blood analysis came back, and they look very good." He opens his briefcase and shows me the photocopies.

"You're O positive and so is the perpetrator—but that's okay; forty percent of the population is."

"So what's the good news?" I ask.

"The fibers don't match."

"The hair?"

"Right. They found one pubic hair in her bed that belongs to a black man, but it doesn't match hair from anywhere on your body. Their own crime lab says so, which means that we don't have to hire our own experts."

"Can I go home now?"

"I'm sure it will be soon. The live lineup failed, and now the physical evidence doesn't match. The victim was very clear that she never had a black man in her apartment, let alone her bed, until the night of the attack. That hair assures your freedom."

The district attorney responds immediately but not by dropping the charges. Instead, he has another set of hair samples taken from all over my body—places where I didn't know hair could grow. He is clearly worried about the fiber evidence, but he wants a conviction badly enough to ignore his own test results.

A week later my lawyer visits me with the new test results.

"Great news, Calvin. The new fibers are just like the first set. There is no match between your hair and the one in her bed—you're off the hook!"

"Can I go home now?"

"Just as soon as I can meet with the D.A. Even if the grand jury indicts, it would be embarrassing for him to go to a trial with this type of evidence."

The next time I see my lawyer, he says the grand jury has issued an indictment, but he still seems absolutely certain that justice will prevail. When I ask him how it went with the D.A., he tells me that things didn't quite go the way we had planned.

"So, what did happen?" I ask.

"Well, the D.A. himself is going to try the case."

The shock registers on my face, and my counsel attempts to explain. "Apparently, there is a lot riding on this case for him, and he is not disposed to dropping it."

"He doesn't still think I did it, does he?"

"Calvin, the only thing that matters to the D.A. is can he win."

"Win? This is a trial for my life, not some kind of debate club! Didn't he read the fiber reports?"

"Look, everything is okay—I'm sure that our case is airtight. We just might have to try it before a jury."

I tell him that I am starting to feel anxious but not worried that we might actually lose. It's just dragging on much longer than I had expected. A trial seems like a lot of trouble to go through just to prove such an obvious case. My lawyer assures me that many of his clients have to go to trial for trivial matters, but the judge usually dismisses the charges when only weak or contradictory evidence is presented.

We are so confident that I never even ask the obvious question, "What if we do lose?" In fact, I hardly prepare for my own testimony at all, because I don't think that the trial will go that far. Besides, I just have to tell the truth; it's best not to overprepare. I don't want to sound rehearsed. The truth, after all, is a simple matter.

Jury of My Peers

On the eve of my trial I try to rest. I read a bit then quietly
meditate in bed until long after lights-out. Shortly after I
fall asleep I am roused by the squeak of the intercom:
"Johnson, your lawyer is here to see you." No one ever
visits this late.

He is dressed in a silk suit and smells vaguely of alcohol
and aftershave. His female companion does not seem to be
involved in legal affairs, and her presence, complete with
sequined evening gown, is disconcerting. As we sit down at
the small table, I am dumbfounded. I can't imagine what
purpose this visit can serve. Surely, he has prepared the
case fully by now; he has been so confident all along.

I am distressed by the strange hesitation in his
movements. It is just hours before the trial, and for the
first time he mentions possible "trouble." It doesn't sink
in right away that "trouble" might mean a lifetime in jail.
I still have faith in the justice system.

"Why are you so tentative now?" I ask him. "All along you've said it was an open-and-shut case – this is not the time to *start* preparing for a tough fight!" I cannot suppress my anger.

The young woman in sequins yawns. My attorney rubs her thigh, as if he's bringing a child back to attention in church. Apparently, visiting his client in jail is not an aphrodisiac. She is bored.

"Are you ready for tomorrow?" I ask him seriously.

He affects a casual tone. "Much of it will be procedural, so we should be covered."

"What does that mean?"

"Everything is fine," he answers. His obviously constrained voice opposes his words, but there is nothing to be gained by pressing him. "Just get some sleep," he says.

I don't sleep a wink. My stomach boils and rumbles till dawn. I pray, I talk to myself, I try to rest, but for the first time I am worried about a conviction. I know that my alibi is airtight, that the fiber evidence excludes me, and that the real perpetrator is clean-shaven. Any reasonable jury, any responsible judge, will not allow the conviction of a man so clearly innocent.

On the morning of November 2, 1983, I am led in chains and prison jumper to the courthouse. At the holding cell the shackles are removed, and I put on a suit. Unfortunately, I had let one of the inmates try to cut my hair, and I have ended up nearly shaving off all his handiwork. It is not a particularly handsome look, but my beard and moustache give me enough hair to appear reasonable.

Inside the courtroom a large pool of potential jurors are questioned by my lawyer, Kenneth Secret, and the district attorney, Robert Keller. It is impossible to ignore the overwhelmingly white majority in the room. In fact, I notice that there are only two black people in the jury pool, and both of them are weeded out as the selection proceeds. I will be tried by an all-white jury. The only black people remaining in the courtroom are my lawyer and me.

It doesn't matter, I assure myself. *There is no reason to suspect prejudice. The color of the jury is unimportant. I just want the very best "tryers of fact."* The accusations against me are so ludicrous, and the evidence so overwhelmingly in my favor, that my only concern is to exclude simpletons who might be swayed by emotional arguments. White or black, I need them to listen carefully and decide honestly.

It is a terrible thing to be judged by strangers who can take away the rest of your life. I had always imagined that such matters are carefully deliberated: the details double-checked, everyone seeking the truth diligently. I am in for a rude awakening.

My easygoing charm and confidence have always made me comfortable with strangers, and I have never really felt the sting of prejudice. I don't have any white neighbors, but my white coworkers have always treated me with respect and fairness. So, I have no reason to suspect that the jurors will be prejudiced—until I look at the chosen twelve. On their faces I see only scowls of disgust. The trial has not even begun, and already they have decided that I am worthy of scorn. A sudden chill nearly shuts down my heart.

All they know about me is how I look and that I am accused of rape, aggravated sodomy, and robbery. While the judge instructs them, I let my eyes survey their faces once again. Every one of them looks back at me with righteous indignation. I lose all hope of a fair "trial of facts." There will be no real trial; it will be about a black man who was arrested by the police for raping two white women. This is 1983, but it might as well be 1923. I am probably going to prison.

Before the trial begins, the jury is removed from the court, and my lawyer asks to examine the indictment against me. This document is the result of the grand jury hearing, which briefly considered the evidence against me and decided that charges were to be brought forward. I was not called to testify before the grand jury and have not reviewed its records.

My lawyer begins reading the indictment at the judge's bench, and his jaw literally drops. The first page wrongly states that I have been previously convicted of "criminal attempt to commit rape, burglary, aggravated assault, sodomy, and armed robbery." Most of the indictment sheet is typed, but those charges are handwritten at the top of the page. It is a frightening mistake, and my counsel instantly submits a motion to "quash" or stop the trial. Because the law forbids trial judges from correcting flawed indictments, a new grand jury will have to reindict me in order to correct the record.

This mistake in the indictment stems from the suspiciously bad paperwork that has plagued my record. My lawyer asks for a minute to speak with me, and I go over the details with him again.

"When I pleaded guilty to the burglary in 1981, the police had questioned me about a series of assaults in the neighborhood. For a while they charged me with those assaults, but the charges were subsequently dropped, because the primary victim stated emphatically that the attacker was uncircumcised. Of course, I never pleaded guilty to those charges, and they should never have been written on my plea record."

Pointing to the charges, my lawyer says, "That is not true. We think there is false information in the indictment, Your Honor. Mr. Johnson was convicted only of burglary, and the remaining charges were dead-docketed by Judge Eldridge in the superior court." He hands the judge the document. "That information is highly prejudicial, and as the court is aware, an indictment cannot be amended by the court. There must be a reindictment, if in fact the court finds the indictment defective."

In our first indication of how the judge will run his court, he overrules our motion. He replies that the jury has not read that portion of the indictment—and they will never hear about it. In his opinion the erroneous indictment doesn't need to be addressed by him at all.

Who will address it, then, I wonder.

The judge finishes his ruling, saying that the previous conviction will come into play only during the sentencing phase; and since he is now well aware that the record is grossly inaccurate, there will be no problem.

As I listen, I know that this paperwork error is a terrible thing that might follow me for the rest of my life. When the government makes a mistake, it doesn't have to fear punishment. Since there are no consequences to suffer, the state can afford negligence; besides, exposure of an error might affect someone's career.

I suspect that the erroneous record is no accident. The indictment reads the way it does because someone wants it to. When I confessed two years earlier to the burglary, I was assured that the rest of the charges had been thrown out. I had no way of knowing that a false record had been entered. Even though my family pointed out the error to the parole board a year ago, no one has fixed the actual record. It would have taken no more than a letter from the D.A., but he, the parole board, and now the judge see no reason to follow up on it.

My lawyer's next motion requests that we be given copies of the victims' statements to police. The prosecutors have a series of weird events that they plan to bring up during the trial—without actually charging me with any new crimes. We don't even have the official police reports of those incidents, but the prosecutors are going to offer them as evidence of "similar transactions." Without copies of those original reports, my defense will be handicapped.

We also request a copy of the original photographic lineup that was shown to the victims. This is important, since three of the four victims who picked out my photo also picked someone else in the live lineup.

For all his arguments about paperwork and police reports, the only concession that my lawyer wins is that the judge will look at the police reports (without sharing them with us) and decide if anything in them is exculpatory. After a few minutes the judge reports that he has found nothing exculpatory in the police reports, and there is no reason for the defense to see them.

My lawyer files several other motions, the most important of which concerns the identification process. The rape victim picked out someone other than me during the live lineup but then claimed that she lied *on purpose* about the identification. It is a strange and convoluted explanation, and we argue that her identification of me in open court should not be allowed. This type of identification during the trial is pure showmanship anyway, since it is obvious that the accused sits at the defense table beside his lawyer.

The story of the identification process is a textbook case of prejudice. The victim, Miss Mitchell, had testified in the preliminary trial that she picked me out from a series of color photos a detective showed her. But the police did not have any color photos of me. They had indeed shown her some color images, but mine was not among them. The only picture of me they showed the victims was a small black-and-white one, the mug shot from my arrest nearly two years before. In that picture I'm sporting a light moustache but am otherwise clean-shaven.

In order for the judge to decide whether to allow the courtroom identification, Miss Mitchell is asked to explain how she identified me.

I listen in amazement as she changes her story. She now says that she identified me from a group of black-and-white photos. She then fudges her initial description of the rapist. Originally, she told police that he had no facial hair, except perhaps stubble. Now she implies he might have had a beard. Of course, the most obvious hole in her identification is that she picked a different man from the live lineup as her attacker. She picked number five; I was number three.

The photo identification was not observed by my lawyer. However, he was able to witness the live lineup. He tried to make sure there was no obvious bias at the viewing, and it was by far the most thorough part of the identification process. The victim was given the opportunity to view us through a one-way glass; we were asked to turn around, to look in certain directions, and to say something. Clearly, this procedure was more informational than a two-year-old, black-and-white photo of me without a beard. We are confident that the judge will rule in our favor on this one, once he hears all the testimony.

My lawyer cross-examines the victim about the lineup.

"Ms. Mitchell, upon what do you base your picking number five out of the physical lineup?

"I don't know — I did pick out number five that day."

"You did not pick out Calvin Johnson?"

"No."

"So, the person that you did pick out — did you base that upon what you had seen at the incident?"

"No, I don't believe — I didn't. I just wanted to pick someone out and get out of there."

"You 'just wanted to pick somebody out and get out of there'? So, at the time that you picked out the person that you did pick out, did you believe at that moment he was the person that assaulted you?"

"Not really."

"You did not?"

"I don't believe so."

"So, are you saying that when you signed the affidavit, when you picked the person and you signed your name to it, that it was not true?"

"More or less, yes, that's about right."

"Are you saying that you lied?"

"Yes, sir." She looks down. "To myself also, probably."

When the prosecutor questions her about this same point, he also asks her why she had identified the wrong man in the lineup.

"Now, why did you give that answer?"

"I just went in, and even though they had told me to take my time and look at each one, . . ." she says and pauses. "I took–you know, I didn't take very much time. I didn't look at each one carefully, and I more or less just wouldn't really look at him in the lineup. I just pushed my eyes away from him and picked someone else."

"At the time that you picked someone else out, did you know that you had not really identified the correct person?"

"I felt like I did." She looks at the judge. "I mean, I felt like I had picked the wrong one."

In every trial there is a dramatic moment when the victim is asked to point to the man in the courtroom (if he is there) who committed the crime. Of course, Miss Mitchell, who misidentified me in the live lineup, had no trouble picking me out in the preliminary hearing, and she accomplishes the same amazing feat now before the judge.

My lawyer tries to point out the utter uselessness of such an identification.

"Ms. Mitchell, at the preliminary hearing do you remember how Mr. Johnson was dressed?"

"No, sir."

"Did he have on prisoner's dungarees?" (It is not hard to identify the prisoner when he is dressed in prison clothing.)

"I don't remember."

"Other than myself, was there any other black man in that room?"

"I don't remember."

"The fact of the matter is, there wasn't. Of course, at the time of that preliminary hearing, Mr. Johnson was sitting there with me at the counsel table, was he not, as he is today?"

"Yes, sir."

The courtroom identification is a sham, but the prosecutor stresses it over and over again, as if it is the gold standard of identification. Since she can pick me out in the courtroom, he contends, I must be the guy.

We continue to press the identification issue using a different tack. The victim's testimony about facial hair is very important, and we again try to convince the judge that her identification is so tainted that it should not be allowed. We explain that we have several witnesses, including my boss, who can testify that I had a full beard and mustache when the rapes occurred. We enter my work I.D. into evidence. This photo was taken around the time of the rapes and shows my well-developed beard and mustache. In contrast, the pictures used to identify me as the perpetrator were tiny black-and-white photos from 1981, when I had no beard. We stress this again, hoping that the judge will act sensibly.

My lawyer, Mr. Secret, asks the victim about her attacker's facial hair.

"Ms. Mitchell, at the time you spoke to the first police officer about the assailant, you were asked specific questions about facial hair; is that correct?"

"I'm sure I was."

"You responded to those questions, 'I didn't recall any facial hair.' Is that correct?"

"I told them I didn't feel any on his face," she says, pausing to recall. "I don't know. He may have had it, yes. I mean, it may have been down here," she says, placing her fingertips on the underside of her jaw. "That's what I said then."

"In fact, you said, 'I don't recall any facial hair. There may have been stubble but no full beard.' Isn't that correct?"

"What?" she seems surprised. "There may have been—or is that what I said?"

He repeats the phrases from her official description. "'There may have been stubble, but there was no full beard.' Is that what you said? Is that what you told the police?"

"Uh-huh, I believe so."

"On the day that you viewed the lineup of Mr. Johnson, he had a full-grown beard?"

"Uh-huh, he had a lot, quite a bit."

"Just like it is today?"

"Similar, yes."

"In fact, the photograph from which you picked Mr. Johnson," Mr. Secret says as he points to one of the sheets of evidence, "this array here, in that photograph he does not have a beard, does he?"

"Right."

I want to scream, *So what am I doing here?*

Next, the prosecutor takes his turn questioning the victim. He tries to equate my full beard and mustache with her "may have been stubble" comment. It is a ridiculous equation, but the judge seems to take his word as Gospel. Somehow, the judge accepts the prosecutor's conflicting statements: the victim got a good look at her attacker; she picked the photo of a man without a beard; in the live lineup she did not pick Calvin Johnson (who has a beard); Calvin Johnson is the attacker.

Everyone who knows me is ready to testify that I had a full beard at the time, but my witnesses (like myself and my lawyer) are black. As much as I want to believe that justice is blind, the simple fact seems to be that race is important to a "jury of peers."

The prosecutor tries to bolster the victim's identification with the following exchange.

"Lori, how long on March 9th did this whole thing take place, your contact with Mr. Johnson?"

(I cringe at hearing my name. I had never met this woman until my pretrial hearing.)

"I'm not sure how long it was — I was passed out for a while, but it may have been, maybe a half hour, more or less."

"And during the period of time that you were conscious, how long did you have an opportunity to view his facial features?"

"If the whole attack was a half-hour, half of that time, maybe."

The prosecutor is satisfied that she got a good look at the man, but the judge tries to insert a modicum of doubt. He assumes a tone that is both understanding and stern, but sympathy seems to get the better of him as he asks her a question. "Ms. Mitchell, these are extremely upsetting charges, and I know that you as the alleged victim are extremely upset. But the court would like to ask you again. You have admitted that you made a mistake in identification one time. I would just like you to realize that you are under oath now."

"Yes, sir."

"And it is extremely important that you know what you are doing, and that you take your time." He looks at her with his brow raised. "Are you sure that you can identify the individual that's here today positively?"

"Yes, sir."

"You are sure?"

"Yes, sir."

"All right. That's all the court wants."

The second pretrial witness is Detective Storey. He conducted much of the investigation, including the original interview with the victim, and the photo lineups. He is also one of the officers who arrested me back in 1981. He and his partner charged me with a rape, but those charges were not pursued, because the victim was positive that her attacker was not circumcised. Somehow, the two detectives still think I did it. "We'll get you next time. Your kind always repeats, and we'll be ready"—the cop's words still echo in my mind. I had been on parole less than three months when they arrested me for Miss Mitchell's rape.

My lawyer questions Officer Storey about the victim's description of facial hair. The detective's evasion is almost comic.

My lawyer asks, "What description did she give you?"

"About six foot, medium built."

"That was the extent of it?"

"Short hair, no accent."

"No accent? Did she say anything about facial hair?"

"She said it was either no facial hair or either light facial hair." He looks disinterested.

"In fact, she said there was either 'no facial hair or there was stubble,' isn't that correct?"

"Well, I consider 'stubble' light facial hair."

"And on the day that you arrested Mr. Johnson, how would you describe his facial hair?"

"Well, he appeared to have a day or two growth of beard."

(I must be the only man in America who can grow a full beard in "a day or two." I knew that the detective might stretch the truth, but it is still shocking to hear his brazen lies under oath.)

My lawyer tries to reason with the judge again. He is eloquent, but I fear he will have no effect. "Your Honor, I think our argument is obvious," he says, and his voice betrays our frustration. "Ms. Mitchell's identification is so — ," he shakes his head, "it just borders upon being grossly unjust for her to even be allowed to take the stand and testify in this case. She admits, Your Honor, that on the occasion she went to a lineup at the city jail, she conscientiously — viciously, I would say — lied that a person she identified was in fact the perpetrator of the crime against her. 'I lied,' she said. So what are we to believe? Is she telling the truth now? Was she telling the truth at the lineup? If so, then why isn't the one she identified standing up here, indicted for the offense of rape?

"You don't have to go into what stubble is in comparison to a beard, Your Honor. If the court takes a look at these photographs, the court can see that the beard is exactly the same as the beard that he has right now. The victim never said anything about facial hair. The initial photograph of the defendant that she picked out was clean-shaven except for a moustache."

The judge listens impassively, and my lawyer continues his plea. "I think that the identification of Ms. Mitchell ought to be suppressed, most specifically based upon her initial falsification. Your Honor, this man is charged with rape, and that jury is going to make a determination on his life."

He points to me and concludes his argument. "She saw him at the lineup and didn't pick him out. She picked out someone else, because 'I wanted to get it over with.' I think that the identification, Your Honor, is so tainted, obviously based on some pressure that she felt to get this thing over with, that it shouldn't be allowed to be presented to the jury."

In rebuttal the prosecutor once again focuses on the in-court identification and on the judge's questioning of the victim. "She has been asked at least three times, 'Do you make your identification based on what you saw of your attacker on March 9th?' She answered, 'Yes, I do, solely on that,' and then the court asked her the question, 'Are you sure?'" He turns to my lawyer: "But Mr. Secret would have this court rule that this is tainted and suggestive, because one day she didn't want to look at the animal that raped her, and therefore she is not qualified to tell this jury who it was." He turns toward me with a look that says, *You are an animal, and I will see you caged for life.*

The judge rules that the victim will be allowed to identify me in court before the jury and that the jury can decide whether she is credible or not. Another win for the prosecution. There is only one last problem to be discussed before the jury comes in. The state has decided not to call the crime lab's fiber expert to testify, so we have subpoenaed Raymond Santamaria, but he has taken ill.

My lawyer explains the situation to the judge. "Your Honor, we have a problem. I have just been informed that one of the witnesses that we have under subpoena who works for the crime lab, that's Mr. Santamaria, is ill. He left work yesterday—went home with a cold. Now they believe he has the flu."

I pray for his speedy recovery, but I am beginning to get sick myself. My lawyer promises to inform the judge as soon as Mr. Santamaria is available. The pretrial is over; the jury reenters the courtroom.

Lori Mitchell is the first witness. Since she is a prosecution witness, Mr. Keller questions her first. Her testimony begins with information about her address and place of employment. She is a manager at Waffle House.

"Now, on the evening of March 8th or early morning hours of March 9th, approximately what time did you go to bed?"

"The best I recall, eleven, something after eleven."

"And do you have a nighttime ritual that you go through, do you recall how you prepared to go to bed that particular night?"

"It may have been a little after eleven. I know I was in a hurry to get to sleep because I had to be back at work before six. I laid everything out that I needed, my scarf, my uniform and all, and then I got in bed. I had set the alarm and put the telephone beside the bed so that I could hear it better, and I was playing the radio. The radio was set where it would play and then go off automatically and the alarm would still be on. I'd done that several times before I went to sleep about eleven-thirty."

"Now, when you went to sleep that particular night, how were you dressed?"

"I was wearing a large T-shirt and a pair of underwear."

"And were those the only garments that you had on?"

"Yes, sir."

"Now, were you awakened before the alarm went off?"

"Yes, sir."

"And how were you awakened?"

"Some—someone waking me up in the night."

"And when you first were conscious enough to know that you were being waked up, were you on your stomach or were you on your back?"

"I was on my stomach."

"And where was this person who was waking you up?"

"He was sitting across my back."

"It was a he?"

"Yes, sir."

"And how was he waking you up?"

"He was pulling on my shoulders and bringing—you know, pulling me up, I guess, to wake me up."

"And do you recall if he said anything initially?"

"Initially, I don't remember exactly what he said, and I couldn't really understand what he was saying. I don't hear well out of this ear, my right ear, and he was speaking more to this way."

"And what was your response when you first woke up at that time?"

"Well, at first I was just—I wasn't quite awake. I was waking up and realizing that I was being woke up and that there was someone on my back, and my response took a few seconds or so. I realized that it was someone I did not know, and that it wasn't anyone I did know, and that something was wrong, you know, I was in trouble. And that was when I went to get off the bed. And as I was coming off the bed, I felt a belt go over my neck. I tried to go to the window but barely made it. I did strike at it, but the belt was around my neck, and he pulled on it and continued pulling. I was struggling, and he continued pulling, and then I was on my knees and the belt was still on my neck, and he was pushing my head into the bed and continuing to pull on the belt until I passed out."

The courtroom is silent except for her voice and irregular breathing. She speaks in a controlled, soft tone, but the horror of her experience is felt below the surface, like a shark beneath a raft.

The D.A. continues. "Now, was a towel present on the bed?"

"Yes, I believe when he was first waking me up, I believe he was trying to get that around my head."

"And did you feel something like a towel around you?"

"Yes."

"Then after you lost consciousness, what is the next thing that you remember?"

She takes a deep and troubled breath. "The next thing that I remember was that he was—I was on the bed, and he was having anal sex at that time."

"Now, how were you clothed at the time?"

"The T-shirt was still on, underwear were half torn off," she answers weakly, as if distracted.

The D.A. is clearly giving her leading questions, but she is so upset by the memory that she begins to stumble.

He asks her, "And at this time, or before this time, as you recall, was there any conversation that you had with him or he had with you?"

"When he had said that—I don't know if it was before then—he had spoke some things." She struggles to gain focus, "I really don't recall right now what they were. . . . I don't remember what he had said before then."

The D.A. tries to refocus his witness. "Let me just ask you this. During this whole ordeal, what do you recall that he actually said to you, regardless of whether he said it before or after a particular instance?

During this whole time that he was in your apartment, what conversations can you relate to this jury took place between you two?"

"I had asked him what he was doing and why was he doing it, and he said that he wanted—he wanted some—he wanted some white—he said that he wanted some white pussy."

Any hope I had of avoiding the race question disappears with that comment. Several of the female jurors unconsciously grimace at me then turn back to the victim.

She continues. "He told me that he had four friends outside, and for me not to touch the phone, and he didn't want to see any police coming there after he left. He said other things, but I didn't hear them or didn't understand them." She pauses to remember. "He said something about coming back, or that he wanted to. One time he was having a problem with his pants and he said something like, 'The darn pants' or something like that."

"All right, Lori. Let me ask you this. Let me go back to the time the leash is on your—the belt is on your neck and you are passed out. The next thing that you recall, there was anal sex?"

"Yes, sir."

"And is that the first sexual activity that took place?"

"That I—"

"That you recall?" the D.A. finishes the sentence for her.

"Yes, sir."

"Now, was there anything used during the commission of that sexual act in the form of any cream or anything of that nature that you recall?"

My lawyer objects to the obviously leading nature of the questions—"Your Honor"—but the witness continues, "Not then."

My lawyer repeats himself, "Excuse me, Your Honor."

"Just a minute, Ms. Mitchell," the judge says to her.

Mr. Secret continues, "I understand clearly what we are dealing with, but I would particularly ask the district attorney not lead the witness."

The judge instructs the D.A., "I understand this particular situation, Mr. Keller, and I'll give you some latitude to lead, but try not to lead totally."

"Yes, sir, Your Honor."

The witness resumes her testimony. "He didn't use anything then or if he did, I don't know it. Like I said, when I came to, he was already . . . He . . . when he pushed me over and he finished . . . he finished pulling, ripping the underwear off, and he put some cream on hisself and me then."

"Where did he put the cream on you?"

"On my genital area, on my genitals."

"And I need for you to be just a little bit more specific, if you could."

"Vagina and, you know, the entire area."

"And then what happened?"

"He had vaginal sex."

A collective sigh of disgust rises from the jury box.

"And approximately, if you could tell me, how long do you think he had been in the apartment about at this time?"

"About a half an hour altogether. At that time, it was about twenty minutes."

"And at that time, what was the lighting situation in the room?"

"At that time all the lights were out. The lights were out, and the bathroom light was on, and it shone into the room."

"And after the vaginal sex, what then occurred?"

"He got up, and he still had the belt around my neck. He stood, and went a few steps over by the light, and with the switch he turned on the light, and I was standing there next to him. I felt like then, that he was going to let me see him, and I was afraid he wasn't planning on leaving afterwards. I looked at him. And then he turned it back off, and he took a pillowcase off one of my pillows. I don't know why, and then he put the pillowcase over my head. And he was looking for something, and he got down on the far side of the bed away from the door, and I was still with him, and he was looking under and beside the bed, too. And then we—he led me downstairs, and we were standing at the bottom of the stairs.

"Then he told me to go back upstairs and get on the bed, and I did. I stayed on the bed—I went upstairs and went on the bed, and when I went past the banister, I had picked up my pants, and from the edge of the bed I got some underwear from my drawer and put those underpants on, and I just stayed there on the bed for a minute, and then my curtains fell, and then I thought he had come back. Then I got the keys to my car and left."

Another sigh from the jury, this time one of relief.

"How long was the pillowcase on your head?"

"Ten minutes."

"When you went back up the stairs, as you just said, when he told you to go back upstairs, was the pillowcase on or off?"

"It must have been off."

"Did he come back up the stairs?"

"No."

"And what was missing from your purse?"

"I'm not sure exactly how much it was, not a lot of money, it was twenty, twenty-five. I don't even know really for sure, between twenty and thirty at the most, probably."

"And did you suffer any injuries as a result of this attack?"

"I—just a lot of bruises and scrapes, and my neck was scraped. I had a scrape on my leg, and I had a lot of bruises on it."

It is a harrowing tale, and I feel as bad for her as anyone else in the courtroom does. But I am anxious to get on with the I.D. evidence.

Mr. Keller finishes his direct examination with questions about the witness's initial description of the attacker. "Lori, you say your curtains fell?"

She nods affirmatively.

"And then you got up off the bed, and what did you then do?"

"I left."

"And where did you go?"

"Waffle House."

"And did you talk to anybody there?"

"Yes, sir."

"And who did you talk to?"

"I talked to my sisters, and there were two police units there."

"And what type of description did you give the police about the person?"

"A black male, medium build. I didn't really tell them how tall he was. I just told them, you know, according to where he stood when he stood next to me, how tall he was. I still don't know how tall that would be."

"How tall are you?"

"Five three."

The D.A. changes his line of questioning and begins to focus on the victim's description of her assailant. She describes his voice and says that he didn't have a southern accent, that he had an "educated voice." The D.A. asks her to explain.

"What do you mean when you say, 'educated voice'?"

"He didn't use a lot of slang. What I mean is, he didn't use a lot of street talk, and he didn't have a southern drawl."

She might as well say a black man with a college degree who was not born in the South.

"And how else did you describe him?"

"He was medium, about medium built. I told them he wasn't heavy, but he wasn't skinny. He was, you know, about medium build."

I do not doubt that she was raped and that a similar attack, probably by the same man, occurred just down the road. Listening to her testimony, it is impossible not to be moved, and it is obvious that she has the jury's sympathy. Unfortunately, that sympathy turns to utter contempt when members of the jury occasionally glance at me. I have learned that there is no proper response to such glares. At first, I try to be impassive, but that seems ridiculous in light of the consequences. So I just look away.

I pray that the jury is not so steeped in sympathy for this woman that they will believe her incredulous identification. I look forward to the technical, nonemotional testimony: the fiber evidence that will exonerate me, my alibi witnesses, the description of the clean-shaven perpetrator. But the testimony of the victim is so powerful that I realize it may seal my fate. The jury will never forget the distraught white woman confidently identifying the black "animal" (as the prosecutor put it) who raped her. The truth will have a tough act to follow.

Since the prosecutor has called the victim as a witness, he gets to address the issue of the live lineup first. He hands her a photo and asks if she recognizes it. The eyes of the jury are glued to her, but at least she is no longer discussing the actual crime.

"Yes, sir. This is the lineup photos."

"Now, did you identify someone at that lineup other than the person that you have just identified today in court?"

"Yes, sir."

"And why did you do that?"

"I was just—wouldn't allow myself to look at him fully in the lineup. I went in and I looked, but I—as I continued looking, I just refused to let myself look at him anymore, and I just picked another person."

It sounds ridiculous to me, but the jury hangs on her every word; she is pathetic and vulnerable. The prosecutor continues his questioning without spending any more time on the live lineup. He asks her about the next time that she saw me.

"Now, did you have occasion to see him again?"

"Yes."

"And where were you when you saw him that time?"

"Clayton County, at the courtroom."

"And was Mr. Secret present, his attorney?"

"Yes."

"And did you identify him at that time—not Mr. Secret, but Mr. Johnson—as the person who attacked you?"

"Yes, sir."

"And that is just after you had identified someone else in the live lineup, is that correct?"

"It was afterwards, yes."

"Ms. Mitchell, how do you know today that that's the same person that attacked you on March 9th?"

"I know. I know it's him." She looks dead at me, and I pray that she might free me from this terror by admitting some doubt. "I know it's him. . . . I know I'm right. I know that's him."

"What about that man today causes you to remember, or think, or positively say that he's the one?"

"I know that's him. That's his face, his eyes, the whole thing. That's him."

"What about his eyes?"

"That's him, I mean, they're predominant, you know, they stick out."

In order to bolster the identification, the prosecutor attempts to show that the victim is familiar enough with black people to distinguish between individuals. That's why he mentioned that she had identified me at the pretrial hearing, while I was sitting next to another black man, my attorney. To further demonstrate her familiarity with blacks, the prosecutor asks about her coworkers and customers at the restaurant. "Ms. Mitchell, I have only two more questions I need to ask you. During your period of time working at the Waffle House, did you have an occasion to work with many blacks?"

"Yeah, there was . . . one particular time I managed a store that was mostly black, ninety percent or more sometimes, in customers and employees."

"So, in ten years with Waffle House, you have come in contact with numerous blacks?"

"Yes."

"Male?"

"Yes, as much as anyone or more than some probably."

My lawyer tries to introduce evidence that Ms. Mitchell has an arrest record for using multiple aliases and passing bad checks, but he withdraws when challenged and focuses instead on the identification issues.

During his cross-examination, he stresses the importance of my beard and her misidentification at the live lineup. He reminds the victim of her statements before the trial. She tries to blur those descriptions.

He confronts her directly: "When you spoke with Detective Storey, he asked you specifically, did he not, 'Did the person who assaulted you have facial hair?'"

"I don't know if he asked me specifically. I don't remember. . . . I told him he may have had a beard that come up under his chin. I didn't feel it."

The next issue that my counsel addresses is my exoneration in the live lineup. He tries to establish that a live lineup is better than a photo lineup of old pictures, prepared by detectives who had arrested me in the past.

He begins by cross-examining the witness about the live lineup. "You went into the room, and there is a one-way glass, is that right?"

"Uh-huh."

"In fact, they told you it was a one-way glass before—"

She cuts him off, "Yes, they tell you it's a one-way glass."

"—and they gave you other instructions about how to view the lineup, look at them one by one. Isn't that correct?"

"Yes, sir."

"You went into that room and did not pick Calvin Johnson, did you?"

"No, I did not."

"Calvin Johnson was in that lineup, wasn't he?"

"Yes, he was."

"But you did pick someone other than Calvin Johnson?"

"Yes, I did."

"And when you picked that person, at that moment, you knew he wasn't the person that assaulted you, is that what you are saying?"

"Yes."

"And that was not truthful, of course?"

"In my mind now there was. . . ."

For a moment it looks as though she is going to admit some doubt. My lawyer tries to get her to continue the thought.

"Excuse me. Did you say that in your—"

"—No," she is still considering her full response, and I have some hope.

My lawyer tries to coax her without leading, but she collects herself and then says firmly, "I picked the wrong one, and I knew it."

Mr. Secret sighs and resumes his original line of questioning. "You realized, of course, that the person that you picked was being accused of a serious crime?"

"Yes, I do. It was—"

"And you signed a statement saying the person that you picked was the person that assaulted you; is that correct?"

"I believe it is, right."

"Are you telling this jury that at the time that you picked him, you knew he was not the man who assaulted you?

"I knew that—I knew he was over there just like I know he's over there out of the corner of my eye now."

"But you didn't pick him?"

"No, I didn't."

"Why?"

"Probably because the same reason I don't like looking at him right now."

"But you picked this photograph out here, number three, didn't you?"

"I did."

"Why did you pick number three out of this photographic lineup?"

"It wasn't—" she stops and then begins again, "I picked it."

"You picked it out because you believed that was the person who assaulted you?"

"I knew it was him."

"You walked into a room where you see six people standing, and you see the man that you know assaulted you and you do not pick him out?"

"I didn't."

I pray that the jury is paying careful attention.

"Now, the date that Calvin Johnson was in that lineup, and on the date of the preliminary hearing, did Mr. Johnson have a beard, do you recall?

"Yes."

"But the photograph that you picked out as being number three; he does not have a beard in that photograph does he?"

"No, he doesn't"

"He did have a beard in the lineup, didn't he?"

"Yes."

"He did have a beard at the preliminary hearing?"

"Yes," she answers and sighs with fatigue.

The pattern should be obvious to the jurors. The attacker did not have a beard, and I do. The victim picked a photo of me without a beard as her attacker but did not pick me out at the lineup with my beard. We have a slew of witnesses and photos that will prove that I have been bearded continuously since before the rapes. *Please God, let them not be swayed by sympathy for this woman.*

My attorney finishes his cross-examination by returning to her supposed lie during the live lineup. He reminds her of what she said in the pretrial hearing about picking someone else in the lineup in order to "just get out of there."

She answers him defensively: "I don't know what my exact words were. I was very scared at the lineup. I did want to get it over with. I may have said I wanted to get it over with. I wanted to get out of there."

"And basically you want to get this whole ordeal over with, isn't that right, Ms. Mitchell?"

"I want to make sure that Calvin Johnson is either put someplace where he can't do it again, or he is helped where he won't do it again."

"The fact of the matter is, Ms. Mitchell, you just want to get somebody–"

"–No, I don't."

"–Is that right?"

"I don't want that."

He points to the lineup photograph. "Isn't that why you picked this person out of the live lineup at the city jail? You wanted to get somebody, isn't that right?"

"No."

"You are seeking revenge, isn't that correct?"

"No, I'm not interested in revenge."

"The person you picked in the lineup did not assault you, nor did Calvin Johnson assault you."

"Yes, Calvin Johnson did."

"As a matter of fact, Ms. Mitchell, you don't know who assaulted you."

"I know exactly who assaulted me." Her silent stare is like lightning before the thunder.

Trial by Ordeal: The Verdict

I am the patient anesthetized, and the lawyers and judge are my surgeons. My instructions for the trial are clear: keep still, remain passive, and don't show any emotion. When the gavel bangs at the end of the first day, I move sedately to the holding room and don my prison clothes. The guards attach the chain around my waist, the ankle shackles, and the handcuffs. Once I am deposited back into the crowded jail, I try to force myself to relax. My lawyer said to get some rest: I need to look and feel my best for the jury.

The next morning my counsel seems to have other cases on his mind already. I get the impression that the trial is nearly over, and it is not going well. The district attorney looks as though he's ready for a press conference: happy, ambitious, well-rested, and relishing the starting gavel.

Before the jury is seated, my lawyer strenuously pleads with the judge that they should not hear from the next group of prosecution witnesses. He points out that I have not been charged with any crime in relation to their stories. In order to decide the matter, the judge asks the prosecutor what each witness will talk about. The stories are surreal.

Barbara Newsome will be one of the witnesses. She lives in Lori Mitchell's apartment complex and claims that a few hours before Miss Mitchell was raped, a man came to her door saying that he was Jim and he needed to use her phone. Since she didn't know any Jim, she refused to let him in. Later that same night, she saw a black man staring in her window. The man was obscured by bushes, however, so she could see him only from the eyes up. The prosecution claims that I am Jim.

The district attorney admits that no crime was committed by "Jim"; in fact, there isn't any physical evidence that he even exists. Though Miss Newsome had seen the man only from the eyes up, she chose my photo from a lineup of six pictures the rape investigators showed her. That is proof enough for the prosecutor. He dismisses the fact that Ms. Newsome picked out another man in the live lineup.

My lawyer argues that the live lineup is more relevant than the photo lineup, since the picture of me, unbearded, was out of date, black-and-white, and less than one and a half inches square. More important, the photo lineup was conducted by a man who was sure that I was guilty, and it was not witnessed by my counsel.

The district attorney responds with his favorite tactic. He tells the judge that Ms. Newsome is prepared to identify me in open court and will swear that I am the man. It is a sham, but the prosecutor acts as if it is a scientific test; the judge, as usual, seems inclined to take his side. Our cross-examination will be like trying to disprove a ghost.

Jackie Hinton, the day's first witness, has another spectral tale. On March 7 she finished her shower around 8:00 P.M., wrapped herself in a towel, and went to the living room. There, she was shocked to find a black man. She rushed back to the bathroom, put on a robe, and ran to a neighbor's house. She didn't call the police until the next day, after hearing a scream from another apartment. When the police arrived, Miss Hinton suddenly remembered that she had seen the intruder at the Stop-n-Go hours before he mysteriously appeared in her home.

The detectives, who were already certain that I was the local rapist (and apparently a peeping Tom), showed her their lineup of six, small, black-and-white mug shots. My photo was the same year-and-a-half old image they had used before, and I am very suspicious about how it was displayed for her. To me, the more important piece of evidence is that she picked someone else in the live lineup. That procedure allowed her to look long and hard at me (with a beard and in full color) from several different angles. She also observed my whole body, posture, movement, and even my voice. And most important, my lawyer was present to make sure that there was no obvious coaching.

My counsel does a good job arguing against the photographic lineup, but the judge does not find the pattern of misidentification disturbing. He does, however, ask the prosecutor why the testimony of the two women is needed, since no crime had been committed in the Newsome case, and no assault occurred in the Hinton story. The prosecutor responds that these witnesses demonstrate in the accused a "lustful disposition," and "a bent of mind." The judge is satisfied by this, and our objections are overruled.

The final witness we object to is the second rape victim, Karen Robinson. It is obvious to everyone that the same man committed both rapes, but I am on trial only for the rape of Miss Mitchell. We have not examined any of the evidence concerning the second rape and are not prepared to defend against it. Miss Robinson was attacked in Fulton County, just across the border with Clayton County, and her allegations will require a trial there. The two victims underwent similar indignities, and there are many consistent factors, such as the use of a pillowcase and belt around the victim's head and neck. If the second rape is brought up here, we'll have to defend against it, but I cannot be acquitted of it at this trial. My lawyer explains all this to the judge, but as we have come to expect, he sides with the district attorney and allows all of the state's witnesses to testify.

The jury is called back into the room, and they take their seats — scowls intact. The prosecutor calls Miss Hinton to the stand and questions her about the shower incident. "After your shower, did anything unique happen?"

"Yes, sir. I heard the front door shut, and I went out of the shower to see what it was. There was a man standing there in my living room."

"And how would you describe the man?"

"He was a black male. His eyes, you know, they stunned me real bad when I walked out the door and looked at him. He was sort of medium build."

"And how were you clothed when you left the bathroom?"

"I had a towel around me."

"And what did you do?"

"I went back into the bathroom and shut the door and locked it, then I grabbed my robe and ran out the door and across the street to my girlfriend's house."

"Now while you were in the living room, in the towel, did you have any conversation with this person?"

"Yes. He said, 'Is Jim here?' or, 'Does Jim live here?' I can't remember exactly how it was he said it."

"And what was your response?"

"I don't know, I didn't give him a chance. I just ran back in the shower."

She describes how she had seen this man earlier at the Stop-n-Go and how she picked out my photo when the detectives came around.

With dramatic seriousness the prosecutor asks her if the man is in the courtroom today. Unsurprisingly, she picks me out from among the two black men at the defense table. (The courtroom identifications are becoming an ever-more farcical formality.) When asked about my appearance, she says that my beard is "fuller now." What she really remembers, she says, are my eyes. So the prosecutor asks her to describe them.

"What about his eyes?"

"I don't know, there's something distinct about them." She pauses, and I wait to hear more, but that is her complete description.

My lawyer doesn't even bother questioning her.

After a brief adjournment for lunch, court reconvenes at 1:30. Karen Robinson, the second rape victim, takes the stand. Although I am not being tried for her rape, the jury is allowed to hear her complete testimony. It's insidious. If they decide that she is telling the truth, they will convict me; but if they don't believe her, I can still be tried for her rape in Fulton County. After some formalities the district attorney directs her to the night of the assault.

"I'll ask you whether or not you had an occasion on the night of March 6th, 1983, to go to sleep? Did you go to sleep that night?"

"Just for a little while."

"Approximately what time did you get to bed that night?"

"I was out on a date, and I got home about one o'clock."

"And do you have a particular ritual that you follow when you go to bed? Do you do certain things, and did you do them that night?"

"Yes."

"And what did you do that night, getting ready to go to bed?"

"I took my TV into my room, along with my cats. Then I turned out the lights, locked the doors, and went to bed."

"Now, when you went to sleep that night, how were you dressed?"

"I had on a short outfit."

"All right, and when you say a short outfit, how many garments did that—"

"—I had on my T-shirt and my shorts."

"So you had on two pieces of clothing?"

"Yes."

"Now, were you awakened that night prior to when you had planned to get up?"

"Yes."

"And can you describe approximately what time that was?"

"It was probably around two o'clock."

"And what do you recall about how you were waked up?"

"I was woken up by someone strangling me with a belt around my neck," she says. Her voice fades with the last word.

"And what is the first thing that you recall that you did?"

"I woke up screaming and asking to be let go."

"And did the person that was doing this to you, did he say anything when you screamed?"

"He told me to stop screaming, and if I didn't, he was going to hurt me."

"And what did you do?"

"I was quiet because I didn't want to get hurt."

"And did he say anything else at that particular time?"

"He told me to take off my clothes, because he wanted to have sex with me, and I was crying and whining and shaking and everything, and he tried to get me to stop."

"And how did he try to get you to stop?"

"Talking to me and trying to comfort me."

"And do you recall what he might have said during this time?"

"He said that he wasn't trying to hurt me, he just wanted to have sex with me."

"All right. Now, did you recognize this person at the time?"

"No. I had never seen him before."

"Now, at this time, were there any lights on at your apartment?"

"I don't keep my lights on, because there is a house behind me that always keeps their porch light on, and that casts a light through the house. And my TV was on. I always leave my TV on, but the brightness on it had been turned down."

"Was there any other lighting at this time?"

"No."

"Now, what happened next?"

"He raped me." Her voice is firm, and the room is silent; it seems as if everyone has stopped breathing for a second. She continues, "Then he just took me through the house trying to look for things, and he made me give him orange juice, and he made me put back the window that he came in through."

"Now, when you say that he raped you, what do you mean, Karen?"

She pauses, looking for suitable words, and realizes that there are none. "He took his sex organ and put it in mine." A member of the jury shuffles nervously.

"All right, and was there any other sexual activity?"

"Just rubbing me and penetrating me and stuff."

"And was there any difficulty?" The district attorney obviously knows every detail of her story, and he leads her through it, making sure that the jury gets a vivid picture of her horror.

"Yes. He couldn't get it in, and he looked for cream and stuff."

"All right, Karen. Now, was any cream ever used?"

"No. He couldn't find any."

"Now, you said earlier that there was something around your neck. What was around your neck?"

"It was a belt."

"All right. Was it one of your belts?"

"I don't think so."

"And how was it around your neck?"

"It didn't clasp with buckles, it loosened by sliding, and he just kept on tightening it, tighter and tighter."

"And then, after he had the sex activity with you, he led you around the house?"

She nods yes.

"Now, how would he have led you around the house?"

"First, he took my pillowcase off of my pillow and put that over my head, I guess because I couldn't see him, and then he led me around the house with the pillowcase on. And he had a little flashlight, a pen flashlight that he used to look around the house with."

"And did he do anything else with the pen flashlight?"

"He just looked at my body with it."

"Did he say anything when he had the pen flashlight and was looking at your body?"

"Yes. He commented I had a nice body."

"Now, what else occurred while he was in your house?"

"He just looked around my house and led me around to the refrigerator, because he wanted something to drink. He made me give him something to drink, made me give him some orange juice, and then he . . ." she breaks off, and fatigue passes over her face. "I kept on crying, and I wanted to go back to sleep, and he wouldn't let me ever go back to sleep. Then he asked if he could come back, and if I liked black men, and where I worked, and what my phone number was, and he was just trying to make conversation." She pauses to collect her thoughts. "Then, and then he turned around to look — looked like he was trying to make sure he didn't forget anything, and that's when I ran out of the house."

The prosecutor knows that there are more details for her to tell, and so he continues leading her through the events. "Now, what about this window? You said something about a window."

"He broke in through my front window and took it all the way out. He also took the plant that was in front of it all the way out, and then I guess he crawled through the window and came into my bedroom."

"Karen, how do you know he came in your apartment through the window?"

"Because he told me he came in the apartment through the window. He told me I should have it fixed to where nobody could get in."

"And then he wanted *you* to put the window back in?"

"Yes."

"Were you able to?"

"I couldn't do it because I was shaking, and I was crying, and I was too nervous, so he took the window from me and put it in."

"Now, how would you describe any clothing article that he had on?"

"He had on blue jeans, and he had on an army fatigue jacket, and he had on a sweater that had ridges down the front of it. There were just ridges all the way around it, and that's all."

The prosecutor continues to ask about his clothes and finally asks about the attacker's hands.

"He had a glove."

"Did he have on one glove or two gloves?"

"Just one glove."

"What kind of glove was it that you recall?"

"It was a driving glove, you know, the type you see people driving with in sports cars. It was tan, and it had little holes in it."

"And did you have to—other than the sexual act—did you have any other contact with him?"

"I tried not to. He made me hug him and kiss him and put my arms around him and stuff like that."

"Now, if this were," the district attorney points to his own jacket, "if my coat were a fatigue jacket, how did you hug him?"

"I put my arms around outside, but he didn't like that, so he made me put my arms around the inside of his jacket."

"So you had to hug him inside?"

"Yes, around the waist."

The prosecutor is trying to establish that she got a good feel of the perpetrator's body and garments. He will try to link the attacker to some of the clothes they confiscated from my house, but the matches are very poor. Most of the impact comes from the simple, but moving, narrative. An innocent woman was raped. She is not an actress; she is a victim forced to tell her story to a group of strangers. Physical evidence, no matter how compelling, cannot match a victim's testimony for dramatic impact. The story is mesmerizing, and the prosecutor knows how to bring out all the key points.

"Approximately how long was he in your apartment?"

"He made me look at my watch, because I lied and told him that my boyfriend lived with me and that he was a fireman and he had a gun and everything. And I told him he'd better get out of my house or he'd kill him if he caught him in there. So he made me look at my watch, it was three fifteen, so he'd probably been there about forty-five minutes."

"Did he take anything out of your apartment?"

"I left before he did. But when he went in my purse, I know he took money."

"When did he go into your purse?"

"When he led me around the apartment, he looked at lamps and everything. It was after he raped me, and I remember that he went in my purse, asked me if I had money, and I told him I didn't, because I didn't think I did, and he said I was lying and everything, and he took my money."

"And approximately how much money was it?"

"It was just twenty dollars."

"And when you ran out of the apartment, what did you then do?"

"I ran out of the apartment, and I hid in some apartments – somebody's porch up the street. I just hid in the corner, praying that he wouldn't see me. And he kept on hollering out the name that I told him my name was, Ann. He hollered it out, 'Ann, Ann,' like that."

"And then what did you do after you were on the porch?"

"I waited there just a little while, and I heard some voices, so I ran to a house and there was some people in the house having a party. I ran in their house, and I called my mother."

Unlike all the other witnesses Miss Robinson did not pick me out from the black-and-white photos, but she did pick me in the live lineup.

It is still hard for me to believe that I looked like her attacker, because of his lack of facial hair and because the other rape victim picked another man in the live lineup.

I do suspect that Miss Robinson had been coached during the investigation. Her testimony was polished, and there are many troubling aspects of how the police prepared her. For example, she had been invited to Lori Mitchell's preliminary hearing (though no one admits to having invited her). My lawyer was shocked to see her there, and he objected to her presence on the basis that it might affect her testimony. But the court allowed her to stay, so she heard all of Miss Mitchell's testimony before her own pretrial hearing. This could have easily corrupted her memory.

I wonder if she was somehow told that she had picked the "wrong" photo. Maybe she was shown some other photos of me before the live lineup, or perhaps she was coached by one of the detectives about how I might appear. Even if she wasn't coached, cross-racial identifications are notoriously unreliable. Maybe it was just an honest mistake, but whatever the reason, my face is now ingrained in her memory as the attacker.

I remember the day that they arranged the lineup. There were seven of us who looked roughly similar. It was nerve-racking, because I knew that my life depended on the honesty of strangers and their ability to remember. I also knew that I was the only real suspect in the lineup. When I heard that one of the victims had picked someone else, I was relieved. However, it turned out that the guy had a perfect alibi: he had been in prison when the rapes occurred. After four lineups for different victims, I worried that luck would begin to play a role. I reasoned that if one victim could pick a man who had been in prison during her ordeal, then eventually someone would pick me. Seven men, four lineups: the odds were against me. Lori Mitchell picked another man (number 4), Barbara Newsome picked someone else (number 7), Jackie Hinton picked no one, but Karen Robinson picked me.

Was it just bad luck, or was she influenced by someone? The only thing that I'm sure of is that not one of the men in the lineup was the rapist. Maybe she just felt she had to choose one of us. There is no cost to the victim for her error, but for me it means the possibility of a lifetime behind bars.

I listen silently as my lawyer gently cross-examines Miss Robinson. He does not attack her credibility or deny her violation, but he does strongly suggest that she has been coached. He wants the jury to know that she was prepared by the prosecution to answer a certain way. He begins by discussing her unusual appearance at Miss Mitchell's pretrial hearing.

"Now, after you viewed the lineup, several days or maybe a week later, you were asked to come to a preliminary hearing in the case of Lori Mitchell, is that correct?

"Yes."

"And at that hearing you heard Lori Mitchell testify, in detail, to everything that happened to her in the assault?"

"Yes."

"Would you say that having sat in the hearing for Lori Mitchell's case had a great impression upon you?"

"No, sir. I had already made my testimony to Lieutenant Wilkerson, who had it recorded."

"But the reason they asked you to come to that hearing was to prepare you—"

"—Your Honor, I'm going to object to the form of the question," Mr. Keller, the district attorney interrupts. He realizes that coaching a witness is not allowed; "preparing" a key witness has serious implications. He objects to my lawyer's question by saying to the judge, "'The reason they asked'—how can she testify as to the *reason* they asked something?"

My lawyer rephrases the question: "Did they tell you, Ms. Robinson, why you were there?"

"Because they wanted me to know what I was going to have to go through. Because they didn't think I was as strong as they wanted me to be."

"And they told you that they wanted to *prepare* you for your hearing?"

"They wanted to show me what I was going to have to do, what it was going to be like for you to question me, and for me to have to say what happened."

"Did they say, 'prepare'?"

"I don't believe so."

My lawyer produces, over the objections of the district attorney, a certified copy of Ms. Robinson's own pretrial hearing. He asks her to read her testimony from that hearing in order to refresh her memory. He wants to know if she said that the prosecutors had invited her to the other victim's pretrial hearing to help "prepare" her.

She looks at the pages and reluctantly agrees. "It says 'prepare' me for my–"

"–and, of course, that was the truth on that day?" my lawyer interrupts.

"Yes, it was."

"So you were there for them to *prepare* you for your hearing?"

"Yes, I guess you could say that."

Miss Robinson is a very confident witness. Even when she makes a mistake, she usually corrects herself with grace. But at times she deviates from the questions, and twice she directs rather crude comments toward me. These comments, and her actions, emotionally impact the jury. I worry that her small outbursts will interfere with their ability to be "tryers of fact." Her first off-the-cuff remark comes when the prosecutor asks her to identify me in open court.

"Karen, let me ask you this. I'll ask you to look around the courtroom, and ask whether or not the person who attacked you is here."

"Yes, he is."

"All right. Would you please look at him and point him out?"

"He's sitting there," she makes a quick gesture toward the defense table.

"Karen, of the two people that you pointed in the direction of, can you tell me which one you were pointing at?"

"It's the man with the beard sitting right there," she sneers at me. *"You'll get your time."* The courtroom is silent except for the stenographer, who quickly records her four words. I remain impassive. She is trying to bait me, and I can do nothing but sit still. I play dead while the wolf attacks. The witness is a good speaker, good-looking, and like all the jurors–white.

She has the jury on her side the whole time, and I am glad when her testimony finally ends. At least she has not succeeded in getting me to respond to her hostility. The judge tells her that she may step down; he then inquires about the next prosecution witness. She leaves the stand slowly, as if she has more to say. The prosecutor stands by his table, looking over his notes.

"Your Honor, we'll call Barbara Newsome," he tells the judge as Miss Robinson takes the last step from the witness box.

They say that time slows down when terrible things happen, but that is not always the case: sometimes the moments skip and jump. As she leaves the stand, I am only peripherally aware of Karen Robinson heading in my direction. Suddenly, she lunges at me and curses, "You stupid bastard!" Once again, only the stenographer's keys can be heard.

My lawyer immediately asks for a short recess, and the judge calls for a fifteen-minute break. I am too dumbfounded to press for a mistrial, and my lawyer has been made timid by the loss of every major motion so far. He and I hardly speak during the break.

After Miss Robinson's angry outbursts, Barbara Newsome is almost comic relief. It seems silly to have this woman testify about a man who only looked in her window, but the district attorney manages to stretch it out with ridiculously detailed descriptions of the window itself, including several photographs, which are entered into evidence. The witness lives in the same complex where Miss Mitchell had been raped, and she tells the court that when she heard about the rape from her friend Radar Jacks (who works in the police department), she told him her story of the peeping tom. The prosecutor asks her to tell that story to the court, and so she begins her tale from the night of March 8, starting from when she heard an unexpected knock at the door. She is an animated and rather comical speaker.

"There was a black male's voice came across and he said, 'My name is Jim. I want in,' and I said, 'No, you can't come in my apartment, you'll have to go away.'"

In fragmented sentences she explains that the man asked to use the phone, but she refused him. After that, she gave him a couple of seconds to leave and then went to the window to make sure that he was gone.

"He was standing right at the same position where I was standing, in front of the window, and he was coming across the bushes fixing to reach for the window to pull it up. Fortunately enough, they were locked."

"And what part of that person could you see?"

"His eyes."

"And what else could you see?"

"His hair, nothing really from here up," she says, holding a hand up to her nose. "I mean nothing from here down, just from right about here up."

"All right, when you saw that person, what did you do?"

"Well, it scared the living daylights out of me, for one thing, and I told him, I says, 'I've already told you, you'll have to leave.'" She wags her finger. "I said, 'Now get away from my window,' and he drew back a little bit, and he shook his finger in my face and he said something to me—but I don't know what."

The district attorney continues to press for more details about the eyes at the window. "Now, Barbara, how would you describe the person at your window? What can you tell me about that person if I asked for a physical description?"

"It was a black male, approximately twenty-five to twenty-seven. Five foot nine, five foot eleven—somewhere around there, because he was bent over, so I can't give you a true height."

"But he was a black male?"

"Yes, sir. He had an afro, but it was short to the head, it wasn't long and bushy, in other words."

"Now, after he shook his finger at you, what action did you then take?"

"I immediately closed the drapes, because I didn't want him looking at me. He frightened me terribly, his eyes were so—they're strange. I closed the window—the drapes I mean, and I ran upstairs to make sure that he was going to leave. I was about to get my mother up when I looked out the window and he had totally vanished. Gone completely, so I didn't wake my mother up."

Ms. Newsome had picked me out of the old photos but chose someone else at the live lineup. Of course—now, eight months later, she has no trouble picking me out at the defense table.

We had not planned to question this witness, because her story is so weak, but her testimony takes a dramatic turn which forces our hand. The district attorney asks her if I look different now, compared with how I looked that night.

"What's different about him now?" the district attorney asks.

"His hair is cut off, and he does have a beard now."

I look at my lawyer, and we have the same thought; how could she say anything about my beard? She saw the man only from the eyes up.

The district attorney freezes. Even he can't let that comment slip by. "I thought you said you couldn't see past—"

"—Well, I'm sorry, I did. I did not *remember* the beard, is what I meant. I'm sorry."

He tries to recover his witness. "What about the eyes?"

"The eyes are the same."

"Are you sure that's the same person—"

"Yes."

"—who was at your door?"

"I'm positive."

"Is there any doubt in your mind?"

"No, sir."

My lawyer questions her briefly about the beard comment, about the live lineup, and about her friends and relatives on the police force. Then he lets her go, thinking that the jury could not possibly be swayed by her strange testimony.

Finally, all the victims' testimony is over. Now, we can move on to the physical and scientific evidence that can exonerate me. I pray that the jury will allow reason to prevail.

The prosecution calls Linda Tillman of the State Crime Laboratory. She is the serology, or blood-typing, expert on the case. She explains that the semen recovered from the victim's body and underclothes belonged to a man with type-O blood. Forty-four percent of Americans are type O, and I am included in that group; it is the most common blood type. Furthermore, she tells the court that the rapist was a "secretor." Secretors are people who release their blood-type markers in other body fluids: saliva, sweat, semen, or vaginal fluid. Ms. Tillman testifies that both the victim and the assailant were secretors. Eighty percent of the population are secretors, and I am one of them. That is all she can tell with state-of-the-art technology in 1983.

Because the serology evidence is so general, the fiber evidence becomes the key to my freedom. What we need is some scientific proof that does more than simply reduce my odds of having committed the crime; it must actually eliminate me from the pool of suspects. The fiber evidence can do just that, but the state's fiber expert is still sick, and I can only hope that he will recover over the weekend. We do not expect the trial to go beyond Monday.

Court adjourns on Friday afternoon, and I smile at my mother. With that simple expression I try to reassure her that all will be well. When I meet with my lawyer, his face conveys the opposite message: all is lost. We both try to be upbeat about the fiber evidence, but neither of us believes that the scowls of the jury can be changed by mere science. Emotional impressions, prejudice, and the need to punish a bad guy are the downsides of the trial-by-jury system.

Being returned to the county jail for the weekend is demoralizing and dehumanizing. I change out of my suit, and back into my prison jumper. I hold out my hands for the cuffs, get shackled, and am returned to a cell.

Although my family had been just a few feet from me in the court-room, there was no time to converse with them, and now I feel completely alone. I pray during the night and read from the book of Philippians. The Apostle Paul talks about his arrest and keeps mentioning his chains. It occurs to me that the traditions of prison have changed little in two thousand years, and I have many things in common with Paul. As I try to sleep, I am comforted by the image of the innocent apostle in chains, but I am also haunted by the jurors' eyes, always seeming to mock my plea of innocence.

On Monday there is another incident that could lead to a mistrial. The jury is never supposed to see the accused in chains or handcuffs: that is considered prejudicial. But as I am being led down the hallway, the jury is milling around, and they all see me in my prison clothes and handcuffs. I tell my lawyer about the incident, but he decides not to exploit it.

Later, we discover yet another reason for a mistrial. We hear that the jury foreman works as a judge magistrate in Clayton County, a fact that should have disqualified him from the jury pool. By the time we find out, it is too late to pursue, except on appeal. The trial resumes with the jury obviously anxious to finish by 5:00 P.M.

The first witnesses are two of the detectives who investigated the case. Since we didn't bring up their role in my previous arrest, we can't bring up the fact that one of them said, "We'll get you next time." Under direct questioning by the prosecutor, the officers tell the same story that the state's other witnesses have told. My lawyer listens carefully, takes a lot of notes, and seems quite anxious to cross-examine them. He asks Detective John Storey about the live lineup during which Lori Mitchell picked someone other than me.

"Was the guy she picked out arrested?"

"Not by us."

"He was indicted for raping Lori Mitchell?"

"No, sir."

"Yet, she picked him out?"

"Yes, sir."

"Now did Barbara Newsome also view that lineup?"

"Yes, sir."

"She picked out number seven, is that right?"

"Yes, sir."

"And is number seven Calvin Johnson?"

"No, sir."

"Did you arrest number seven?"

"No, sir."

"Did you charge him with the crime?"

"No, sir."

"Even though someone positively identified him as the perpetrator?"

"That's correct." The detective explains that number seven had been in jail at the time of the crime and so couldn't be a suspect.

Next, my lawyer questions him about the initial description of the perpetrator by Ms. Mitchell. "You asked Miss Mitchell if the perpetrator had facial hair, did you not?"

"Yes, sir."

"And her response to that question was, 'I don't remember a full beard. There could have been some stubble.'"

"Yes, sir."

"What day did you arrest Calvin Johnson?"

"On the fourteenth."

"That was five days after the alleged incident took place, is that right?"

"That's correct."

"And on that date, did Mr. Johnson have a full beard?"

"I didn't see him that day. I didn't personally arrest him."

"You didn't see him that day. You saw him at the lineup on the sixteenth, correct?"

"Correct."

"And on that date, did he have a full beard?"

"Yes, sir."

"Just like he has today?"

"No, sir. It's a lot further along than what it was on the lineup."

"A lot further along," my lawyer says incredulously, "but he did have a full beard?"

"Yes, sir."

The prosecutor calls the other detective, Mike Wilkerson, and asks him about Karen Robinson's description of her attacker.

"The victim gave me a description as a black male, approximately six feet, six foot three, two hundred pounds. I think she said something about a beard."

My lawyer cross-examines him on this point, and the detective requires a bit of prodding to refresh his memory. "When you talked to Ms. Robinson, she did not say anything about facial hair, did she?"

"No, I don't think so."

"You asked her?"

"No."

"You didn't ask her anything about facial hair?"

"Well, I might have. I can't recall if I did or didn't. I asked her several things."

My lawyer picks up a copy of the detective's testimony from the pretrial hearing and hands it to the witness. "If you will begin at line two here, Detective Wilkerson, to line six. Does that refresh your memory?"

"Yes."

"So I will ask you again, did Ms. Robinson tell you anything about facial hair?"

"No."

"And you specifically asked her the question about facial hair?"

"Yes."

"On the day that Mr. Johnson was arrested, did he have a beard?"

"Yes."

"Similar to the one he has now?"

"Uh-huh, yes."

Finally, an honest answer, but the equivocal descriptions given throughout the trial have probably confused the jury. It is clear to me from their testimony that the detectives have an interest in convicting me. I remember again how they told me that they'd get me after the rape charges were dropped in 1981. The detectives still believe that I committed that earlier crime, even though the victim was sure that her attacker was uncircumcised. The memory of their threat makes me sick: *We'll get you next time. Your kind always repeats, and we'll be ready.*

It appears that they are now willing to bend the truth (or be forgetful) in order to convict me. I am glad that my lawyer has read the pretrial transcripts carefully, but I am not sure if the jury even cares about the obvious contradictions in testimony. The judge calls for a short recess before we begin the defense presentation. When we return, I will be the first witness.

I used to be a radio announcer, and I graduated with a degree in communications from Clark, but I am still terribly nervous. I have no idea what an effective defendant should sound like. I have been advised to be passive: "Just relax. Don't make too much eye contact with the jury. Speak to the person who asks the question." I worry that this advice may be wrong, but I'm not sure that anything I say—neither style nor content—will matter anyway. The jury's faces already indicate conviction, and their frequent glances at their wrists presage a speedy verdict.

My lawyer questions me about my activities from March 5 to 9, 1983. I explain that my schedule was very regular. On weekdays I'd wake up at about 4:00 A.M., and my dad would drive me to work at the courier service. I always clocked in before 5:30 A.M. and got out at 12:30 in the afternoon. Karen Robinson was raped early on Monday morning, March 7; Lori Mitchell was raped early on Wednesday, March 9. Both attacks occurred about 3:30 A.M.

I testify that during the night of March 5th, I stayed at my girlfriend's house. I was there all night, and that is the night that Jackie Hinton found the man in her apartment as she got out of the shower. My girlfriend and her mother both corroborate my alibi.

On Sunday, March 6, my family had gathered around the TV to watch Georgia football star Herschel Walker play in his debut game with the New Jersey Generals. Later that evening we had supper together and then watched some more television. I called my girlfriend, just as I did every evening, around 9:45, then went to bed around 10:00 or 10:30.

My mom testifies that she had a bad week (with back pain) and had stayed awake on the couch each night, so as not to disturb my dad. On the days of the attacks she never went to bed until after we left the house in the morning. There is no reasonable way that I could have left the house without her seeing me. During both of the rapes, my mother was spending sleepless nights on the couch, and I was asleep in my room.

On Monday the 7th, I got up as usual about 4:00 A.M., and went to my parents' room to make sure my dad was up. I ate a quick breakfast in the kitchen, then said good morning to my mom, who was awake on the couch watching TV. A little before five, Dad drove me to work, and I clocked in by 5:20 A.M. Ms. Robinson testified that she looked at her watch in the midst of her ordeal at 3:15 A.M. Our homes are at least a fifteen-minute drive apart, and if the car had been moved, my mom would have certainly noticed.

On the night of the second rape, the one for which I am being tried, I tell the jury that I was at home watching TV with my folks until about 10:00 P.M. As usual, I called my girlfriend just before I went to sleep at about 10:30. The next day I got up at 4:00 A.M., woke my dad, and punched in at work by 5:20. Once again, Mom was awake on the couch when I got up. She had passed another sleepless night with the television on, and I remember feeling bad for her.

There isn't much else for me to say, and I finish without any dramatic flair. Innocence is dull.

On cross-examination, I am asked about our dog, my afternoon workouts at the gym, and other details of my schedule. The district attorney keeps asking how long I've lived at my present address and had my present job. I think he wants me to mention that I had once been in prison, but I answer his questions truthfully without offering any information about that previous incident. (He cannot discuss it unless I bring it up, since it has no bearing on the present case.) He also keeps asking me if my beard grows fast. Naïvely, I answer "yes." How fast it grows doesn't really matter—it was already full when I was hired by the courier service in January; the rapes occurred in March.

We put my boss from the courier service on the stand just to certify my work I.D., which shows me with a full beard in early February. My boss corroborates my facial hair.

Our last planned witness is Raymond Santamaria, the crime lab's fiber expert who had gotten sick. When he doesn't show up by late morning, we start worrying. The judge grants an early lunch recess, hoping that Mr. Santamaria will show up during the break. My lawyer orders sandwiches, but I cannot eat a thing.

Raymond Santamaria arrives just as the judge is deciding what to do about his absence. We call him to the stand immediately and begin with questions about his qualifications. He explains that he has been with the state crime lab for three years. He has a degree in forensic science and is qualified in the microanalysis of hair and fiber evidence. My lawyer points out that he works for the state and has testified in more than forty cases. Mr. Santamaria tells the court that he received the victim's bedsheet, hairs recovered from the crime scene and victim, and hair samples taken from all over my body.

He begins his technical testimony by explaining how he uses a special comparison microscope in his work. This scope allows two samples to be viewed at the same time, side by side. It's like two microscopes joined by an optical bridge. The science of microanalysis is quite advanced, and racial identifications are routine. In order to determine whether a specific hair was contributed by a particular person, the scientist examines its physical properties such as texture, length, pigmentation, and the variation in diameter of the hair. He describes how a trained person can easily tell hairs that have been cut from those which are naturally tapered; and how the anatomical source of a hair can be determined. "Pubic hair is generally coarser in texture," he explains. "The shaft diameter varies significantly as opposed to head hairs, and the pigmentation generally varies also in pubic hairs."

Mr. Santamaria does not explain why my hairs were sampled twice, but both analyses exonerate me. The Negro hair found in the victim's bedding does not match mine. That was clear from the first analysis; however, instead of releasing me, the prosecutor made me go through the plucking procedure a second time. When the second hair analysis corroborated my claim of innocence, the prosecution decided to ignore its own expert, and we had to subpoena him.

My lawyer hands Mr. Santamaria the evidence bags from the case and asks him to describe them. "This package here is a Ziploc plastic bag, labeled 'pubic combings of victim.'" He puts down the bag and picks up another. "And there is also a bag labeled, 'known pubic hair of victim,' and 'known head hair of victim.' These three items were in a rape kit that was submitted to the crime lab. Also submitted was a Ziploc plastic bag labeled, 'known pubic hair of suspect, Calvin Crawford Johnson.'"

There is also a second bag of my pubic hairs, a bag of my head hair, a bag with three Caucasian head hairs, and one Negro pubic hair recovered from the victim's beige bedsheet. Mr. Santamaria himself recovered the hairs from the sheet. My fate is tied to the one pubic hair.

He continues, "The Caucasian head hairs from the sheet *did* match the victim's known head hair. The one Negroid pubic hair *did not* match the known pubic hair of Calvin Crawford Johnson."

This is the key piece of physical evidence that I have waited for, and through the mouth of the state's own expert I am exonerated. The district attorney, however, is not deterred. During his cross-examination, he concocts a wild tale about how this random Negro pubic hair ended up in the bedsheet of a woman who had just been raped by a black man. First, he tries to cloud the issue by pointing out that two other hairs were found in the bedding and that Mr. Santamaria could not determine their origin. These other hairs also do not match any of mine, but the fiber expert was not sure of their origin or type. Next, the district attorney asks Mr. Santamaria a series of questions that allude to unlikely origins for the hair that exonerates me. The prosecutor's wild speculation violates one of the most important principles of investigation, known as Occam's razor: the simplest explanation is preferred over more convoluted ones. It's obvious to me that the district attorney is playing to win, not to uncover truth.

"Could you tell me whether or not that hair could have come from Lori Mitchell if she used a public restroom and transported that hair onto the bedsheet?"

"That would be possible, yes," answers Mr. Santamaria without any enthusiasm.

"If the sheet was laundered at a public facility, could the hair have originated there?"

"Yes, that's another possibility."

"If blacks had lived in the apartment six months earlier, and that sheet touched the floor and the hair had been on the floor, could it have gotten on there?"

"Yes, sir."

My lawyer tries to get the expert to discuss his opinion of such remote possibilities, but the district attorney objects before we can get this line of questioning off the ground.

The final testimony of my trial is from the victim herself. The state recalls Lori Mitchell to ask her how this Negro pubic hair might have arrived on her bedsheet.

The district attorney explores his nonsensical theory. "Prior to March 9th, 1983, while residing at that location where you were living, how did you have your clothes laundered?"

"I took them to the Wash, Dry, and Fold service on Riverdale Road."

Then he asks her a question that I'm not sure he knew the answer to: "And while you were living in that apartment, did you ever have the occasion to have a male Negro visitor come to that apartment?"

"No, sir."

That is how my trial ends. The evidence of truth is discarded as an accident left on her sheets by the laundromat, and truth itself is replaced with a lie put forward by the state of Georgia. The judge instructs the jury about the case, "the people versus Calvin C. Johnson Jr." They are reminded that I am innocent until proven guilty. He tells them that the burden of proof is on the state, and that if even one of them finds reasonable doubt, they should resist a guilty verdict. Many of the jurors peek at their watches or look up at the clock. When they begin deliberating it is about 5:00 P.M. They are done by 5:45.

We are called back to the courtroom, and I know that my worst fears will be confirmed. The reading of the verdict is a mere formality: the jury had decided my fate the very first day. I am found guilty of rape, guilty of aggravated sodomy, and guilty of burglary. The cuffs are placed back on, and I am returned to the county jail. The jury gets home before supper.

One week later I am brought back into court for sentencing. To add to my utter humiliation, the district attorney points out that my parents had been in the courtroom during the whole trial and that I had committed this horrible crime even though I came from an intact and obviously supportive family. He says that I am a threat and that I had been paroled only because the prisons were overcrowded. He chooses not to mention my model behavior and exemplary parole. Instead, he emphasizes the brutality and dehumanizing nature of rape, and he even brings up the second rape (for which I have not yet been tried).

My lawyer attempts to point out that I was tried for only one crime. He also asks the judge to ignore the writing on the indictment, which falsely reports prior convictions for "criminal attempt to commit rape, armed burglary; aggravated assault and rape." (That "incorrect paperwork" will cause me trouble for the next sixteen years.) My lawyer ends our case with the traditional words, "That is all we have."

I am called to the podium, and before he pronounces sentence, the judge asks if I have anything to say. I clear my throat and say what is in my heart.

"Yes, sir. I would like to say one thing to you, Judge Boswell, to Mr. Keller, and to the detectives involved, Detective Storey, Detective Harper back there. With God as my witness, I have been falsely accused of these crimes. I did not commit them. I'm an innocent man, and I just pray in the name of Jesus Christ that all this truth will be brought out. The truth will eventually be brought out. That's all I have to say to the court in Clayton County here today, Judge."

I am not the penitent rapist they desire. To them my claim of innocence is just an aggravating circumstance. By retaining my right to appeal, I appear unredeemable. They don't understand that I was not thinking of my legal options when I spoke, I was thinking about God.

"Mr. Calvin Crawford Johnson, with regard to indictment number 12-22011-3: Count one, the offense of rape, it will be the judgment and sentence of this court that you be sentenced to the state penitentiary for your natural life." I look over at my family and see my mom crying. . . . all has been lost. I mouth the words, "It'll be all right."

In addition, the judge gives me fifteen years for count two, aggravated sodomy, and fifteen years for count three, burglary. It is a shockingly stiff sentence, and not at all in line with a first offense for rape and aggravated sodomy. His harshness is explained by his next comment: "The court also notes that this is your second burglary under Code Section 16-7-1B. Further the court notes with regard to count two (aggravated sodomy) that this is a recidivist indictment, and the order will so reflect."

"*What?*" I turn to my lawyer. I can't believe that the judge has gone back on his promise to ignore the errors on my indictment. Even the prosecutor has admitted that the ludicrous charges from my first arrest had been dropped. The truth is that I have never committed, nor been convicted of, any sexual or violent crime. My lawyer and I can't believe what we have just heard.

"The sodomy charge is a recidivist charge?" my counsel asks in shock, his brow knit in frustration.

"Correct," responds the judge. "It is all recidivist, very honestly, but I'm taking note that the second count is particularly a recidivist indictment."

My lawyer persists, and approaches the bench for an off-the-record discussion, which produces no noticeable result.

I am about to serve a life sentence, plus fifteen years, for a rape I did not commit, and it is considered a repeat offense, because of another rape I did not commit. I want to scream, but they would just club me. Instead, I remain silent, because I am now the permanent property of the prison system, and I have to obey its rules.

They lead me away in my orange prison jumper, while the men in suits prepare for their next case. I am still not used to the sound of chains around my body, and I look at them with a brief feeling of panic. The ordeal has taken its toll, and I am weak from the loss of hope.

A Last Chance for Justice

The first new lawyer I contact tries to discourage me with
the facts: "You've been convicted of the exact same crime,
same M.O., just a couple of miles from the first attack. Do
you realize that the first conviction will be reported to the
new jury, and they will be compelled to assume that you
committed that rape? Mr. Johnson, no one is acquitted
under those circumstances. You already have life plus
fifteen years. A second conviction will ruin any chance of
parole – ever."

I am adamant. "I am not guilty, and if I can prove that
I didn't do the identical crime in Fulton County, they'll have
to grant my appeal in Clayton."

He politely declines to take the case.

At home, Mom and Dad, already deeply in debt from
my legal bills, do what they can for me. My older sister,
Judy, is working in Washington, and my younger sister,
Tara, is studying at Fisk University. When Judy heard that

I had received a life sentence, she said simply, "What's the next step?" But Tara, a teenager in college, took the news quite hard: my parents had shielded her from the details of the accusations against me, and her shock at the sentence is profound. Then four months after my sentencing, Mom has a stroke and is incapacitated for several months. The family obviously has a number of challenges besides my incarceration.

After Mom recovers, she and Judy begin the search for an attorney who understands my reasoning. They find one who agrees that an acquittal in the second trial is the only way to prove my innocence, though he, too, warns me of the possible consequences. I am looking at a second life sentence with no chance of parole. The sensible thing is to forget about the Fulton County case and just work toward parole, but if I really want my name cleared, my only option is a second trial.

Unfortunately, Fulton County has no interest in trying me, but I continue to insist. My new lawyer, Michael Hauptman, contacts the district attorney and reports back to me. "They think you're crazy—you're asking for double life. As your attorney, I again have to warn you that your chances—"

"I am innocent. I don't care whether the truth has a good chance or a poor chance. The truth is my only chance."

Unlike my first attorney, the new lawyer tells me to make eye contact with the jurors. During the first trial I was meek though honest. After a year in prison I have no trouble summoning up the courage to be bold. He also advises me to address my answers to the jury, not the person asking the questions.

"Look at the prosecutor when she asks a question, but address your answer to the jury. They are the ones who will decide your fate." He warns me about the prosecution's strategy. "Because you are taking the stand, they will be able to discuss your previous conviction as a matter of character. They will use that conviction as a powerful weapon against you, and they will probably put both victims on the stand."

The trial proceeds much like the first one, but when I take the stand things are different. At one point I am misquoted by the female prosecutor. It is a blatant falsification, and I say so.

"You're a liar, I never said that."

The judge warns me about the tone of my response.

"If she says that I said those things, she is a liar." I am angry.

The judge warns me again, "Mr. Johnson —"

"If she claims I said those things, she's — a — liar." Calvin C. Johnson Jr. has risen to his own defense.

The evidence and testimony are practically identical to the Clayton County trial. The only real difference between the two is my demeanor, and the fact that the prosecutor can cite my conviction in the Clayton rape. There is one other subtle difference, which has nothing to do with witnesses or physical evidence; it is a difference only skin deep. I have a mixed-race jury this time (five whites, seven blacks), a white lawyer, and a black judge.

The jury deliberates for more than a full day, and they obviously take their responsibility seriously. When we are called back into the courtroom for their verdict, I already know that it has gone much better than the Clayton County trial, but I can hardly stay in my seat when the foreman rises.

"Not guilty," he says loudly, for each and every count.

Justice is done, and I am ecstatic. I hug my attorney and ask him when I can go home. "Soon, I hope," he says, "soon."

My father and the victim's father are both in the courtroom when the verdict is read. As he is leaving, the victim's father approaches my dad.

"I'm glad your son was acquitted," he says to my surprised father. "There's something funny going on with this case." He doesn't elaborate, but to my dad it is powerful confirmation of the obvious. Pops had been a lawyer, and he knows injustice when he sees it.

They didn't allow cameras in the courtroom, but there was a sketch artist from one of the town papers who sat in the front row the whole time. He was quite taken by the case and had drawn a detailed picture of me as I testified. At the end of the trial he gave the drawing to my lawyer, who promised to give it to me as soon as I was released. My dad calls it "the perfect picture of anger." I give Pops a quick hug before I am rushed back to the holding room, where I exchange my suit for overalls, cuffs, and shackles.

Once again I am ready to start my life over. It is 1984, and I am twenty-seven years old. Fulton County has exonerated me, and I am exhilarated. Praises to God flow from my spirit like a river. On the bus back to jail, I shout out a sermon that lasts nearly an hour. Every man on that bus praises God, and the Spirit's fire burns bright in our hearts. We must have been quite a sight, a bus full of men in irons headed for prison, whooping and hollering, clapping our cuffed hands. *Hallelujah! Soon, soon, soon I will be home, AMEN!*

But for weeks after my acquittal, nothing happens. And then it gets worse. The Clayton D.A. resists our calls to reexamine my conviction, then the appeals court rejects our motions outright; everyone seems to get used to the idea of my serving the full sentence – innocent or not. It is maddening. From behind bars I can do nothing. I need people on the outside to be convinced of my cause, to have faith in justice, and to find the answers to vague questions of law and science.

However, with my mother's increasing illness, my family's resources are depleted, and their energy zapped. I come to realize that my dad and sisters have their own lives to manage, and I am not the only priority. After a few months of everyone telling them that my case is hopeless, my rally cries raise little excitement. Still, they do what they can, and I am grateful. But I begin to wonder, *Where is God in all of this?* The happy preacher on the prison bus was just a naïve fool. I'm not asking for a miracle – only simple justice. If the legal system just worked properly, I could be out in a month; but it isn't working. So where is God?

When frustrated men are in conflict there is a cycle of escalation that is hard to resist. As tensions between me and the guards build up, the officers begin to show their authority. They group around me and make references to throwing me in the hole, or bark out orders with increasing volume. This behavior is meant to intimidate, but it only provokes a man who is close to the edge. Bolstered by the false strength of anger, I lose all fear.

One day, one of the guards and I get into it: just some posturing, but I don't back down. When we leave the road crew and board the bus that evening, the other prisoners smirk at me; they are so sure that I'm gonna end up in the hole. I don't care.

The next morning one of the trustees stops me as I head to the bus. Six-Six earned both his name and his prison vocation by virtue of his tremendous size. The guards rely on him to keep the work teams functioning, and the men respect him because he is just.

"Man, you got to calm down," he looks into my eyes. "You know they wrote you up last night, and you would be in some big trouble if someone hadn't interfered." He raises his brow, and lowers his head to my level. I just stare at him.

"Look, I'm not gonna stick my neck out for you no more. You've got a bad attitude, Johnson. Next time, that discipline report won't be lost in delivery."

I take his advice and try to play the good prisoner. I shouldn't be here, but losing control is just going to make matters worse. Somehow, I'll find a way to clear my name.

One day, I run into a man who had been on the bus the night of my acquittal. "Man, what happened, I thought they found you innocent? What are you still doing here?"

"Well, I had those other charges from Clayton. . . ."

"But you're innocent." He seems genuinely concerned. "It was the same guy did both of those rapes—they know that."

"Yeah, well. . . ."

"I know it, too," he mumbles, and looks away from me.

"What?—What do you know?" my heart stops.

"You know how guys talk. . . . I just know that you didn't do it." He walks away with his lips shut tight, shaking his head in disgust.

He will never tell me what he has heard. He is no snitch, and he is scared of revenge. Once again, the truth is suppressed.

Care of the Body

In 1985 my road crew is pressed into swamp service, and
I find myself swinging a bush axe once again. My right
hand grows numb from the repetitive grasping and swinging.
Every night my wrist stings, and I don't have enough
strength even to grasp a pencil. On days when my hand is
really irritated, the axe slips away from me, and we have to
stop the line so that I can retrieve my tool.

Part of the natural action of the axe is that the head
snaps and pops back as it arcs. One hot morning I hit a
large branch and the axe pops so violently that the handle
cracks and stings my palm. I yell so loudly that the men
around me think I've been bitten by a snake. The work line
stops cold. I drop to my knees and yell again. The boss man
comes down to take a look. "Six-Six, get Johnson ready for
the infirmary."

When the doctor asks me what happened, I tell him
about the constant numbness in my palm and the pain in my

wrist. He diagnoses it as possible carpal tunnel syndrome and refers me to a specialist at the prison hospital in Augusta. The next day I read up on the syndrome. I want to make sure I have all the appropriate symptoms.

The specialist is a young man with a very calm demeanor. He gently examines my hands, turning them over in his soft warm palms. Then he explains in an even voice that he will have to assess the nerve damage. I have no idea what the test will be, but I am quite relaxed by the young doctor's bedside manner. Quietly, he takes out a sharp needle and immediately sticks it into my ring finger. It stings like a bee, but I feign total numbness (a textbook symptom). Then he stabs it again – deeper, and then again, until blood runs freely. He continues stabbing – alternately probing then piercing, the whole time watching me. I remain silent, though the pain is excruciating.

"Did you feel that?" *Stab, stab.*

"Umm, no. Maybe a little."

"How about that – anything. No? How about here – deep in the crease under the knuckle?"

"Kinda, like a twitch maybe."

"Hmmm . . . Let's try the palm."

By the time he is finished my hand looks like a pincushion. He writes out a diagnosis and places it in my bloody fingers.

"Mr. Johnson, I recommend that you be taken off the landscaping crew, and be given some other type of labor."

"Yes, sir."

"You're not to swing a bush axe for at least six months. Do you understand?"

"Yes, sir."

I return to Wayne County and present my medical orders to the guard. The next day I am awakened and told to get on the bus with the rest of the chain gang.

"No, sir, I have a medical order from Augusta, it says – "

"I don't care if you have the surgeon f'ing general in your pocket, get dressed and get on that bus."

Not wanting to risk a disciplinary report, I politely board the bus and cut brush all day with my pinpricked hand.

Back at the dorm I again try to explain my situation, but the guards ignore me. This goes on for weeks, until I get an appointment with the physician's assistant (P.A.) assigned to the prison. I figure that he will surely honor the specialist's prescription, but he turns out to be just as doubtful of my injury as the guards.

"Look, whatever that specialist in Augusta said is not binding here," he says and looks over my hand as if it were a piece of dead meat. "I'm accountable to the warden about the inmates of this camp, and your condition does not mandate reassignment."

"Doctor, look, if that axe slips again someone might be seriously hurt."

"I'll treat whatever injuries might arise." He scribbles some notes on my chart. "Meanwhile, you should get some sleep, and don't overexert your wrist."

"Sir, would nine hours of swinging an axe be considered overexertion?"

He says nothing and dismisses me.

Although I have no faith in the system, some of the older inmates convince me to file a complaint. Just as they had predicted, it is denied at the prison counselor level, and at the appeal level, and at the warden's appeal level. But I decide to pursue it with the state authorities. I didn't realize it, but by filing that complaint I became a major concern of the Wayne County correctional authorities. It turns out that wardens and prison staff hate being investigated. Although most of these investigations don't result in changes, they do force the workers to behave themselves during the investigation. In general, workers don't like to be observed by outsiders, and this is especially true in the criminal justice system.

Six-Six is smiling when he finds me in the yard.

"Johnson, congratulations. You got the P.A. reassigned."

"What?"

"Old Doctor Frankenstein is gone. Maybe the warden didn't want Internal Affairs snoopin' around him too much."

"Maybe Doc just wanted a change in scenery."

"I don't know about him, but I hear you might get a change of scenery—real soon," he says, laughing.

"What did you hear?"

"Not much, but I won't expect to see you on the work bus no more," he says with a smile that shows his enormous white teeth.

The appointment comes as a complete shock. I had always wondered what the warden's office looked like, but I never thought that I'd find out. My grievance is still under appeal at the state level but apparently the result has already been decided—I am being transferred. For some reason the warden wants to tell me so himself.

He is a good old boy who is clearly unaccustomed to being investigated. His tone with me is at once polite and condescending, in that combination peculiar to old-time southern bureaucrats.

"Johnson," he begins, "you are going to be leaving my work camp soon, and I don't want to see you here again." He says each word very slowly, as if there is far more meaning than is being conveyed on the surface. "I hope that your work issue will be resolved quickly." He turns to look out the window. "That's all." He dismisses me with a nod toward the door, and I move to leave. "One more thing, Johnson." I turn to face him. "I mean it when I say I don't want to see you in my camp again."

I turn around and walk toward the door with an irrepressible grin. It is harder to suppress my scream of delight than it had been to ignore the doctor's probing needle.

The reward for my injury is a transfer to Men's Correctional Institution. Men's C.I. is a special prison where those with physical limitations are incarcerated. It houses the handicapped, the old, the infirmed, and a few well-bodied men who keep it running.

The arrival at a new prison is always a surreal experience, but this one is amazing. The yard area is filled with men on crutches and in wheelchairs. A blind man walks slowly along the perimeter, swinging his white cane in a rhythmic arc. The more I look, the more I am convinced that I have entered the Twilight Zone. As I stare at the tall wire fences surrounding these broken men, I think of a cage for injured birds.

Settling into the routine of Men's C.I., I try to pinpoint the differences between this place and the other institutions. The biggest change seems to be the relationship between the guards and the prisoners. While it is a prison in every sense, the guards here are used to dealing with the sedate personalities of their charges. It is a far cry from the violent world of maximum security.

When I need to get a new splint for my arm, one of the guards drives me into town and escorts me without the use of handcuffs. He obviously doesn't know that I am in for a violent offense; otherwise, I am sure that he would have cuffed me. I feel no obligation to inform him, as I am glad to have my wrists free. We walk down the sleepy main street and into a free-world medical office. Apparently, the officer knows a woman who works in the back room, so he goes behind the curtain, completely out of my sight—which means that I am out of his.

I am alone in the waiting area, three feet from the door. It is a mind-bending temptation.

He remains back there for a very long time. At one point a woman walks in, looks behind the counter, and seeing no one there, leaves to continue her shopping elsewhere. She probably just popped in to chat with the receptionist during her free time. *Free time.*

Freedom is just outside that door, I think to myself: the freedom to drop into a store or walk down a road. I wonder whether this opportunity to run is fate finally bringing me some good luck. But I also wonder if it is a setup, a way to add extra time to my sentence—or maybe even shoot me. I would run, except that I know that a fugitive can never go home, never contact his family. So, I resist the temptation, but I will look back on this moment for the rest of my life.

Even though my hands continue to ache, I am generally fit. They keep me very busy with every sort of odd job at Men's. But it is comparatively mild work, and I enjoy my time in this convalescent home with bars. Everything seems to move much slower here, and for a change, I actually have the energy to read at the end of the day. Even better than that, I discover that there are weights and a basketball hoop for physical training. I become an enthusiastic user of both—perhaps a bit too enthusiastic, according to Shortstop (I assume his nickname stems from the fact that one of his legs is much shorter than the other.)

"Now, Johnson, you got to slow down," he explains, as we rest against the yard wall.

"Slow down?" I laugh. "This place is plenty slow enough for me."

Shortstop looks concerned. "That may be," he says, wiping his forehead with his ever-present hankie, "but you know, they watch you here. Young guys like you don't last long."

"I'll be all right," I say.

He lowers his voice. "They're takin' notes all the time, son—especially when you lift weights." He mimes the actions of a weightlifter and smiles. "Now, you listen to me, you don't have to lift them all the way over your head to build muscles." He shifts his weight and looks back toward the tower. "That's what I heard them say, that you lift them big weights way over your head."

"Look, I don't care. They can watch me all they want. I just came here to get away from Wayne County. If they move me—they move me." I leave him resting against the wall and go shoot some hoops.

There is an active Christian fellowship at Men's, and in early 1985 they ask me if I'd like to join them, but I have no use for such things. I have quit praying, quit reading the Bible, and won't go to any church service for any reason. I get along with everybody okay, but I don't need to be social, and I don't need God. I say it all politely, but the message is clear to the religious prisoners: *leave me alone.* They respect my wishes. I am a walking time bomb, and no one wants to light my fuse.

One of the kitchen guards loves to bark out orders and yell at folks for no reason. We call him Boots on account of his spit-and-polish footwear. The name is especially funny, because, except for the boots, the man is a total slob. He always comes in late, messes with the food, and never smiles; fortunately, he stays clear of me. I can ignore his constant haranguing as long as it is directed toward others. But eventually, he turns his attention to me.

"Johnson, what the hell's a matter with you—you lazy, good-for-nothin' idiot. You drop another peel, and I'll have you in the hole till there's not a black hair left on your black body," he says, laughing. "You'll be older than Shortstop by the time I let you out, boy."

He is surprisingly light, and it takes no effort to hold him against the wall with my left forearm. I lift him in that manner so that we are about the same height and our eyes can meet; of course, this means that his feet are now dangling. I point the index finger of my free hand in his face and say, "As long as we are both in here, don't you ever – *ever* – talk to me like that again." I gently lower him to the ground and go back to my work.

We never exchange another word, but the following week I receive my transfer order. On the morning that the bus comes to take me away, Boots arrives early for work. His footwear is shining extra brightly, and for the first time, he is smiling at me.

On the bus the driver reveals nothing about my destination.

"I sure hope I'm not going to one of them tough work camps like Mount Vernon?" I offer in the form of a question.

No answer. He keeps quiet through the entire drive and remains silent as we clear the gates of Mount Vernon Correctional Institution.

My anger has won. I am back deep in south Georgia once again, not forty miles from my former prison. Although I hadn't completely lost control, it is clear that my anger is becoming dangerous and unhealthy. It has cost me a bed in the relatively peaceful Men's C.I. – a fact that, unfortunately, just makes me madder.

Mount Vernon is the place where young prisoners are often transfered after they've done some time in Alto. Once in Mount Vernon, these boys form gangs based on their hometowns and ethnicity. I want no part of the gangs, and they seem to respect my independence.

At first I am put to hard labor, but eventually I am assigned to the print shop, where I make signs and stickers. I learn how to silkscreen, and I work in the art room creating decals for police cars, fire engines, and ambulances. My media skills are helpful in the darkroom, and I am good at stenciling the prints. I enjoy the work, and it makes life a bit more tolerable. My folks come to visit every couple of months, but the trip takes them several hours, and I hate to see them look so tired on visiting days.

I am able to keep my temper at Mount Vernon and don't receive any disciplinary reports. So when I ask to be transferred to a prison closer to Atlanta, my request is eventually granted: I am moved to River State, only two hours from my parents' home. The proximity to my family makes their lives a bit easier, but I soon discover that there are new challenges to contend with.

At River State Prison the term *criminal justice* is indeed an oxymoron. It is a high-security location housing men who have been convicted of serious crimes: murder, bank robbery, rape. But it isn't the violent offenders that we fear the most at River State—it is the guards, who have a reputation for being especially brutal.

River State is also unusual because of its peculiar design. The prison is set up like a three-piece compass. There is an East building, which houses several dormitories and administrative offices, and two other dormitory buildings, called North and South. These separate brick-and-concrete structures are curiously linked by a series of underground tunnels. The tunnels are fairly narrow and serve as constriction points, where inmates are made to walk single file. At night the tunnels are normally empty, except when the guards come for a specific man.

As soon as I arrive at River State, my cellmates explain the peculiar habits of the guards. Ice, who claims that his name refers to diamonds, is an older inmate with fine white hair. He starts out fairly loud and agitated, but as he gets serious, he slows way down. By the time he tells me about the tunnels, he is nearly whispering.

"The guards don't take nothin' from nobody," he says. "If they even *think* you're sassin', they take you in the tunnels and beat you to within an inch of your life."

Peanut, a scrappy young man with an odd-shaped afro, adds grimly, "They did it to Cool last week. His face swelled up so bad that his eyes shut close—he's still in the hospital."

Ice continues, "They didn't even stop when he was down. They just kicked him like a dog."

"What about the prison counselor?" I ask.

Ice laughs. "Might as well be the warden's boyfriend."

When you are watched over by men with guns day and night, you take a serious interest in their moral framework. Corrupt guards are the greatest danger to the peaceful operation of a prison. Eventually, the men will fight back, and men who have no recourse to justice often act like animals.

Bullies are the same wherever they are found: in the sandlot or in the prison, guards or inmates. They always go for the weak, and they have no respect for the rules. I know it is important to show the guards that I won't cause any trouble, but they also need to know that I won't be pushed around. Defense is always proactive behind bars; you can't wait for something to happen to prove that you'll fight back. Your reputation with the guards (and the convicts) is best established before trouble starts. Fortunately, for us long-time convicts, a reputation follows you through the system. Everyone knew a little about me before I arrived at River State, but I still work to establish a presence in the first few weeks. I work out at every opportunity, and I never joke around.

Because of its proximity to the state capital, Rivers has a lot of volunteers from Atlanta congregations who provide church services. These functions are well attended and make a big difference to the morale of the prisoners. One popular feature of the services is that women are among the visiting holy. The prison grapevine reports which groups have the prettiest female participants, and these are always the most popular meetings. Just the chance to see women attracts many a hardcore atheist to church. Some of the men devise a rating system, which has nothing to do with the quality of the theology and everything to do with the qualities of the women. Even my own hard heart begins to soften toward religion as my friends tout the particular advantages of going to a certain service. It is a strange type of evangelism, but it is effective. "Man, you need to go to church tonight – they got some *pretty* girls in that church."

When I finally attend one of the recommended services, I discover that my dormmates had been truthful. There are indeed plenty of pretty women at the meeting, and they sing sweet music. The allure stays with me for a while, and I attend exclusively the denominations with pretty girls. Eventually, however, my conscience speaks up. *What kind of hypocrite are you? You're no better than those poor heathen idiots—going to church just to see the pretty women. You turned your back on God—now you're going to church just to stare at ladies?*

My conscience successfully shames me. I hate being a hypocrite, and even the sight of beautiful women can't soothe my feelings of duplicity. Once again, I leave the church – completely this time. All that talk about forgiveness and joy just makes me sick anyway. I dismiss God in my life with a simple question: "What kind of God allows this to happen?"

I spend time in the weight room whenever possible. There is dignity in exercise, and it is something that I can control: a goal I can set, accomplish, and outdo. Prison life is a great incentive for keeping a muscular appearance. A small group of us spend a great deal of time lifting and working out. We are a silent encouragement to one another, and the unspoken competition allows us to be men.

As soon as I arrive, I remove my shirt and fix the weights. Each week I add an extra curl or a few more pounds. My arms tense and bulge with every flexion, and I am proud that the fatty meals have not ruined my health. It is a bit annoying that we are constantly watched by the guards, especially since no one ever makes trouble in the weight room. It is a peaceful sanctuary for testosterone and sweat: the prisoners police each other here, and we guard this privilege jealously. Without using any intimidation, the weight room is reserved for men who are serious lifters. Most us of were star athletes in high school; some were even professional players. When I consider the wasted potential in this room, I get worked up and have to add more weight.

Sometimes there are female guards posted around the room, and occasionally they stare at us with what seems like longing. We hear them talk. Most of them are married, stable women with a government job and a fat, lazy husband. One woman with glasses comes by each day to watch us lift – not because it's her job, but because we are strong. I am less flattered than annoyed, like a lion in a cage.

One day when I come to lift, Big Nick is smiling; he doesn't usually put on a happy face in the weight room.

"What's up?"

"You know that old guard lady with the glasses?"

"The one in the booth?"

"Yeah, that's the one." He looks over at the window, which is crowded with walkie-talkies. "She ain't gonna be watchin' us no more."

"What happened?"

"Seems she wasn't just watchin' us – she was in there playing with herself," he tells me, laughing. "The sergeant came by to see her last night, but she didn't hear him on account of the weights banging – and her daydream." He laughs again. "He caught her red-handed with her pants undone, and her other arm up her shirt."

"Imagine that," I say.

"I'd rather not," he replies, then begins his squat-thrusts.

So much for the dignity of exercise.

River State Rebellion

Whenever Ice and I work in the kitchen together, he tries to inject a little levity into our day. His favorite games always involve the female guards.

"Johnson, hand me that fruit—no, not the apple, the banana."

It's the end of the shift, and we are putting away the food and wiping down the counters. At this time of night there are always plenty of guards around to make sure we don't pilfer any knives or leftovers. Their night shift coincides with clean-up time, and they are often hungry. Occasionally, there are some morsels that are considered edible by free-worlders, and Ice loves to share them with the women. Most guards will accept only fresh fruits or vegetables (the actual meals are eaten purely for survival.)

"Officer Butler, would you like something to eat?" Ice asks Miss Butler. He is being particularly ingratiating. "Some fresh fruit perhaps?"

She almost smiles. "What do you have?"

"How 'bout a nice, ripe banana? I have one left from the pudding," he says, holding out the perfect fruit by its stem.

"Sure," she answers casually.

At first I don't realize it's a game; then I notice that the man with a broom stops in mid-sweep and the guy at the counter stretches his neck to watch. The female guard opens the top of the fruit with her painted nails and peels it about halfway down. Then she unconsciously licks her glossed lips and breaks a piece off in her mouth. The men try to act nonchalant, but their interest is obviously focused on her every move.

Ice comments on her performance after she leaves. "She really knows how to eat a banana, she's one of the best," he says. He smiles and closes his eyes like he's just been kissed.

The next day he tries the same trick on a different guard.

"Would you like a nice, ripe banana, Officer Duval? I have one left over if you'd like."

"Yes, thank you, I would," she responds.

He hands her the long fruit with a smile of anticipation.

"May I have a knife and fork, please?" she asks.

"What?"

"A knife and fork," she repeats, "to eat the banana."

"Ma'am, nobody eats a banana with a knife and fork. Besides, we've put away all the cutlery."

"Well, my folks are from France, and we always eat with a knife and fork," she explains, holding out her hand for the implements.

"Johnson, give the lady a knife and fork," he says to me as I wipe down the counter; his disappointment and contempt are thinly veiled. Under his breath he grumbles, "Never gonna give no damn French guard a banana again. . . . I thought those people were supposed to be sexy. . . . knife and fork—shoot."

After a while the tedium of kitchen work begins to irritate me. There is no real satisfaction in this labor, because even though we prepare the food, we hate it. The meals are always fatty, the meat inedible, and just about everything is boiled and tasteless. When the last dorm begins eating, it is our signal to start the cleanup. Extra guards file into the cafeteria, and they check to make sure everything is in order. Whenever there are leftovers, Ice asks the senior officer to announce it to the men.

"There's seconds on tonight's meat," shouts the guard.

"You eat it," a voice says from one of the tables.

"Who said that?"

"You eat it," now from another table, perhaps at the far end.

"All right, I want to know who said that!"

Silence. The officer turns his back.

"You eat it!" "You eat it!" "You eat it!"

Before he can turn around, a half dozen anonymous men have added to his frustration. "I bet you won't say that to my face," he says as he bangs his nightstick into his palm.

"You eat it," someone says from the middle of the room.

"If I find out—"

"You eat it!"—left side.

"—who is saying—"

"You eat it!"—right side.

"—I'll—"

"You eat it!"—middle.

"I'm gonna lock you all down!"

"You eat it."

Ice knows some of the important details of my history, and he watches out for me the first month. One afternoon as I'm lifting weights he asks me, "Johnson, you spend a lot of time in the law library, right?"

"I'm not a prison lawyer," I answer, "but I read a lot. Filed my own paperwork, that kind of thing."

"Make sure the guards know that you read and write," he says as he watches me load my weight. "They usually pick on the illiterates—guys who don't know their rights and can't file a complaint. They never mess with me, because I have my GED, and my daughter still comes to visit. She's gonna be a lawyer," he adds with pride.

As soon as I have some free time, I make sure that I am seen in the law library. While I am there, I casually discuss with Peanut a grievance that I had filed in a previous prison. A guard overhears part of our conversation, and a precious seed is planted in the grapevine.

The grievance protocol in Georgia is designed to eliminate frivolous lawsuits. There are several layers of complaint and appeal before a grievance even leaves the prison walls. At each level the paperwork and regulations get more complex, and this increasing difficulty serves as an effective deterrent. Most inmates discover that they must hire a lawyer early on, or quit. The result is that many prisoners are compelled to drop appeals due to confusion or financial constraints. Fortunately, there are "prison lawyers" who can help out at reduced rates. Some of these men have actually practiced law on the outside, but most of them are simply schooled by experience. A short filing can cost between twenty-five and forty dollars, but even at those rates many men are kept out of the process.

The first level of complaint is the prison counselor. He investigates the initial report and always deems it "without merit." Next, the prison committee, and then the warden, are given an opportunity to reverse the counselor's finding (to my knowledge this has never occurred). Then, once the formality of internal denials is complete, the case can be heard by an appeals judge. Summary denials are the rule here also, and that effectively discourages all but the most diehard inmates from legal recourse.

I explain to Peanut that the complaint I had filed was about my carpal tunnel syndrome. At the time, it seemed like a strange legal route to take, but I've been told that my experience was actually fairly typical. After the usual rounds of denial, my appeal was finally scheduled to be reviewed by a judge. I was brought to the federal district court in handcuffs, looking forward to my day in court. But instead of the courtroom, I was led to the judge's private chambers. There were four men in that room: the judge, me, and two lawyers for the state. The judge listened to both sides, and then decided that my case was "without merit." I could have appealed to yet another judge, but I had made my point; and I had already been transferred by the warden to a new prison. So, I let it drop. The main reason for filing a complaint is just to let the staff know that you are not easy prey. The mere initiation of paperwork is sometimes enough to keep guards within the legal bounds of their employment. I hope that just the rumor of my past legal action might insulate me from abuse at River State.

It doesn't take long for me to witness the guards' excess. Within weeks of my arrival, they are already picking on a new inmate who had arrived with me. Just as Ice had predicted, the latest victim is not someone likely to file a complaint. Slim is a young tough who is not very intelligent, and completely illiterate. I begin to worry about Slim when a guard yells at him for cutting line at lunch. It might have been an innocent mistake, but he and the guard exchange some words. Slim should have kept his mouth shut, but instead he started explaining himself to the guard. The guard told him to shut up, and Slim swore at him. That would get you a week in the hole at any other prison, but at River State it just earns him a cold stare.

On Friday night, we see the guards lead Slim away in cuffs. They take him down toward the east door, and we all fear the worst. As we watch, Ice shakes his head with the resignation of the long-incarcerated. But Peanut is still a teenager, and he cannot contain his anger.

"They're takin' Slim down in the tunnel—and they're wearing gloves!"

Another young inmate is equally indignant: "Man, we're not gonna take this shit anymore! They can't just beat somebody up because he can't write."

A man who lives near the east door shouts to us, "I can hear him screaming—man they're killin' him in there."

"Those bastards!"

The young men are overheating, and I know that it is just a matter of time before something huge happens.

It is a week before we see Slim again, but his face is still swollen, and he bears the scars of prison stitches. The guards snicker as they bring him back to our dorm. He is cowered and silent. As I watch him move stiffly to his bunk, I decide that I won't just sit by and watch them kill this young man.

The next day at lunch I stand behind him in line. "Slim, you wanna file a complaint?"

"Man, I don't know how to do that stuff," he says. He doesn't bother to face me; since the beating he keeps his eyes downcast.

"I'll help you out," I say.

"Can you write?" he says and looks at me briefly.

"Yep, and I've filed a couple of grievances before. Even went all the way to a judge once."

"Did you win?" His face betrays no emotion.

"The guards left me alone—"

"Just because you filed?"

"As soon as they heard Internal Affairs was coming down, they quit messing with me."

"What do I have to do?"

"I'll write it up, you just have to sign it—an X will do."

He doesn't turn around again, but I hear him say, "Thanks, Johnson."

For the next few days I spend every minute I can writing up the forms. The rule in most prisons is that you can have only your own legal documents in your possession. You aren't allowed to work on papers for another inmate, so prison lawyers have to operate clandestinely. The pros get around this by never filling in a name. I follow their example and prepare Slim's paperwork without writing in any of the key identifiers. When the papers are nearly ready, I tell Slim to meet me at lunch. All he'll have to do is supply some details about himself and sign the document. I can just imagine the look on the guards' faces when this illiterate inmate files a brief written by a communications graduate.

While I work on the forms, I have to be especially wary of snitches. Since I am relatively new in this prison, I am not really sure whom to suspect. I avoid anyone who talks to the guards more than absolutely necessary. In my experience the only men who talk to them regularly are snitches—scum who would frame their own mother for a chocolate bar. Snitches earn their rewards by telling the guards what they want to hear. Sometimes it's true, and sometimes it's a lie. Either way, a snitch's word is taken over anyone else's. Most snitches are rewarded with extra privileges, but I've heard of some who have been released through unexpected sentence reductions. Some snitches actually begin to feel like police officers: they get cocky and start acting as if they're a part of the management. It must be a powerful feeling: a single note passed to a guard can remove the accused from his dorm and lock him down in solitary, "pending investigation." Sometimes the investigation is "pending" for months – months of no visitation, no exercise, and no fresh air. But the snitch usually gets his in the end. Either the dorm catches on and punishes him, or he gets too cocky and the guards drop him. Eventually, the system lets him know his place – he is a guard dog and nothing more.

I take every precaution against snitches and remain confident that I have succeeded. However, I sense there is trouble when I see two guards smiling at me.

Damn a snitch, I think to myself. Perhaps someone did overhear me talking to Slim or saw me writing up his complaint. It's so frustrating, because we are so close to filing: I just need his signature, but the guards' stares make me anxious. Still, I am determined to finish what I have started. Perhaps they don't know how close we are to filing; maybe they won't interfere in time. I pick up a tray and get in line behind Ice and Peanut. I try to spot Slim, but he is nowhere to be found.

"Ice, where's Slim?" I ask, casually.

"Didn't you hear?" He grabs a stale roll and slides his tray along the rails.

"Hear what?"

"He was transferred today," Ice says, glancing at the guards who are still staring at us from across the room. "Reidsville," he continues. "They were in a big hurry to get him out of here." He looks down at the folder I am carrying. "At least he got away from these animals."

Peanut shakes his head in disgust and says under his breath, "Don't worry, we're gonna get those bastards."

"I hope he finds someone to read his mail for him," I say as I throw his file in the trash.

That night, Ice explains to me that what happened to Slim is a popular tactic at River State. If a knowledgeable prisoner starts helping an illiterate, the guards merely ship one of them off – and if internal affairs shows an interest, the staff scatters everyone involved. There are never any witnesses at River State.

Prison is all about the control of actions and possessions. Surprise inspections and confiscation of contraband are a routine part of life. If you leave an item on your bed and there is a surprise inspection, it can be confiscated – even if it's something as innocuous as a library book. You cannot receive packages, except at holidays; and you are subject to search and loss of privileges at any time. These things occur in the best prisons, but at River State the guards devise new ways to add to the humiliation of incarceration. They seem to take our stuff for no reason; and instead of assigning work that gives us a sense of purpose, the clear intention of much of our work here is punishment.

Each day from my dorm window I can see an example of the guards' creativity. In clear view of all the prisoners, they have established a special work team, "the Stump Crew." Their job is to remove large stumps and then bury them completely. The catch is, there is only one gigantic stump, and it is endlessly excavated and reburied. The goal of this futility is to break the men's spirit while the rest of us watch. It makes me furious just to hear their shovels, and I would probably attack any guard who subjected me to that torture.

The young men are always talking about beating up guards or burning the place down. When Slim was transferred, I was nearly as mad as they are now, but I have seen enough to know that violence and destruction just breed more of the same. Most of the young men's ranting is just talk, a way for them to vent frustration without risking punishment. But as things get worse at River State, the older prisoners sense that trouble is coming.

Flagrant injustice always leads to open violence, but before the dam breaks there are plenty of small breaches in the peace. At River State, these breaches are perpetrated by both sides. The prisoners take glee in pulling one over on the guards, and they have devised several outlandish annoyances. For example, if a guard puts down his keys – even for a second – they are likely to be stolen and tossed out a window. Such a mishap can cost the guard his job. Another favorite tactic is to subtly vandalize the lockbox. We pass those boxes in the hallway several times a day, and they contain the logbooks and other items the guards need to access every few hours. The boxes open from underneath, and it is possible to place a substance there that will transfer to the guard's hand as he reaches into the lock. Boogering the lockbox is a specialty of one inmate, who has earned the nickname Boog for his trouble. Boog loves to watch the guards try to shake off his prodigious snot.

As fall progresses there are more serious attacks against the guards. In one dorm room several prisoners hurl batteries at a guard. While this may seem to be inexcusable and animalistic behavior, it is to be expected, since the guards treat the men like animals.

Although most guards do their job without malice, the few who abuse their power destroy the morale of all. Officer Doyle is one of the bad apples. The inmates in my dorm become upset with him after he confiscates many of their favorite possessions during two searches in a single day. While conducting these searches he overturns a number of beds and damages what scarce property the men have. He doesn't find any serious contraband either time, but he smiles as he flaunts his authority.

When he returns to search the room for a third time that day, the men form a human wall at the door. He calls for backup, and fortunately, his supervisor recognizes a volatile situation.

The supervisor looks at us and asks, "What's going on here?"

After a few seconds one prisoner speaks up and says, "He ain't comin' back in here. He busted up all our stuff."

There is a tense moment of silence. The supervisor tells the guards, "Go on and leave, I want to talk to these men." It is a brave and smart move, but it only puts off the inevitable. Within a week Doyle is assigned to other duties.

The cold weather brings more discontent in the poorly heated cells, but I try to stick to my mantra, CCC: *cool, calm, and collected.* I refuse to let the guards get to me, and since I am not easily riled, there is no fun in it for them. I've discovered that kindergarten rules of the playground apply to the guards as well – they won't bother you so much if you just ignore them. This strategy works for the most part, until one of the guards brings up my conviction.

We had just returned to our room when Officer Roth comes by and starts chatting. There are only a few of us in the dorm, because it's just before supper and most of the men are still coming back from their jobs. Officer Roth is talking about a sex offender course that will be offered in February, but no one is really interested. Out of nowhere I hear him say, "Well, Johnson's a tree-jumper."

I freeze. Those words could change my life in prison—no one knows why I am here, and sex offenders are scorned behind bars.

The next night after work, I wait for him in the hallway. I am in an area where there are no cameras, and there is no one else around. I figure that the hallway will still be clear when he performs his rounds, and he and I can have a little talk about discretion. Suddenly, I see him round the corner—now it's just him and me. I stand before him and block his way.

"Johnson?" he senses trouble but doesn't panic. He knows that I am a reasonable man, a model prisoner.

"Don't you *ever* come around here telling what I'm in for."

He begins to shake and stutter. "I, I, I, I'm sorry."

I move out of the way and let him pass. The conversation is over.

The next day I pass him as he talks with a group of guards, and he respectfully calls me "Mr. Johnson." I never trouble him again, and he never mentions my sex-offender status.

The way the compound is set up, there are about four hundred prisoners in the North building, and three hundred in the South. We sleep seventy to a dorm, and each building has either two or three floors of dormitories. The two opposing dormitory buildings are separated by the main courtyard, under which are the infamous tunnels. If the prisoners in the opposite building are being particularly loud, it is possible to hear them through the windows. Usually, that only happens around the holidays, when the inmates are especially frustrated.

On Christmas Day, the warden hears us shouting between buildings and decides to call in the Special Tactical Units. These elite guards are dressed like modern gladiators: they wear armor, carry shields, have face masks, and swing their nightsticks like medieval mace. In response to our holiday noise they parade up and down the hall, shields in place, electric tasers ready—cursing worse than prisoners. Their mere presence is sufficient to quiet us down. We have all heard about their particular brand of crowd control, and most of us want nothing to do with it.

The New Year starts with several beatings by the guards, and as the weeks of winter wear on, the few staff members who oppose the miscreants either quit or are transferred. Without any substantial opposition the guards enjoy unbridled "authority," and their disregard for human rights becomes even more blatant. The prisoners are without reasonable recourse, so unreasonable alternatives gain appeal. Rioting is not the most effective method of complaint, but sometimes it's the only form available.

Peanut is the first to notice the smoke: "There's a fire in the North building! Hey, everybody shut up! They're shouting something."

All the young men run to the windows, crowding to catch a glimpse of the mayhem. We hear shouts and crashes across the courtyard.

"Which dorm?" I ask.

"Two North."

"That's Flash's dorm," Ice says, thinking of an old friend.

Peanut shouts, "Hey, Flash, yo! Two-N, what's up?"

The older men hang back, fearing the worst, but the young men stomp about, and some rip off their prison shirts in a small act of defiance.

Peanut turns to us from the window. "They're burning the place down, they're not going to take it anymore!" He smiles at the spectacle of the fire.

"Go, North! Burn it down!" a disorganized chant begins to spread.

The young men leap, shouting that we should join in the mutiny. There is no argument, no attempt at persuasion. It is too late for organized thought; the crowd takes on its own spirit. We older men move further away from the windows, but the younger ones begin to smash things.

The first item that comes down is the detested intercom. It is the ultimate symbol of incarceration. From dawn to dusk it barks out our fate. We wake to its buzzing, and put our lights out like children when it commands darkness. When it calls our name, we go wherever it directs, "Lawson, report to the counselor. . . . Jones, to the security office."

It is not enough to merely pull it down—the intercom is splintered until a coil of orange wire runs from its side. A young man jumps on the flattened speaker. Next into the pile are the mattresses, laundry carts, anything that can be smashed or ripped. Most of the heap is metal, and there is not a lot to burn, but it is clear that the men are building a bonfire.

"What's going on in North now?" asks Ice.

"Riot squad's arrived."

"Oh, shit," Ice says to no one, "now look what you've done."

The young toughs stand by the window shouting threats to the guards.

"Come in here, and we'll castrate you. . . . We'll burn you along with the mattresses – you bastards!"

Peanut relays details to us, like a play-by-play announcer. "They've entered the North building. . . . they got the bullhorn out. . . ." Then he turns to the inmates near him. "We better hurry and get this fire going."

As the young men leave the windows to engage in more effective destruction, we get our first glimpse of the North building. Just about every dorm now flashes with orange flame and billowing smoke. We can see televisions ripped from the walls and tossed into the fire – even the much beloved pool tables in several dorms are reduced to timbers for the flame.

Ice is disheartened by this rash stupidity. "You think we're ever gonna get TV and pool tables in here again? Those fools will be older than me before that happens." He looks around at the dorm with disgust and begins filling his lockerbox. "Once that goon squad gets in here, all hell is gonna break loose. Those boys may be talkin' that stuff now, but when the guards start crackin' heads – they'll be quiet as sheep." He looks over at my stuff. "Save what you can," he says.

The tactical forces move through the halls of the North building with all deliberate speed. It isn't often that they are allowed to perform their special service, and like all well-trained troops they are anxious to use their skills. As their armaments become visible in the courtyard, the baiting of the rioters becomes pathetically ludicrous: "We're waiting for you suckers, we're gonna kill you!"

The prisoners are basically unarmed and completely disorganized. It is truly maddening; we are all going to pay a serious price for this comedy.

"They're smashing the radios," Peanut says, and he looks suddenly worried. Apparently the young men had not considered that their own dear property might become a casualty.

The special agents are well organized and methodical. Their strategy is apparent by their movements: they plan to empty out each of the three dorms in succession, traveling from North to East, and finally South. We will be the last building taken. The men at the window can see the operational details. As each unit approaches a dorm, they give a warning for the "uninvolved" to come forward. Compliance with this order is no guarantee of safety, since everyone is clubbed as they exit. After this initial "clemency," the officers go on a rampage, smashing whatever possessions they find, and beating men indiscriminately.

The scene in the stairwell is worse. All of the prisoners there are handcuffed with plastic wire, and the guards move them along by brutally shoving them or kicking them in the back. Everyone at the top of the stairs is pushed so hard that they fall face-first down the steps. With their hands cuffed, they don't have the ability to break their fall. Their blood mingles with the water from broken pipes. While we can see only brief snapshots through the window, it is clear that we are in for some rough treatment. I am determined to protect myself as best I can.

As always, Ice provides excellent advice. "Put on all the clothes you own. It's going to be a cold, rough night." He has obviously taken his own counsel and looks forty pounds heavier. Adding to his bizarre appearance is the strange bulge created by the prison sheet that he has tucked into his pants. He catches me looking down at the protrusion in his groin.

"Emergency padding," he explains. "They are not going to treat us like gentlemen."

I follow his lead, and we pad ourselves with everything we can; then we stow our precious radios in the footlockers, hoping to protect them from the angry troops.

"Come on, you bastards, we're ready for you!" A few fanatics still bait the guards, but most of the men don't want to watch the onslaught. The crowd at the window diminishes significantly as the troops enter the ground floor of our building. Skinny, who weighs four hundred pounds, is trying to hide under his bed, but his great size merely elevates the mattress and adds a pathetic aspect to the pandemonium.

"What's burning now?" one of the older men asks.

"Looks like everything—except the honors dorm under us."

One of the hooligans shouts, "Let's go get 'em!" and twenty men take up the cry.

The boys are now frantic—they have burned everything in sight, so the prospect of destroying an unspoiled dorm is like blood to sharks. In seconds, they construct a makeshift battering ram from the steel remains of bed frames. With this primitive tool they manage to smash through our door, and then bust the stairwell lock. Even though there is noise coming from every side, we can hear them dragging the metal ram downstairs. Through the floor we feel them smashing their way into the honors dorm. Once the door is down, their war cry fills the air as they make their way to the beloved pool table in the center of the room below us. Then comes the now-familiar sound of a large object being torn from the floor by a dozen angry men. Finally, there is one loud shout in unison, and the table strikes with such force that the concrete building shudders. Nothing will be spared.

Seconds later, the riot police arrive on our floor. We hear them try to enter the first dorm room. Those prisoners have taken a much more serious approach and have barricaded themselves in the smoke-filled room. Their ingenuity costs them a tear-gas attack. One prisoner is hit directly with a canister and loses consciousness—we never learn his fate.

Once the barricade next door is finally smashed, the guards move in to that room with a vengeance. They send the men into the hallway, cuffed and coughing; many are bleeding from the head. The prisoners are shoved and kicked down the hall from guard to guard, and then finally pushed down the stairs. The advantage to being on the second floor is that we have a few extra moments to insulate our bodies. The disadvantage is being pushed down the staircase with both hands tied behind our backs.

"Shit!" Peanut turns to us with ashen blankness. "They threw a man off the balcony!"

I try to imagine the safest exit strategy. I know that even in chaos, planning is an asset. While the young men become more and more agitated, some of us older guys actually become much more calm.

The troops move up to our door and shout unintelligibly. Shine, the bald prison barber, keeps shouting back at them, "Don't hurt me, don't hit me, I'm the barber!" Skinny is now shaking his entire bed frame and has apparently wet his pants. Ice and I have put on every stitch of clothing we can find. Ice guesses that the guards will be most vicious in the dark recesses of the dorm, where we have spent most of the riot. We decide that it is worth the risk to move closer to the door, and we prepare to meet our attackers face to face.

When the broken door swings open, I hear the bullhorn screeching, and through the smoke, I see raised nightsticks. I know they will strike everyone within reach. Although my instinct is to cover my face, I think my only chance is to look them straight in the eye. At least the ones I know can be held accountable by my stare. I square my shoulders and walk out with calculated dignity. The nightsticks begin to swing: the guards crack open the heads of men on either side of me. Perhaps it is just my good fortune to be spared, but I did look every one of them in the eye.

In the hallway my hands are tied tight behind me with a plastic cord, and I am shoved toward the staircase. At the top of the stairs stands Officer Doyle, now infamous for utter cruelty. I watch as he kicks each handcuffed inmate helplessly down the stairs. Several men are injured so badly that they can not continue unassisted. I stand as tall as I can and approach him with purposeful steps. Most of the men try to run past him; some of them even preempt his kick by diving down the stairs themselves. But I decide to slow down and stay with my game plan. When I reach him, I look him straight in the eye. With the other guards I did this to hold them accountable—maybe to wake their conscience. With Doyle it is strictly a threat. My look means one thing: touch me, and I will risk my life to kill you later. He lets me pass unmolested.

Outside in the freezing January night, everything is turned upside down. We are shoved into the mud and told to lie still, arranged like paving stones on the ground. The sod has turned to mud, churned by our feet and the leaking water from dozens of broken toilets. We lie face down in that cold, foul ooze for hours. Unseen guards occasionally come by and snatch necklaces from prone inmates. My own gold chain is pulled, but it does not rip; the thwarted thief walks away cursing. When I recognize the western boots of a decent guard, I ask him to loosen the gouging metal from my neck. To my surprise he removes the necklace and gently stuffs it into my shirt pocket.

We lie that way until the afternoon, soaked to the bone, hungry, and denied movement – even for bodily functions. Eventually, they figure that they have to feed us, and so we are brought into the dining hall for sandwiches. We are forbidden to speak, but no one is in the mood for talking, anyway. Since we are all handcuffed, a remarkably unhappy staff is forced to do the jobs normally assigned to inmates.

When we finally return to the courtyard and see the destruction by the light of day, it is a parable about anger. Our possessions have been destroyed, our privileges burned, but nothing has been gained. And yet, in the end, there is an element of justice. The attention that the riot draws does not bring privileges back, but it does force the guards to stick to the letter of the law for a while. In the aftermath of the riot every man suspected of having actively participated is relocated or punished. We who remain have the unpleasant duty of cleaning up their mess. Layers of grime and soot are scrubbed from every wall and ceiling. The floors are washed and buffed by hand until they glisten, and for months we work to remove the sour smell of smoke and mildew. Worst of all, when each day's hard labor is done, there is no television, no pool table, no distraction of any type to covet.

The in-house attempts at an investigation are rather lopsided. The convicts are summarily moved out and punished, but the guards continue on, undisciplined. There is no serious investigation until the man who was thrown from the balcony launches a major lawsuit. Suddenly, Internal Affairs swoops down with a battery of agents who interview every man in the prison.

The Internal Affairs interrogation room holds the promise of long-delayed justice. I await my appointment eagerly and prepare pages of notes about some of the atrocities perpetrated by the guards. When I enter the office, I am greeted by Detective Morrison, a well-dressed black man with an earnest face. He offers me a seat and seems interested in my version of the events. He picks up a pencil as I begin to tell him about Slim and the tunnel, and how I attempted to help the young man file a grievance before he was transferred.

"Excuse me, Mr. Johnson," he says. He looks over his notes as if he is trying to find his place.

I realize that I have probably been speaking too quickly. "Sorry, Detective Morrison." I smile apologetically. "I'll slow down."

"What happened in the riot?" he asks me, smiling back.

"Sir, the conditions that led up to it—"

"No, I want to hear about the riot itself. What was your part in it?"

"I didn't really have a part in the riot, sir."

"But you saw others, right? What were they doing?"

"Well, the guards were—"

"Can we stick to the convicts? Who were the leaders? What about this Peanut character?"

I can't believe what I am hearing. "I thought you were here to investigate," I reply.

"I am here to find out what happened and who was involved."

"Whose side are you on?" I ask.

"Are you going to answer my questions or not?"

Everything is suddenly clear to me. "Who are you anyway?" I ask indignantly. "I didn't see any badge. Where's your I.D.?"

He reaches for his wallet before realizing that I am interrogating him. "Who do you think you are, Johnson?"

"You don't know who I am!" I say defiantly. "Maybe I'm Officer Johnson of the F.B.I.—here to investigate you."

"Get out of my office!"

"How do I know this is *your* office," I say as I get up. "I thought they were sending a real investigator!"

As a result of the official inquest, several more convicts are punished. Every one of us loses possessions and privileges, and we know that we will spend many more months cleaning up the mess. The riot hasn't really changed the guards, but the media attention has forced them to watch their step. The man who was thrown from the balcony foolishly drops his lawsuit and returns to River State partially paralyzed. The one dorm that had remained calm throughout the riot is able to maintain possession of the last pool table at River State—until it is removed by the warden two months later.

The Board of Pardons and Paroles

I walk into the room and see them all seated at the table,

smiling. It is like an audition for a play, and I am in
costume. They are dressed in the clothes of the free world,
but I am in my prison blue-stripe. On my shirt, in letters
as big as my hands, it says, "State Prisoner," and I am
suddenly aware that no matter how much I have groomed
myself, I am still just another convict.

"Mr. Johnson, on behalf of the parole board, I want to
welcome you here. We'd like to begin by asking you to share
with us about how you have been spending your time."

I describe the skills that I have acquired and the books
that I have been studying. They already know my discipline
record is excellent and that I am considered a very reliable
worker. They ask about my family and seem to be aware that
my parents and sisters are willing to help me in every way
possible.

The members of the board wear the benevolent smiles

of priests or nurses as they listen attentively, occasionally taking notes, or complimenting my prison record. But then they get to the heart of the matter.

"Mr. Johnson, how do you feel about your crime now?"

I hesitate. *My crime. My crime?*

"Mr. Johnson . . . can you at least tell us what happened on the night of the activities for which you were arrested?"

"Well, . . ." I stutter, "I was arrested and convicted on a rape charge, but the man who did the rape also raped another lady in Fulton County, and I was found innocent of that crime –"

"But what about the crime for which you *were* convicted? Can you tell us anything about that crime?"

"I can only tell you what I heard at the preliminary hearing and the trial – even then, I've blocked a lot of it out."

They are obviously disappointed.

"I . . . I was not there when the actual crime took place. I could tell you what I heard at the –"

"Mr. Johnson, do you have any remorse, or even regrets about the crime?"

"I've already told you, I wasn't there, but I feel bad for the lady, it was a terrible assault –"

"Mr. Johnson, was the victim white?"

"Yes, sir. She was a white lady."

There is a silence as several board members jot down some notes, then a woman speaks.

"Have you enrolled in the Sex Offenders Program?"

"No, ma'am, I don't think that I need to do that, because I've never committed a sex crime."

The chairman takes charge again. "Mr. Johnson, is there any crime to which you will admit?"

"Well, sir, I broke into a house some nine years ago. I was caught and pleaded guilty. I did my time, and the record will show that I was a model prisoner, sir. I am truly sorry."

"But you were also indicted for rape and aggravated sodomy at that time."

"Sir, those charges were dropped."

"Well, it says here. . . ." he puts his finger on a particular line, "that you were indicted, and confessed—"

"No, sir, that's not true. There was an error in the documentation, and it was supposed to be cleared up. The parole board was made aware of that in 1983, sir."

"Well, nonetheless, Mr. Johnson, you have been convicted of several crimes, and you don't seem to want to tell us about any sex offenses in which you have taken part?"

I am crestfallen. My shoulders drop, and the polite, optimistic expression passes from my face. "Sir, I have already told you. I did not commit those rapes. I was found innocent by a jury in Fulton County, and it was the exact same type of attack." I do not mention that the second jury was mixed race, since the parole board is mostly white.

"Mr. Johnson, thank you for your time, and we will inform you of our recommendation in writing after we deliberate."

"Thank you, sir."

A few weeks later, I get a letter from the parole board. "You have been thoroughly and carefully considered for parole. . . ." Of course, I am denied; but this time the board has recommendations and expectations for me. They expect me to participate in the Substance Abuse Treatment Program, and they recommend that I volunteer for the Inmate Sex Offender Counseling Program. "Satisfactory participation in such a program will not guarantee your release at your next consideration, but your failure to participate in such a program will be looked upon with considerable disfavor by the board."

There is no way that I will ever get paroled without attending their class.

Prison Industry

Each morning at breakfast the warden stands by the door looking us over as we eat. Though he never says a thing, the message is clear. We are his boys, and this is his plantation. It is a sickening feeling and hardly an inspiration to swing an axe or work in the shop all day.

At breakfast it is easy to identify the three types of workers. The first group includes the swamp men; they are muscular and silent. They eat ravenously, because their work is hard and because many are so tired at the end of the day that they go to bed without supper. The second category of worker has only one member – he is the "warden's boy." Happy as a lapdog, he will spend his day shining shoes or dusting the office; maybe the warden will take him out for a ride or fishing. He is in a class by himself, and we all despise him. The third group of workers is the most interesting. These men work just as hard as the swampers but look even happier than the warden's boy. They are the seamsters of Prison Industry.

The tailors are the envy of all other convicts. They are the most handsomely dressed fellows in prison. They wake up an hour early to crease their uniforms before the bus arrives; their hair is trimmed, waved, or curled, and they look as if they are going out on dates. I am one of them.

Prison Industry, or PI, is the only motivated workforce in the prison system. I waited four years to join the ranks of those who sew state clothing for institutions throughout the South. We toil all day using outdated machinery, but every one of us finishes his quota—no matter how high it is raised. I have become so proficient at sewing that I usually finish my work an hour before the bus leaves for the dormitory. Underwear, shirts, even pants are no problem. I have earned a well-deserved reputation as a man who can sew suits out of socks.

What would inspire hardened convicts to become master tailors? Simply the oldest motivation known to man—there are women present.

The factory floor is a huge warehouse with row after row of sewing machines on tables. The machines are paired so that two sewers are close enough to pass work between them. One prisoner does the rough seams, and his partner finishes the piece by adding buttons, elastic, or other details. The pair works so closely that their thighs occasionally make contact under the table. For the one hundred and fifty men in the back room this is just an inconvenience, but to the elite sewers of the mixed-gender front room, it is one of the sweetest perks in prison life.

There is always activity and noise in the factory. Machines hum along—or thump to a stop if the cloth bunches or a needle breaks. Runners move from station to station, ferrying products from one assembly area to another, and the repairmen in their neat prison clothes move from machine to machine nursing and coaxing the antique contraptions to squeeze out one more day's use. There are always stacks of cloth on the tables and boxes on the floor. Scraps are everywhere, and no matter how diligently the sweeps work, the factory floor is a chaotic jumble of cloth, boxes, and cut threads.

During morning and afternoon breaks we stay at our tables and are allowed to chat. The female prisoners are our mirror image: similar but different. They have known the same type of life, been hardened by the same indignity of bars and punishments, and yet, they are still ladies.

Until I arrived here, I had forgotten the value of female company. There is no substitute; no privilege compares, and no punishment is more severe than her denial. In Prison Industry, I learn again to treasure a woman's held hand.

We are told by the guards that touching beyond the hands will result in suspension or eviction. A single violation can cost two weeks in the hole. Kissing can cost you months apart, and anything more erotic than the meeting of lips results in permanent expulsion from PI. A man would gladly spend two weeks in the hole for ten minutes with a woman, but the risk of losing his coveted PI assignment is enough to keep him in line; or at least it is enough to inspire ingenious deceptions.

I had been afraid that my classification as a sex offender would have voided my request for the sewing detail, but mercifully I was allowed to try out. Probational employment in the sewing pool has all the benefits of PI except that you work in the back room — without women. This is obviously meant to inspire competition, and it works well: after six months of prodigious effort, I am promoted to the front room.

Even though it is forbidden, physical romance thrives under the watchful eyes of the guards. As in every prison situation, the rules and the exceptions have to be learned in PI. Fortunately, there are honest men who try to school the new recruits.

"Now, let's say you have a lady friend and you want to get a kiss," a prisoner named Smooth-Black explains. "Just don't do it in front of the guards — be sneaky. Make yourself some friends who can fake a distraction."

I soon learn that distractions are the most valuable commodity traded in PI. Like castaways, our ingenuity is the result of necessity. We fashion every conceivable camouflage and generate countless varieties of cover-up.

At first, I was completely naïve about prison girls. After several years of all-male company, I was overwhelmed by the sight, smell, and mellifluous sounds of female humans. Although I had been a bit of a ladies' man when I was younger, I always tried to be a gentleman, and ladies responded well to my kindness. So, my first day at PI I was well groomed and on my best behavior. In the cafeteria I was thrilled when a young woman struck up a conversation. I put on my most polite airs, and she genuinely seemed to like me. Within ten minutes she made me feel like a million bucks—talked me out of half my lunch and almost got my watch, too. But I learned quickly.

Prison is the ultimate in poverty, and poverty is a tremendous incentive for con games. In PI, I discover that opportunism knows no gender bias—if anything, the women seem to have the upper hand. I watch them manipulate men the way a sculptor molds clay. They understand that male prisoners need to feel like men again, and many of us are willing to pay any price for that privilege. What is it about being in the company of a beautiful woman that makes us feel so good? Whatever it is, the men of Prison Industry absorb it and become addicted.

My reaction was probably fairly typical. I went from being naïve and getting ripped off by the girls to playing their game, only better. In no time I evolved from being a wide-eyed, sloppy inmate to dressing fine and talking like a player. I made promises about the future in order to secure favors in the present. If a particular girl stopped giving, my attitude was "no problem, that's cool," and I moved on to another.

I remember one poor gal who had a thing for me. She was new to PI, and like all the new girls she looked like a caricature of a butch inmate. That's the way they all start out—just as tough as the men. They walk like men, swaying at the shoulders instead of the hips, and some of them even tug at their crotches the way that young men do. But after a week in PI, they transform into women. I am amazed at the effects of a single trip to the prison beauty shop. Gone is the ever-present, turned-around baseball cap, and instead we see the luster of well-kept, feminine hair. The beauty shop even seems to change their voices, which start out baritone and masculine-sounding but eventually soften to gentle or sultry tones.

When I saw the transition in this particular girl, and noticed the way she always ended up close to me in line, I knew I had a live one. By that time I had come around to the prison dating etiquette. It is all about getting. This girl didn't have much to give, except small tokens of her affection and a fine gold necklace that she wore every day. As a player, I had my target.

I started out soft, just showing my appreciation for her necklace, the workmanship, the color, the weight of the metal. But when she didn't give in, I went straight for the heart. I told her that if she really loved me, she would give it to me.

I wear that chain like a trophy. It is more than just gold; it is status and conquest. I feel good about my love trophy, but I also have occasional pangs of conscience. The thing is, no one resents a player in prison. It's expected. In fact, my cunning seems to attract some of the women who openly flirt with me.

There is one woman, however, who is friendly but irksome. Something in her manner is distressing, though I can't put my finger on it. I have wondered what she is in for, but because of my label as a sex-offender, I am especially reluctant to ask. Then one day at lunch, she walks by and smiles. After she's gone, some of the women at my table begin talking about her.

"She boiled her baby—cooked him in a pot!" Puddin' is hunched down, whispering with hushed excitement.

"That's sick!" exclaims another girl who had killed her own husband. "Why would anyone do something like that?"

"She fed it to her husband," Puddin' says with a shudder.

Even in the moral vacuum of prison society, the rules of engagement begin to bother me. After a few months I am both bored and disgusted with the types of relationships that I have formed in PI. My first step toward decency is to stop exploiting the weaker girls. I am actually happy when I finally meet someone who can out-manipulate me.

Shennita is one of the brightest women I have ever known. She's never been to school, but she learned everything the streets could teach her. At a very young age she mastered the "oldest profession on earth." She has pulled off all the classic cons and even devised several inventions of her own. She has no one in the free world who cares for her, and she has survived purely by daring and bluff. When we first meet in the cafeteria, I am pretty sure that she is playing me—I think that maybe she is after *my* gold necklace. But her smile is so disarming that soon my guard is completely down. Within a few weeks we request to sew beside each other, and thus begins our secret partnership. It is obvious that we are well-matched players, and we decide to join forces in order to con some of the new guys in the back room. Our inspiration is equal parts entrepreneurism and entertainment. We are a good team, and our partnership is both exciting and profitable. It's not long before I develop strong feelings for her.

Like most of the men in PI, I am overcome with the symptoms of prison love. There is an incredible mixture of puppy love and crazed lust. I try not to delude myself; this is not the real world. This relationship with Shennita would not have even started on the outside, but in prison it has become intense — even overwhelming. I dream of nothing but her night and day.

I actually look forward to work each morning. I rise an hour before my cellmates and attend to details of hygiene that I have never before considered. Each hair on my head is pressed into place, and even my moustache is scanned daily for errant fibers. I press my uniform and fluff the light blue pocket hanky that matches my prison stripe. I wear jewelry and practice several expressions in the mirror. I find the best side of my face and decide to sit so that it is presented to my partner. My boots are shined, and I have traded Christmas candies for some fancy laces. I am not alone in my obsession: walking to the bus in the morning, I notice that some of the men are actually smiling.

Shennita and I enjoy our game of conning the new recruits, and we take our new roles seriously. She is used to having a strong man direct her work, so I usually call the shots. I identify the quarries, and she bags them. When I tire of her attending to some poor creature's ego, I direct her to instigate an argument and break with him. We prey on the men in the back room, because she sees them only during lunch. These probationary tailors are the most anxious convicts in the penal system. All day long they are so close to women that they can smell their perfume through the vents. However, for all their proximity, they are allowed interaction only during lunchtime. We have turned this situation to our advantage and devised a con that is both amusing and enriching. Shennita is so good at what she does that we are swimming in cigarettes and candy, commodities that can be traded for anything else we need. We have become comfortable in our excess, but for the sake of a challenge, we decide to move on to bigger things. She's been flirting with a well-heeled dope dealer, and now we're angling for jewelry and money.

In the lunchroom I watch her from a distant table. She walks through the crowd like a mink among dogs. Everyone watches as she passes. She is beautiful, but more than that, she knows how to move and carry herself. A pretty woman is like a fishing lure; actual beauty is important, but carriage and motion are what catch the fish. I try not to stare. If her mark sees me looking, he'll suspect a con, and the game will be over.

When she finally sits next to him, he beams. Soon the two of them are laughing. Gently, he touches her arm — and suddenly I find it harder to smile at the game. When I see him lean over and whisper in her ear, I decide that I've had enough; all the jewelry in River State is not worth the price. Even in this corrupt affair, jealousy is a powerful force.

Back at our machines, after lunch, I murmur to her that it's time to quit him.

"Quit who? That old boy is going to bring me earrings next week."

"I don't like him — drop him."

She hands me the pants that she has been sewing. I scoop two buttons into my palm and run my thumb along the seam to the fly.

"He's got a lot of money." She speaks almost seductively, then coyly smiles with her lips together.

I accidentally prick my hand on the needle but don't even hesitate in my stitching; it takes too much effort to shut down the automatic work of my body. Our quota has nearly doubled in two months, and we are now more machinelike than the machines we operate.

"Just quit him tomorrow," I say. My right hand skirts quickly down the left leg to attach the elastic.

"Damn. . . ." she says under her breath.

I pause to examine our work and sigh. It's obvious that we've been distracted. The two legs are joined into a single large cylinder, perfect for someone with one central leg.

I start to throw it toward the "rejects" box, but she intercepts my wrist and aims it toward the "finished" pile.

"Good enough for prison work," she says with rare seriousness.

Our next morning is tense, but it is important for me to show no emotion. Since she is observant, she probably notices that I am wearing my best prison shirt and that I have put on a few drops of precious cologne. We say very little, and when the bell for lunch sounds, she gets up silently.

As usual I do not acknowledge her at lunch. Instead, I sit by myself beside a small group of unattached men. The room is filled with the muted voices of happy couples.

There are sporadic outbreaks of laughter from pockets around the room, and some of the girls can be heard like birdsong above the flirtatious prattle. Then a noise catches my ear, and I turn instinctively. Shennita has raised her voice. She is standing beside the seated rich prisoner, her right hand on her hip, her left dismissively flexed toward him. She is causing a scene that the guards may find intolerable. Under my breath I say, almost unconsciously, *"Calm down, girl,"* but it is too late. Everyone is looking at her, and what little conversation continues is focused on the arguing couple. I am tempted to create a distraction, but it would be most foolish to draw attention to myself: there can be no speculation among the backroom men that she and I have something going on. We have conned a dozen inmates in this room, and I do not need twelve sex-teased convicts angry at me.

I catch a little of the tirade but focus my eyes on the mashed potatoes and brown sauce that have congealed on my plate.

"— You two-bit hustler. You think you're some kind of pimp? I'll be damned if...."

I see the guard shift on his feet, and I fear the worst for Shennita. Then suddenly she shuts up. I am amazed by her intuition. She calmly extracts herself from the table, and all eyes watch as she crosses the room in her most indignant yet graceful march. I freeze in mid-chew when I comprehend her intention.

There is an empty seat next to me. I listen as she walks across the room, then sits down beside me. "Please pass the salt, Johnson," she says. Her right hand reaches toward me, and her left holds a sandwich.

Now I know how Abraham felt when he finally admitted to Pharaoh that Sarah was not really his pretty sister but his wife. Just as Abraham must have worried, I worry if I will survive the night.

This becomes the climax of our relationship. Even though Shennita has shown me great respect by breaking from her lucrative sugar daddy, something between us is gone. It's not easy to mix business and love in Prison Industry.

Before I started my prison sentence, Beth's mother took me aside and gave me a bit of advice: "Son, don't ever compromise your manhood in there." I knew what she meant: no matter what the temptation, don't get involved with homosexuality in prison. Once I was inside, I would hear other guys joke about how cute someone's butt looked in the shower, but I knew that any concession to such temptations would be dangerous.

It is true that there is sex in prison. In a dormitory of sixty men, there are likely to be some who enjoy each other's physical company. I was surprised to find how many of these men receive special attention and favors from gay guards, but I was never molested or even hassled by unwanted advances. There were plenty of guys who tried to flirt, but I made it clear that I had no attraction to them, and perhaps my size and demeanor discouraged further attempts. While it's true that weaker men are targeted by sexual predators in prison, a man who is willing to be independent and defend himself is generally safe.

We all struggle with our sexuality. Conjugal visits are illegal in Georgia, and forced celibacy is an unwritten part of every sentence. There are plenty of rumors about rich inmates receiving special favors, and the degree to which wealthy prisoners (and the warden's boy) get conjugal visits is a matter of great speculation. However, most of us have had to survive on just a kiss during visiting hours to sustain us through the years.

Sex with a visiting girlfriend or wife is difficult and dangerous, but it is not unheard of. Usually it requires bribing a guard: a little something for him to turn his head while two people enter a bathroom together.

But the punishment for such acts is so severe for both prisoner and guard that most men simply serve their time without any sex. Prison Industry, however, begins to change all that.

▦ Lunch has just ended, and we are starting the afternoon shift. Smooth-Black is manic as he looks around the sewing room.

"Johnson, just stand here with Snakebite and Q.T., while I get freaky with Miss Puddin'." He gives me a friendly smile: "We'll do it for you and your lady friend next week."

Snakebite, a young man with two deep scars on his neck, looks worried; he is easily intimidated by Smooth's cool assertiveness. I just want to mind my own business and not get involved in schemes that could lead to expulsion, but the temptation to comply is difficult to resist. Smooth-Black could talk the white off rice, and his promise to do for me and my girl next week is a powerful inducement.

"Peanut's gonna talk to ole Miss Nelson while we go at it," Smooth continues, assuming we will all go along with his plan. "You fellas just stand here and block her view in case she turns around."

We arrange ourselves according to his direction, but something just doesn't feel right. "Oh, man, I don't know about this...." I say, getting cold feet.

"Just do it! Come on, Johnson! Shoot, I've waited twelve years for this!"

"Yeah, and spent a thousand cigarettes on that girl," Peanut adds.

"Shut up, Peanut. If you *could* get some, you would, too."

"What you're gonna get is four minutes of fun and a lifetime of genital warts." We all laugh.

"Shut up. Now see, Miss Nelson just came in – go talk to her. The rest of y'all just stand up – and look busy!"

Since he started grooming himself, Peanut has become one of the handsomest, smoothest-talking brothers in the joint. He knows exactly how to charm the newly divorced guard. Smooth-Black has arranged this distraction and choreographed his blind perfectly; all that's left is to consummate the plan.

As we watch Peanut converse with the guard over a box of clothes, Snakebite, Q.T., and I poke at the old sewing machine. We stand around it as if working on a stubborn motor. Smooth-Black lowers his seat nearly to the ground. His cigarette-collecting girlfriend grabs a pair of scissors and cuts a small flap in the crotch of her prison pants. She is, of course, an expert seamstress and will be able to sew up the hole in the bathroom before the evening search. In a few seconds she straddles Smooth and begins moving quietly over him. We have our backs to the couple, but the novelty is magnetic and each of us looks briefly over our shoulder to see how it's done. The sounds of the chair and the rhythmic, soft exhalations are both comic and erotic. I look over at the guard; she is twirling her hair.

"Damn, Peanut is good—he's got her all twisted up," says Snake-bite.

"Smooth's not so bad either," adds Q.T. with a snicker, "—for an old dude."

We all laugh through our mask of serious work and continue "fixing" the machine. There are one hundred and forty-eight seamsters not having sex in the room, but it has taken the coordinated effort of a dozen or so to allow Smooth-Black his two hundred and forty seconds of bliss.

There are other ways it is done, and sometimes a guard is involved. Occasionally, a female prisoner disappears for a few moments, and coincidentally a male guard is absent at the same time. Some prisoners go for the very risky: cooccupation of the bathroom. And I have even seen prisoners wedged between sewing machines and the wall. There is not a lot dignity in these conjugations, but sex in the workplace happens everywhere, and the act lends itself to absurdity.

After a while I tire of the sewing-room shenanigans. I know that I need a change, and kitchen work will allow me more freedom of movement. Although women are not allowed to be kitchen workers, I still enjoy their company at lunch, and they occasionally pass through en route to other tasks. As a kitchen celibate, I am happy. I flirt a bit with the gals at lunch but avoid the more serious aspects of relationships. Then one day a new woman walks through the kitchen carrying a basket of rags. She is tall and thin, with regal cheeks and full, expressive lips. There is something very pleasant about her, something cheerful and genuine in her subtle smile. I nod briefly as she passes by, and I can feel her looking at my back as I stir a cauldron of steaming pasta. A smile crosses my lips – but I catch myself. I am not getting involved with another prison girl. Then she starts singing.

For a minute I think that Gladys Knight is doing time: "I'd rather live in his world, than live without him in mine. . . ."

Her voice is perfect – better than the radio. I stop my stirring to listen for a moment. I will never hear a sweeter sound. There is a lot of talent in prison, but Songbird has the sweetest voice I have ever heard. In the kitchen her pure tones resonate, and the man chopping onions twenty feet away silences his blade. After she has picked up all the rags in the room, she leaves us, and for the rest of the shift, no one speaks.

I look forward to her brief visits, and finally get up the nerve to request a song.

"Do you know anything by Anita Baker?" I ask.

"Only the whole catalog. What would you like to hear?"

"Giving You the Best That I Got." It is a thrill to request a song.

"Mmm, my favorite," she says with a sigh. She licks her lips and closes her eyes.

As she sings, I forget that I am in prison, that she is a stranger locked up for who knows what, that I am an angry man. For a few moments I just close my eyes and listen. I hold still as a baby in his mother's arms. Her voice is so sophisticated, her phrasing so perfect that we could be in a concert hall. When she is done, all I can manage to say is thank you. I am hooked on her singing.

I ask some of the women about her and am told that when she sings in the shower, inmates crowd into the bathroom just to hear. It is not the type of adulation normally given to artists, but it is a form of true gratitude. She brings music into our time-wasting dungeon that is more beautiful than anything any of us have heard in the free world. Because we have something good with us, it brings out something good within us. Her voice is a comfort.

When I discover that she is in for killing her husband, it doesn't change the way I feel about her. In prison you learn that murderers are not necessarily the worst people. Sometimes they are just normal folks, caught in violent situations, who make bad decisions. The difference between people who pull a trigger and those who don't can be a few seconds of tragically bad judgment. Many inmates do their time and return to society no more likely to kill than the rest of us. That is my impression of Songbird, but perhaps I am unduly influenced by infatuation. I feel like a high school boy wondering if she likes me.

One Friday, on my break, I go to the storeroom and she is there. It's one of those rare moments when two people find themselves alone, stare into each other's eyes, and exchange something that alters the relationship forever. I am pleasantly surprised by the way that she welcomes my embrace; in a short time we are pressed up against the wall, locked in a passionate kiss. It seems that our frustrations at being locked up and our pent-up hunger for love mix and burn like explosives in our kiss. There is a special urgency behind bars, where every embrace is a risk, every kiss forbidden.

In order to spend more time together, we both request transfers to the front sewing room. We sew side by side each day and become good friends. It is not the most physical relationship that I have ever had with a woman, but there is a sensuous aspect that few men will ever experience. I have often wondered if Anita Baker or Barbara Streisand sing to their lovers. Do they hum as they cuddle at night or give private performances over a candlelit dinner? Songbird sings gently into my ear as we work each day, and it drives me crazy. They say that every baby loves his mother's lullabies, and I can remember my younger sister being calmed from hysteria by my mother's singing. But I would have never guessed that a grown man can be just as pacified by a woman's sweet song.

▣ While I am getting to know Songbird, the entire Prison Industry begins to unravel. Some female prisoners complain about "sexual harassment" by the guards, and the press starts to get interested. At lunchtime, it is all that anyone talks about.

"It's like the last days of Vietnam around here," says the Colonel, an old warrior who possesses recognized wisdom.

"What are you talking about?" Smooth-Black asks. "You don't think they gonna shut us down, do you?"

The Colonel pops his heart medication into his mouth, pausing dramatically to swallow before responding. "I was posted at a remote field station at the end of the war. We hadn't seen much action, but then in 1970 Nixon started peace negotiations, and everyone knew that the war was ending. So, every guerilla who spent the war carrying a sixty-pound rocket on his back decided that he might as well get rid of the weight. We were in the middle of nowhere, and there were thousands of guerillas who all wanted to fire their mortar before the peace. As soon as Nixon announced that the truce would begin in thirty days, all hell broke loose. We went from getting hit once a month to receiving four hundred rockets a day," he says. He lets his arm sweep around the room. "This place is going down. . . . just look at what's going on."

His prophecy proves true. The men, and even more so the women, become terribly anxious to make out. It's as if mating season is coming to a close. Women who had played hard to get and been more interested in money than sex now change their priorities as the end seems near. Couples become less concerned with the rules, and every time a guard turns his head, a wave of kissing and petting sweeps through the room. Gifts are exchanged openly, and men who had been models of calm and restraint give in to manic passion.

One couple has us stand and block for them in the usual manner, but there aren't any scissors within reach, so the girl just pulls down her pants and sits on the man's lap. We keep our backs to them for a long time, but the couple seems interested in much more than a quick union. Soon their chair is banging against the wall – its spring squealing in rhythm. We urge them to hurry. "Wrap it up – come on, let's go!" But they pay us no heed. I can't believe their brazenness, but the panic of the final weeks drives people to extremes of risk and passion. As a result, many couples are caught, and the hole is filled with men who go out smiling.

Tonto, a prisoner who wears a western-style turquoise necklace, takes the biggest risk of all. He has fallen for a girl who is HIV-positive. Although they have courted for several months, they've never consummated the relationship. Condoms are not allowed in prison, even though prisoners have a high HIV-infection rate. He approaches us at lunch and asks us to arrange some boxes on the floor near our machines. He and the girl plan to lie behind the cardboard wall.

"Tonto, you can't do that, man." Smooth-Black, who has one of the largest libidos in the joint, does not usually urge caution, but even he knows that this is an absurd risk.

"I love her, man. This is going to be our last chance." Tonto is both anxious and resigned to fate: "She's got twelve years left."

"Did you get a condom?" I ask.

"Are you crazy, where the hell would I get that?"

"The guys at the store can get anything."

"Look, they may close this place down any day now—I need you to do this for me."

A cardinal rule of prison life is to mind your own business, but we know that this could be his death sentence.

"Tonto, are you sure?" Smooth-Black shakes his head, trying to find a way to reason with him.

"Just do this for me—all right? After lunch."

When a man loves a woman, and he has one chance to make love, he will risk everything for her. We pile up the boxes, just as he asked, and we even stand around them for extra protection.

Every day the mania increases, and I become so sick of the whole scene that I request a transfer out of PI. I will certainly miss Songbird, but the Colonel is right; it's all going to end soon anyway, and I'd rather go out on my own terms.

At lunch I am flooded with requests to help set up distractions, but there are too many of them, and I am forced to turn some down.

"But Johnson, you've got to create a distraction." Smooth is more agitated than I have ever seen him. "How about a small grease fire?" he asks.

"You know I'm not in the kitchen anymore."

"How about one of your friends, then?"

"Smooth, I can't do anything for you today."

He turns to the Colonel, who has maintained his dignity throughout the chaos, never taking part in our shenanigans.

"Colonel, you got to help me."

"I am not risking my parole for your sex drive, Smooth."

Smooth is so anxious that he appears angry. "You're always talking that old war stuff! I ain't never seen no bravery from you." He goes straight for the heart. "What would the boys in the platoon think of you now? You're just full of talk—you ain't no he-ro."

I can tell by the frozen look on the Colonel's face that Smooth has succeeded in making him mad. The Colonel, like me, slows down on the rare occasions when emotions well up. He seems as calm as ever, but his eyes flit about. Smooth should have known better than to bring up the dead who served under the Colonel's command. He had been suicidal over those memories, and I can't believe that Smooth would open this wound for the sake of his own pleasure. The bell interrupts him as he begins to speak again.

Lunch is over, and I move away from the two older men, sensing that further conversation will bring only trouble. I am sick of the games that people play just to get sex. I am nauseated by Smooth's willingness to shake up an old man to get five minutes with his girl. As I walk back to the sewing room, I hope that Smooth hasn't distracted the Colonel from taking his medication. The old man nearly died six months ago, and we all remind him to take his pills with each meal.

Back at the machines Songbird hums "Amazing Grace," and I forget about Smooth and his frustrated passion. I forget about the Colonel's bruised pride and the twelve pairs of pants that must be finished before I get a break. I just close my eyes and smile. I'm back in church with my mother; she has me wearing my brand-new, scratchy wool jacket. I am a bored little boy, but my father's watchful eye lets me know that complaining or slumping in my seat will get me a whipping. The church is beautiful. It is Easter; the women wear flowers and pretty dresses. My mother's eyes are riveted to the altar, where the pastor's daughter, all in white, is singing. The church is silent, and not even a breath from the congregation is heard. I catch only glimpses of the singer through the forest of adult heads and ladies' hats. Then I hear her voice, "Amazing grace, how sweet the sound. . . ." My mother's hand squeezes mine in light affection, and I look up to see a tear rolling from the corner of her eye.

Suddenly Songbird stops singing—Tonto is shouting.

"—The Colonel had a heart attack! Get the doc, get the doc!"

Doc is a man who went to medical school and fell in love with drugs. I run to the kitchen, where he works.

"Doc, let's go, the Colonel's down!"

We race to the center of the factory, and I push the onlookers out of the way. Doc rips open the Colonel's shirt and listens to his chest.

He calls to the nearest guard, "Get over here! Hold up his head!" The guard moves quickly, and soon a circle of prisoners forms around the beloved old soldier; some are praying. Everyone in the circle is ready to assist, but there is only one man who knows how to save a life.

I realize that I am just adding to the crowd, so I push my way past the ring of concerned friends and through the perimeter of the curious. Once I get outside the crowd, I see a carnival of sex. There are several couples in chairs, and one pair partially covered in cloth on the floor. It is a sewing room orgy—no opportunity will be wasted by the desperate lovers. I see Smooth-Black. He is not alone—he has gotten his wish.

Within a half hour the Colonel is rushed to the hospital, and the sewing room returns to normal.

On the bus home I think about the day's events. "This place is going crazy," I say, without wanting to start a conversation. "Thank God my transfer goes through next week."

Smooth has his eyes closed and looks exhausted. "I don't know how I'll live without my sweet Puddin'," he moans.

"Is that all you think about?" I reply in disgust.

"No," he deadpans. "I'm also thinking how can I get those six cartons of cigarettes I promised to Doc and the Colonel." He raises a hand to give me a high-five and laughs. "We got you good!" Then in a poor imitation of me, he quietly screams, "Ahhhh! Colonel's having a heart attack! Ahhh! Ahhh! Colonel's having a heart attack!"

It was all a con—one last big distraction before they closed the place down.

Sex Offenders Program

Innocence is a liability in prison. The whole system is
predicated on the notion that every convict is guilty.
Consequently, all programs to rehabilitate criminals are
directed toward repentance, which is required for parole.
Staunchly defending one's innocence is seen as recalcitrance,
further proof of a reprobate mind. I know that what the
authorities want is a confession. My years are not sufficient
to pay for their error; they want contrition. The carrot that
they hold out is early, or at least timely, parole.

For men like me there is a special counseling course, the
Sex Offenders Program, to help us look more palatable to
the parole board. The course is voluntary, but anyone who
wants to get out must enroll. The public has been sensitized
to sex offenders, and the state is now reluctant to release a
man without having attempted some type of reform. Sex
offenders are seen as especially likely to repeat their crimes.
Murderers are released without much fanfare, but a sex

offender is so feared that his neighbors are often warned before he moves in.

For many years I wouldn't even consider entering the program. I didn't tell anyone why I was in prison, and I just wanted to do my time quietly until the truth came out. But as Mom gets sicker, I begin to change my mind. While I try to remain patient, time is ruthless in its assault against her.

It's tough on Dad, too. He no longer tells friends about his son. He knows that I am innocent, but he is a practical man, and this is a difficult matter. The questions are too hard to answer, and few people would believe that a black man duly convicted of raping a white woman is really innocent. Many of my father's closest friends don't even know that he has a son. The thought of my nonexistence gives me a feeling of evisceration—I am empty.

My family has done everything that they can to hasten my release. They've seen several lawyers whose advice is always the same: join the sex offenders program, guilty or not. It is a sound strategy for release, and my dad recommends that I consider it, though I cringe at the suggestion. His plan is that I should enter the program while my family hires someone to lobby the parole board on my behalf. Their goal is to get me out—clearing my name is not their top priority. I am fortunate to have a family that is willing to pay for my freedom, but the stigma of being permanently labeled a sex offender makes me sick; and joining the program would seal that label.

Whenever Dad visits, he repeats his practical advice: "The lawyer says that your participation in the Sex Offenders Program is very important to the parole board; and C.C., if you play their game, you will eventually get out."

I try to explain to him that it would mean confessing to horrible crimes that I didn't commit.

His response: "Son, just do what you have to do."

I look into his eyes and see the pain of visiting me and the fatigue from tending to Mother's ailments. It is not just my life that is rotting in prison. Perhaps I have been selfish. How can I stubbornly fight for my integrity as if I am the only one suffering. I begin to tell him that I will enroll in the program, but the words get stuck in my throat. I feel ill before I can pronounce the first syllable. All I say is, "I'll do what I can." My decision must show on my face, however, because he pats me on the back as he gets up to leave.

The following day I sign up for the course, even though just writing my name on the roster makes me feel dirty. Our first meeting lets me know that the course will be a form of guided group therapy. They want us to think of our victims as people instead of objects and to vent our anger in more positive ways—"like weight lifting," I suggest in my only comment of the day. I listen politely and keep my mouth shut when it is time to share.

The counselor explains that this is therapy and we are expected to be candid about our sexual addictions and criminal histories: we should try and relax. The more she says it, the more unsettled I feel. Everything for me is inverse. She says that she wants us to be honest, but that is the last thing she wants me to do. When she says we should put down our guard, it means that I must put up mine and act like someone else.

"You are here because you have something in common," she says. But I am sitting among men with whom I have very little in common. The class is like one of those anxiety nightmares, where you show up at school having forgotten it was exam day. I am not prepared—I am not even in the right class.

When I signed up I had not considered the mechanics of deception that would be required. *How can I sit here as if I am one of them, as if I need to learn revulsion for despicable and depraved acts?* I wonder what sort of sickening fantasy of violence will be required in order to pass the course.

At the next meeting men tell stories of serial rapes, rape homicides, child molestations, sexual mutilations, and other violent offenses. These are not fantasies or stories, they are true crimes committed against real people—and some of the men clearly enjoy listening to the others' tales. It is a support group of which I cannot be supportive. I can't even begin to understand the minds of men bent on such activities, and yet my presence indicates that I am one of them. It was one thing to sign up for the course, but it is quite another to act like a rapist. I try to convince myself that my motives are what is important—I want to relieve my family. But I feel like a collaborator, a turncoat who has become a devil in order to save his family—*no, I'm not really one of them, I'm just acting like it, just enough to fool the authorities.* When it is my turn to talk about sexual violence, I pass and wonder how long it will be before they make me speak.

After the third session the counselor asks me to come to her office. "Mr. Johnson, is there a reason why you will not share with the group?" she asks with professional dullness.

"Miss Baines, I want to tell the truth, but I am not a sex offender."

She peers above her reading glasses. "Mr. Johnson, you realize that this is a course for sex offenders. May I ask why you are here?"

"I was convicted of rape, ma'am."

"That is a sexual offense," she says in an even, clinical tone.

"But I'm innocent."

She sighs and briefly considers my comment. "Look, I'm not here to judge." She drops a bit of her reserve and continues, "But I do have to report to the parole board about the group. They will ask me about your participation. I realize that it may be *uncomfortable* for you to talk—"

"I didn't commit those rapes, ma'am. I've never committed a sexual offense."

She is about to say something but stops and looks at me seriously.

"Okay, this is totally off the record, and I will swear that I never said it, but if you don't participate in this group, you are leaving this prison in a casket. You've read the papers, you know they won't allow a recalcitrant rapist back into the community. If you quit the Sex Offenders Program, your parole hearings will become rare and meaningless. This is your *only* chance." She adjusts her glasses and signals that our meeting is over. I leave her office feeling trapped and sullied.

At night, I cannot sleep. I again consider lying—not just attending the program but "participating." I want to ease my mother's pain, but I also realize that becoming an admitted rapist is irreversible. A false confession might get me home before Mom becomes too ill to talk, but I would then have no way of clearing the family name.

What kind of job can a self-confessing rapist get? I ask myself. I hate prison—every single moment behind bars is like having a wasting disease, but escaping these bars by losing my integrity is not the kind of freedom that I desire.

The next day I make another appointment with the prison counselor. "I want to participate in the Sex Offenders Program," I tell her. She smiles. "But I cannot admit to crimes that I did not commit."

The smile instantly fades. "Sorry, confession is the price of admission."

"What about the Fifth Amendment?" I ask. "Can't I claim that admitting crimes to a prison employee puts me at risk of self-incrimination?"

She almost laughs. "Mr. Johnson, we don't report to prosecutors what we hear in counseling sessions."

"It's not that I'm paranoid, Miss Baines, I just want to participate without lying."

"Look, I'm not a lawyer," she says, lowering her voice a bit, "but I could recommend someone who might be able to answer your legal questions. Now, in terms of our Sex Offenders Program, I can't let you participate until you are willing to confess your offenses."

There is obviously no use continuing our discussion about the class, so I change my tactics. "You said you know someone who can answer my legal questions?"

"There's a new program, the Prisoner Legal Counseling Project. It's run by the University of Georgia law school. I don't know anyone who has used their services, so I can't tell you if they are any good, but I do know that the program has ruffled a few feathers, so there is at least a hope." She smiles. "I'll get you the address. Meanwhile, I want you to consider the relative merits of full participation in the program here at River State—"

"Do you think that I could get that address now, ma'am?" I gently interrupt. "I'd like to get started right away—if it wouldn't be too much trouble."

She shakes her head. "You are persistent."

"It's all I've got, ma'am."

She makes a few calls while I wait, and writes down "James C. Bonner Jr., attorney, the University of Georgia."

"Thank you, ma'am. I appreciate your help."

"Good luck, Mr. Johnson."

I have no way of knowing how important the name James Bonner will become to me in the future. It takes me several months just to reach him, but eventually Mr. Bonner helps me find the key to freedom.

With my sister Judy in Cincinnati,
Christmas 1958.

With my family in
Cincinnati, mid-1960s.

With friends in
Atlanta, summer of
1975. I'm second
from the left.

High school graduation night,
Atlanta, June 1975.

With my dad, 1979.

At the Clark Atlanta College
Media Department, 1976.

My graduation from Clark Atlanta College,
May 1980.

In Georgia state prison, ca. 1990.

A visit from my mom in prison,
1991.

Speaking at church in Atlanta, 1999.

On a ministry trip to Uganda,
September 1999.

Visiting my mom in the nursing home with my dad, my sisters, and my nephews, 1999.

Mom at home for the day, Christmas 1999.

With (from left to right) Huy Dao, Jane Siegelgreen,
Peter Neufeld, and Barry Scheck at the Innocence Project,
New York, June 2000.

My wedding, July 2000.

With my daughter, Brianna, at home, 2002.

With my dad, 2002.

Anger

There is a threshold after which math becomes detestable; and no one counts down from twenty-five years. For the lifer prison is a series of shorter countdowns and letdowns. All dates are approximate: release, transfers, parole hearings – everything is subject to change according to rules that no prisoner can fathom.

The men with short sentences are the precision time-keepers of prison life. They are anxious about every lawyer appointment, every visit, and they still have faith in the generosity of the parole board. You can see the days and weeks tick across their faces. To the lifer their waxing grins have all the charm of a stomach flu.

After a decade in prison I am able to entirely suppress the numbers. I try not to keep track of the months until my parole hearing: no mental calculation of the years remaining in a life sentence. But as my sense of time wanes, my sense of indignation grows. Each day I awake to a silent rehearsal of the absurd "facts" surrounding my case.

I am innocent. I have filed appeals at every level, and always I am denied. The parole board sends smiling representatives who give me hope, but during my hearings they ask me over and over again, "What can you tell us about the crime?" Each time I go up, I am denied parole, and rather than shortening the period between hearings, they lengthen it. Everyone urges me to join the Sex Offenders Program, but membership requires a detailed admission of my crimes.

My jaw aches from clenching, but I repeat my silent mantra through gritted teeth: I will not lie, I will not condemn myself as they have condemned me – if I have no hope for parole, so be it. I will not slander myself.

Anger is not a trait I was born with. It began in prison, and it grows each day. After ten years my anger has started to assert itself. For most of my life I took pride in being easygoing, slow to react, and naturally calm. But I have changed. I have become unsociable and quick to argue – but who wouldn't? I wake up each morning to prison bars, in the company of men I would not choose as friends. My time – and my life – are totally controlled and hopeless. As soon as I open my eyes, I am mad. The gnawing in my stomach now accompanies the dawn of each new day.

I am so angry that complete madness cannot be far away. Bitterness is a drug, an addictive substance – it haunts me each minute, whispering its catechism of complaints. As much as I try, I cannot calm the increasing volume of those voices. I cannot reason my way out, because my anger is so reasonably constructed – I am innocent, I have been railroaded, and no one will help me. I have followed all the rules, been patient in my appeals for help – and nothing. Nothing! My case for hatred is airtight, and the facts arrange themselves in my mind without effort. It is consuming me, and I am losing myself. Up until now I have contained the rage beneath a thin shell of control, but now the surface has cracked.

The guards come rattling and banging to wake us up, but I refuse to rise like some sleeping lamb.

"Get up!" they shout.

I mumble into my bed, "Why do they have to bang on the bars? That's not even allowed in zoos."

As they approach, their shouting gets louder: "Come on, out of bed!"

"Shut up!" I shout back. "Why do you have to be so damn noisy!"

"Come on, let's go," the guards drone on.

"Why don't you come in here and get me," I say, baiting them. "And stop all that banging – we're not animals!"

The toughest guard in the group stands beside the door of our cage and addresses me menacingly, "Johnson, I hope you're not making trouble."

"Why, what are you gonna do, lock me down, throw me in the hole – come on!" My voice is loud and clear. "Go on, get a bunch of your friends together – throw me in!"

"Johnson, I'm warning you, it'll be a disciplinary report."

"Lock me down! What's the matter, you lost your keys, you break your arm or something? *Come on and get me!* Here are my wrists – where are your cuffs?"

Eventually the guards realize that their threats hold no sway. I am a man without hope, and such a man has nothing to lose. The guards prefer to discipline those who cower and cry. Their punishments have obvious effects on the behavior of fearful men, but I am beyond both fear and hope.

When my dad calls to inquire about sending a package, the guards refer to me as a "troublemaker." Pops knows that I am losing the battle.

On Sunday I happen to be looking out the window and see his car pull up. Usually, Dad talks with me only a little while and then leaves me and Mom alone until visiting hours are over. Today, he is alone; he must have left at dawn to get here this early. The guard brings me to the visiting room, and I take a seat.

"Where's Ma?"

He doesn't answer.

"Is Mom coming?"

"Calvin, you've got to stop calling and troubling your mother. She is sick. She is a sick woman, and she doesn't need to be shaken up by your complaining."

"What are you talking about?"

His voice rises to full indignation. "She is sick, and you need to calm down."

"Calm down?" I rise from the chair. "What do you—"

"Sit back down and listen."

"I don't have to listen to this—" I turn for the door.

"Listen, or you will not speak to your mother anymore."

Slowly, I return to my seat.

"I'll only say it once. You're not the only one with a hard life. If you think that you can be mad all the time just because you're innocent, you're wrong. You've got to move on. I know you didn't commit those rapes—but the police had your picture for a reason. And with all you had . . . You had no business hanging around with hoodlums and getting in trouble. Do you know what it was like for your mother when you got arrested the first time—do you think her friends came around to socialize? And what do you think it was like for your sisters at school, lying to everyone about where you were—on a trip, working out west. We know you're innocent, but I don't even try to explain to people anymore, who would believe it? It's best to keep quiet and deny them the malicious gossip. Now you need to take it like a man. The whole family arranges its finances and schedules around you—every holiday is spent driving to this prison, and every Sunday we are all waiting by the phone in case you call so you don't waste your fifteen minutes looking for us. We are all doing our best—you've got to do the same. You've got to move on." He pauses and then changes the subject. True to his word, he never brings it up again.

The guards continue to be a pain, but the guys who really get on my nerves now are the short-timers. I have no tolerance for the complaints of men with sentences less than five years—especially since they *are* usually guilty of their crimes.

From the corner of the room I hear one of them whine, "I won't see my wife for three years—"

"Shut up! What are you whining about? This ain't no country club.

I've been in for *ten years*, and I ain't never cried. Nobody here's gonna cry with you, so just shut up!"

Short-timers are insufferable moaners – crybabies. They constantly look at pictures of their children and weep. It drives me crazy.

"Man, can't you stop your silly crying. You're lucky to have kids. *Two years away from daddy, wah-wah.* Just shut up! You committed a crime, so do your time like a man." He is silent as I continue, "They kidnapped me – came into my home and took me away for no reason. I didn't do anything, and I have a *life sentence.*" My words pound like a hammer against steel, "You still think you have something to cry about!"

Over the years at River State I notice a disturbing trend. Each month the proportion of short-term men seems to rise. The result is that the rate of men going home increases from one a month to one a week. This reminder of freedom is more disconcerting than the bars. I finally decide to ask the counselor what's going on.

"We're being converted, Johnson. You and the other lifers can stick around, but from now on we're medium security – more freedom, strictly short-time."

"Then I've got to get out of here."

I request a transfer to Hancock, a long-term prison, because I'd rather spend my time with men who have committed heinous crimes than live among crybabies who come and go. For me there is more peace around those who have quit crying about life on the outside, and I need the stability of an environment where no one leaves. Misery may not love company, but it detests giddiness. My sentence is life-plus, and I am tired of people checking out like this is some kind of damn hotel. In a long-term prison parole never comes before gray hair, and I can deal with just one or two old men released each month.

When my mother finally comes to visit again, I see her from a distance and feel a bit of happiness. They say that men dying on the battlefield call out for their mothers, and I can believe it. She has always been there for me. I sit across from her at the visitor's table and reach over to take her hand. She does not raise it.

As I look to her face to question her reluctance, my heart is wrenched. My mother's face is crooked. She's had a stroke. She can barely talk, and her sweet mouth is set in a permanent frown on one side. I try hard not to cry. I don't know where to look or what to do. No one had mentioned a word of it to me. Am I acting so crazy that they won't even tell me my mother is sick?

In my misery I send home all my photos, my trial transcripts (which I never could read anyway because they made me ill), and everything else that is associated with hope. I begin to accept that I am hopeless and vengeful; it is just a matter of time until I become violent. There is nothing that can restore me – my youth is gone, and with it died the man that I had been. I have become as hard a prisoner as ever there was.

Religion has become my enemy, because faith is the purest form of hope, and hope disgusts me more than anything else. There had been times when religion was a big part of my life, but that light has been completely extinguished. My years on the outside are a cold and distant memory. Occasionally, happy images of the free life surface in my mind, but they quickly shatter like a fallen mirror. Sometimes I try to remember what it was like when I was young: I had a fiancée, a career, and even faith – but that might as well have been a million years ago.

Joy

I wake up as usual and see the bars, the wall, the tired,
smelly men—and I get angry.

"Don't wake me up until it's over," I say to the man
beside me.

"What?"

"Just don't wake me till it's time to go home."

"Johnson, you all right?" he asks.

I bury my head in the pillow and want to cry. I am
not all right at all. I don't want to go crazy, but I am not
all right. I whisper into the pillow, "God, please help me . . .
get me out of this."

The man below me senses there's a problem. "Hey,
Johnson, they got them girls from First Baptist coming
tonight, why don't you come with us?"

I attend the service but not because of the girls. I am at
the end of my rope, and I know I need help. The minister
reads a short scripture: "Come unto me, all ye that labor

and are heavy laden, and I will give you rest. Take my yoke upon you, and learn of me; for I am meek and lowly of heart: and ye shall find rest for your souls. For my yoke is easy, and my burden is light."

After church, alone and on my knees, I pray.

Lord take this burden from me. . . . I can't do it. I have no strength—please Lord, set me free. . . .

There is no instant miracle; the anger and looming threat of madness do not vanish right away. But God does give me a hunger to read the Bible, and in those pages I begin to find my answers. Day by day, verse by verse, it shows me the way to a sound mind: to freedom from bitterness, anger, envy, and hate. The way is prayer. Not just the usual repenting or pleading; my prescription is to pray for my enemies, for those who despitefully used me, for those whom the devil has convinced to convict me.

At church, everyone says the Lord's prayer, ". . . and forgive us our sins, as we forgive those who have sinned against us. . . ." The idea is simple – even trite – when life is good. Small grudges, petty disagreements; these things can be forgiven and forgotten. But how can I forgive the people who have put me in prison? People like the district attorney, who continues to keep me here even though the evidence exonerates me and a jury found me innocent. How am I supposed to forgive that kind of continuing sin? What does that kind of forgiveness look like? It is not simply letting bygones be bygones; I need a new way to forgive. *Help me, God, regain my peace.*

I search the scriptures diligently, and I read every passage that I can find about forgiveness. After a few months I begin to see how it works. In the Bible everything important is accomplished through prayer and love. So, I pray constantly. But still the anger and bitterness do not leave. Finally, one day I reread the sermon on the mount – and I get it. "Love your enemies, bless them that curse you, do good to them that hate you, and pray for them which despitefully use you, and persecute you."

Forgiveness is not just saying, "I forgive you." It is a commitment to love those who hate you, even those who continue to "despitefully use you." I finally understand that I don't need to forget, I need to remember those who keep me behind bars. I need to pray for every aspect of their lives. That is what Christ taught about forgiveness. It is not passive, and it is not easy.

Each day, God shows me more. I have been angry for so long that I'm not even sure whom I am angry at. Through prayer, my hatred is revealed and teased out as if it were shrapnel in my soul. God shows me that I'm not just angry over my stolen youth, but I'm also tormented by my mother's great suffering. I know that the stress of my incarceration has caused her strokes and heart attacks. Because of my suffering, she has endured years of operations, medicines, and pain.

Lord, help me to forgive those who put me here.

And it isn't just those involved in the trial whom I must forgive. I discover that I also need to forgive my fiancée for leaving me. I thought I had put that issue behind me years ago, but now I realize I just pushed away the pain – there is still anger in my heart. She left me without so much as an explanation, and over the years I had forgotten about it. But God doesn't want me to just forget about it. He wants me to forgive her and to pray diligently for her new family. I have to love her as a dear sister in Christ.

Slowly, frustration is replaced by hope, but the battle is not easy. For so many years, being angry has made sense. My anger is based on reality. The bars are very real, while forgiveness and prayer are intangible. It would be easy to stay angry, and yet somehow I know that if I persevere, prayer will free me from all this madness. I continue to pray each day.

As soon as I awake and see the bars – before bitterness can take hold – I get on my knees and worship God. I pray methodically for the district attorney: his family, his children, his travels, holidays, possessions, and of course for his soul. I do the same for the witnesses against me, the judge, the jury, the guards, and my ex-fiancée. I also pray for anyone whom I hold the slightest grudge against. It is ironic that the surest way into my prayers is to offend me. When I finish praying for everyone who has hurt me, I pray, "God, show me who else."

There is still plenty to be frustrated about. The parole board puts off my hearings for longer and longer periods, and I'm told that its members are quite unimpressed with my "jailhouse religion." They still ask me for details of the crime, even though I have told them that I did not commit the rape. In terms of an appeal, no one has come forward with new testimony or evidence. The judge in my case has retired, many of the witnesses have moved away, and I am sure that the evidence is rotting or has been thrown out. I can't stand prison; but like the Apostle Paul, I begin to discover that there is a ministry in chains. Perhaps my example might bring those around me to Christ.

I have learned in all circumstances to give thanks.

Something is different today. I open my eyes and see the usual bars and the same men, but the demon is gone. I am not angry at all. Like a soldier awakened after a bomb blast, I take inventory of myself and discover with joy that I am whole.

"Thank God for the beautiful day!" I say brightly, as I jump off my bunk. The men around me stare. They think it's a joke—it has to be a joke. No one in here is ever joyful.

For the first time in more than a decade, I smile with childish glee. It is amazing. I have totally let go of bitterness, and it is as if a door has been opened in my soul.

"Why are you smiling? You never smile," one of my bunkmates says, just before the guards arrive.

"God has made another wonderful day, and we're alive!" I answer with a happy grin.

"You all right, Johnson?" He looks concerned.

As the guards approach, I stand by the door. Many times before I have been rude to them, and they approach with trepidation.

"Good morning, sir," I say with unaccustomed enthusiasm.

They look at each other.

"I hope you're having a fine day, sir."

"*Johnson?*" the taller guard looks totally puzzled. "*Are you all right?*"

"Thank God we're all alive," I say.

The guards are skeptical of the change, but it's the prisoners who watch with the most curiosity. They want to know if it's for real. Prison conversions are a common occurrence; men get religion in order to get out, get help, or just get along, but everyone in jail wants real freedom.

Prisoners, more than anyone else, are aware of the human condition: they need a way out, one that really works, one that keeps them free.

Their boredom also makes them keen observers, and they are just waiting to see if I will fall. There is nothing funnier than watching the pious tumble, and there is no lack of such humor when new converts are surrounded by skeptical eyes, twenty-four seven. It would be big news if the Holy Roller fell to temptation. They watch me carefully, and there is not much that can be hidden in prison.

A year passes, and the joy in my heart continues to grow. God teaches me to be thankful in all things and to praise him regardless of circumstance. But thankfulness is sometimes difficult, especially when I try to resurrect my appeals. No one wants to take on the case, but I persist, sustained by faith in a God who can do all things.

I write to a number of local and nationally known lawyers, and I receive replies that are completely discouraging. Most are actually form letters, and the few attorneys who do take the time to write recommend that I just wait out the remainder of my sentence. Whenever I get one of those letters, I walk around the prison yard and just praise God. I usually do so silently, but occasionally I sing aloud. The more I praise, the more I am blessed, and the better I feel.

I remain upbeat even though my problems continue to grow. The low point comes when I call home and am told that my mother has suffered another very severe stroke. When I get word that she has fallen into a coma, I become desperate to see her. I am almost in tears whenever I think about her. There is nothing that I can do – I can't even hold her hand anymore.

Her coma continues for weeks, and I get so upset that I can hardly eat the tasteless prison food. I know that I'm in trouble when I begin to suffer insomnia. On my second night of restlessness, I pray until I am exhausted, and then finally fall asleep by softly repeating, "Praise God, praise God, praise God. . . ." The next morning I awake with a sense of peace. Against all odds God gives me the assurance that she will live to see better days. From that moment on, I don't worry about her, and with my inner peace restored, I sleep like a baby.

Her coma lasts one month, and then another, and another, but I remain confident that she will recover. Finally, after four months, she awakes; *she will live to see better days.*

As I mature spiritually, I get involved with church far beyond mere attendance. At Hancock Prison I assist the volunteer ministers, and even join the choir. I can't read music, but I learn the songs by following the highly trained voices around me. I am not as good as they are, but I manage to make my own joyful noise without detracting too much from the harmonies. Many of the choristers become my good friends, and I am amazed by their many talents—not just singing, but song writing, musicianship, poetry, and preaching.

One day, as I'm praying and walking around the courtyard, I hear two inmates talking about Kairos. Apparently, they are going to some kind of meeting with that funny name.

"What's it about?" I ask.

"Oh, we can't explain it, you just have to come," they say, smiling. The more they refuse to explain, the more curious I get. I decide to attend.

Kairos is a Greek word that means time. But it is not like the time that we have on our watches: the Kairos ministers describe it as *God's time* or *when the time is right.* Prisoners are keenly aware of time's many meanings, and the fellowship is aptly named. It is unlike any other prison ministry in that men can eventually go through an entire weekend experience called a Kairos Walk. The walk is an intense series of meetings, studies, and worship services held at the prison over three days.

I attend the one-day introductory meeting and am swept up in the love of the volunteers who give up their weekend to serve convicts. They bring plenty of food and play wonderful music, and they are upbeat without being trite. Some of them are former prisoners who offer testimonies of God's love in the free world, but most of them are just regular guys with jobs and families. The central theme of the day is "The Prison Is Our Community." The word *community* seems foreign at first, but eventually I come to realize that the dormitory *is* our home.

At the end of the day a prisoner who has participated in a Kairos

Walk is asked to give the closing talk. We all know him and admire his exemplary life. His talk is full of hope and inspiration, even though he will never get out of those prison clothes: he has no chance of parole.

"You are needed to serve God and the brethren here," he tells us. "And you must find the lost and the needy in this place and bring them to their shepherd." A few of the brothers shout amen. "It is no harder for you than it is for any businessman downtown. If you need an example to follow, consider the men who serve in both places. Just look around at those who came to serve you today."

After the Kairos meeting, several of us decide to begin holding Bible studies and prayer groups in the dormitories. The first meeting in our dorm has just three men, but the next has six, and the following nine. With nine men we have to be careful not to disturb the peace and activities of the other inmates. Sometimes we stand together and pray quietly; other times we sit at a table far away from the television, so that our dormmates can go about their business.

The fellowship group gives me something to look forward to. Now, instead of waiting to get out and do this or that, I have found my mission within the walls. After dinner each night we return to the dorm for a few minutes before yard call. In that brief time we hold hands (sometimes four or five of us, sometimes twenty-five now), and pray in a circle.

"Anyone have a particular prayer concern today?" I ask before we begin.

Jason, a new transfer, speaks first. "My aunt – she's got the breast cancer, and she can't even visit anymore. They say she's gonna die real soon, maybe even this week. She's the one that told me about Jesus." He pauses and then adds softly, "And my mom just found out she has it, too."

Men are always distraught by their dying parents, and it is a grave humiliation to be denied a visit to your mother on her deathbed. Most men know that their incarceration has ruined their folks' lives, and with their parents' passing, all chance of redeeming the family's honor is lost.

"Father God, we pray for Jason's aunt, and hope that until the hour of her death she is comforted by you. Let her know that she and her nephew will meet again in your kingdom. And Father God, we pray for Jason's mom, that you might heal her before this cancer spreads. We also pray for Jason as he faces these difficult days. Lord, please give him comfort, and sustain him in this hard time."

We pray for the government, the dormitory, the officers, the victims of crime, and those who suffer because of floods and hurricanes. We always close with the Lord's prayer, because its words are so fitting to us.

I try to make sure that the leadership in our dorm rotates, so that all the men can develop their capabilities. Many guys fail once they get out into the free world simply because everyone expects them to. It takes a great deal of self-confidence and self-control to start a new life after doing hard time. Often the only ones who welcome an ex-con when he gets out of prison are the same people who got him into prison. The first job offers are usually criminal—and they are tempting because the con has experience and he is desperate. By allowing the men to be leaders, and even to make mistakes, we help them to develop their sense of self.

As our numbers grow, the prayer group witnesses the power of God through many miracles. Soon, prayer requests are coming in by mail from friends and relatives.

"Listen to this letter from my mom," Jason says to the group, a few months after he joined us. "Remember when we prayed about her cancer? Well, listen to this: 'Thank you for your prayers. They operated, but they could not find any trace of the cancer. It's completely gone.' She's okay, man. She's gonna be okay." Jason smiles. "Praise God!" Although he lost his aunt to cancer, his mother has a miraculous recovery.

We marvel at the power of simple prayers from people like us. By praying for one another, we develop a deep trust and great love among the group. We are honest with one another about our situations, past and present, and as we pray for forgiveness, it becomes evident that most of the men did commit the crimes for which they have been convicted. I don't talk much about my own situation, except to ask for prayer that the truth will come out.

On my own I continue to pray that my name will be cleared. I don't just want to get out of prison, I want the truth to be known. I had said at my sentencing, "I have been falsely accused of these crimes. I did not commit them. I'm an innocent man, and I just pray in the name of Jesus Christ that all this truth will be brought out. The truth will eventually be brought out." I look forward to that day with growing confidence.

I call my sister Tara often, and always ask about my nephews. She tells me about their latest accomplishments and adventures, but I have the feeling that I am a bit of a mystery to them.

"Tara, do the boys know why I'm in prison?"

"What do you mean – I mean – no. I never really talk to them about it, C.C."

"I want you to bring them in."

"To visit you there?" she says, laughing nervously.

"Yes, I want to explain to them what's going on."

"Calvin, they don't have to know all that; they really don't care."

"Tara, they're boys, and their uncle is in prison – believe me, they want to know."

"I don't know, C.C., it's pretty traumatic."

"It's worse if we keep it a big secret. Kids hate family secrets. They'll imagine more terrible things if we're not honest."

I list my nephews as official visitors, and when their security clearance comes through a few weeks later, their mother brings them in. I have tried to imagine what the visit will be like for the boys, not yet teenagers, full of innocence, trusting in our system of laws and justice.

They come into the visitors' room dressed in their Sunday best, but they look a little apprehensive.

"Hi, Jimmy, Sammy, I'm your Uncle Calvin. I bet you're wondering what I'm doing here."

They nod silently.

"Well, the charge against me is rape. That's when a man attacks a woman and hurts her. But I didn't attack any woman. The police made a mistake, and we're trying to get it cleared up."

"How long have you been here?" asks Jimmy.

"Since before you were born, almost thirteen years."

They stand in stunned silence as they try to calculate a wait longer than their very lives.

"So, when are you getting out?" Sammy asks.

"In God's time."

"Oh. Is that soon?"

I laugh. "I certainly hope so. I want to see you guys play ball."

"Can you have a ball in here?" asks Jimmy.

"Yeah, sometimes I play basketball with my friends."

"Are your friends in here, too?"

"Many of these men are my friends and brothers in Christ. We help each other, and sometimes we play ball. And every night we get together to say our prayers."

I let the boys ask me anything they want, and when their curiosity about prison is satisfied, we talk about normal things like baseball and football: the Braves and the Falcons. They promise to send me letters, and I tell them that I look forward to coming over to their house soon.

DNA, the Key
to Freedom

Months pass without a response from Mr. Bonner at the

Prisoner Legal Counseling Project. I try to maintain the

difficult combination of hope and low expectations that

sustains me. I figure that he'll probably send a form letter

at first, but I am prepared to fight on, no matter what. The

letter I sent explained my reluctant desire to participate in

the Sex Offenders Program. I also asked if Mr. Bonner could

write to the parole board about the innocent verdict at my

second rape trial and the irregularities concerning my first

trial. The last thing I asked him to investigate was DNA: a

new forensic tool that few prisoners, or lawyers, know about.

I first heard about DNA in a magazine article about

the British scientist, Dr. Alec Jeffries, who had testified in

a rape case using a technique he developed called "DNA

fingerprinting." In another article I read that a newer method

called polymerase chain reaction or PCR, produced DNA

fingerprints from minute amounts of material—even from

sources that were thousands of years old. That same article mentioned two California scientists, Henry Ehrlich and Edward Blake, who had pioneered the use of PCR in criminal investigations. Dr. Blake was the first American scientist to testify about a PCR fingerprint. That was during a rape trial in 1987—five years before my letter to Attorney Bonner.

I figure that if PCR could be used to imprison a guilty man, then it could also be used to free an innocent one. My hope is that Mr. Bonner will confirm that logic. I try not to get overly optimistic, but I wonder if PCR might be the answer to my prayers. Unfortunately, the technique sounds so high-tech that I imagine it will cost hundreds of thousands of dollars. But if it can prove my innocence, I will find a way to pay the price.

Several more weeks pass, and still no letter. Then, finally, one arrives. The return address reads "University of Georgia Law School, James C. Bonner, Esq." I open it quickly but carefully. Inside, there are four pages of answers to my legal questions.

As I read his responses, I feel the first surge of real hope that I have felt in several years. Not all of it is good news, but finally someone is taking me seriously. He is especially detailed in his comments about pleading the fifth in the Sex Offender Program and cites several examples of case law that he feels are applicable. His conclusion is that the state can probably require an admission of guilt for entry into the program, but that admission may not necessarily end my legal right to a new trial. It seems as though he is saying I can have my cake and eat it, too. I consider taking his advice and rejoining the program, but it just doesn't make sense to admit to a crime now and then fight my conviction later.

No, I have already decided, I will not lie.

The news about the Sex Offenders Program is not what I wanted to hear, but the letter contains a treasure trove of other legal ideas, and Mr. Bonner's obvious concern for me is a much-needed shot in the arm. He concludes his letter:

> In summary, I think you are going to have to decide what you want to do from the standpoint of your personal interests.
>
> The Parole Board does not operate as a court, and it has to presume that convictions are valid. Its usual response to protests of innocence

is to point back to the courts, and you can count on one hand, with fingers left over, the number of times it has been persuaded to set aside a conviction for innocence. I do not think it will be persuaded simply by any letter I write.

I do not know the answer to the DNA question yet. I will have one of my students make inquiries, but I personally think it is not very likely that we will find the physical evidence still preserved.

I analyze his comments. He obviously doesn't have any experience with DNA, and he does not see it as the primary avenue to freedom, but at least he is willing to learn about it. My own view is that scientific methods are better pursued than legal ones. People on the outside generally have faith in the criminal justice system, but my faith in legal remedies evaporated long ago. I have no idea if the evidence has been preserved, or how long DNA will last on a shelf, but if they can extract it from mummies, maybe they can get it from a ten-year-old rape kit. I try not to think about how I would pay for the state-of-the-art tests. *One step at a time,* I remind myself.

On phone day, I call my dad and tell him how helpful Mr. Bonner has been.

"Is there anything I can do to assist him?" Dad asks.

"He said that he needs all the court records and anything in the state archives on my case."

"I'll go to the archives and start photocopying on Monday."

"There's probably a few hundred pages, Pops." I hesitate, not wanting to push. "He says he needs everything."

"I understand."

"Thank you, Dad."

"We'll be coming up to see you next Sunday, if your mother's feeling better, and we'll have a treat for you – Kim's coming along."

My childhood friends in Cincinnati have stayed close to me, especially Kim Robinson, the daughter of my mother's best friend, Marti. We are the same age and played together since the second grade. Back home in Ohio we had sleepovers and teased each other mercilessly. When I went to college at Clark Atlanta, Kim enrolled in our sister school, Spelman College. We both majored in mass communications and even had a few classes together. My girlfriends were often jealous of our close friendship, and I'm sure that her boyfriends felt the same way. But in reality Kim was always just a wholesome pal—one of my "nice" friends. We enjoyed family outings, long drives in my car, and especially just talking as only lifelong friends can.

From the moment that I was imprisoned, my Cincinnati friends stood by me. They believed that I was innocent, and they did all they could to support me and my family. Kim took it upon herself to write to me every two weeks. Her dedication and beautiful penmanship were a source of great comfort to me, as well as a source of jealousy on the part of my fellow prisoners. It was over one of her letters that I had my first prison argument; those cheerful epistles were my precious property, and I allowed no one to read them. When so many others had deserted me, Kim and her folks kept my spirits up, and they always kept their eyes open for a way to get me out.

Once a year I was permitted to receive two holiday care packages: one from my family and the other from Kim and her mom. The list of package requirements and forbidden contraband was byzantine and absurd, but Kim managed to make the parcel joyful even without including such treats as chocolates, Polaroid photos, black pens, cash, and so forth. We were never really sure what the reasons were for all the contraband rules, but we knew that you could lose your mail privileges if you were found in violation. Over the years I heard a number of rumors concerning the origin of each prohibition: Polaroids can be slit and drugs could be stashed inside; the guards use black pens, and they're worried that inmates might try to forge orders; drugs can be mixed into chocolates. Whatever the origins of the rules, Kim learned the ropes early on and sent only permissible items, like hard candies and articles to read.

When I arrive in the visiting room, Kim is seated beside my mom. It is always a treat to see her. "Did you get my package at Christmas?" she asks amid the noise of the crowded room.

"You know I got that package," I answer, managing a wry smile. "I'm sure I wrote you *at least one* thank-you note."

"I heard you have a new lawyer from the University of Georgia—your dad says that he's really good."

"At least he takes me seriously. He's the first one who's not trying to push me into the sex offenders class."

My dad looks away but holds his peace.

"C.C., you don't belong with those perverts," Kim reassures me.

"I don't belong in prison."

She tries to steer away from topics that might upset me. "Do you think this guy can get you out?"

"I will get out. I'm not sure how, but I will get out."

After receiving Mr. Bonner's letter in November 1992, I become the captain and cheerleader of my legal team. That team consists of my sister Judith, who coordinates correspondence, phone calls, and visits; my dad, who does the research and copying; and my mother, who keeps our morale high. I continue to contact other lawyers and organizations that I think might be able to help secure my freedom, but no one offers anything except form-letter sympathy. After so many years in prison, it is hard to get anyone excited about my case, especially since I am not on death row, and they figure that a rapist eventually gets paroled (as long as he participates in the Sex Offenders Program). Mr. Bonner is the exception to the rule, but unfortunately, after our initial correspondence, I do not hear from him again for eight months.

Mail call is always a tense moment, but I am now among the more anxious prisoners. I am in good company: a lot of men nervously await news from loved ones or lawyers. The young guys are still anxious to hear from wives or girlfriends; but as time goes on, the frequency of mail diminishes for most of us, and we all adopt a cooler attitude toward the postman. For the old lifers even the birthday cards eventually vanish, and the gray heads seldom look up when the envelopes are passed out.

"Mail call," the guard shouts. "Sanders, you got mail." A man's face brightens. "Glixon—you, too," he walks up slowly, obviously expecting bad news.

"*David J. Fox!*" one of the prisoners shouts. "Mail for *David J. Fox?*" he repeats. David shouts his own name each day, but no one remembers him ever having received a letter.

"Johnson, you have mail."

I open the envelope from Mr. Bonner with deliberate patience, but my heart is beating against my eardrum. I read the first few lines quickly, and realize that it is not good news.

25 May 1993

Dear Mr. Johnson,

I have probably traveled several thousand miles with your file, thinking that I would have a chance to review it. . . . I have only today finally had that chance.

There was nothing helpful in the 1981 plea transcript. . . . [It] affords no useful basis to show that you were wrongly identified.

I have probably told you as much, but from a *legal* standpoint, I do not think your Clayton conviction is vulnerable. It may have been a bad verdict, but it was one made according to the law.

My heart slows, and I feel the sweat of disappointment form on my back. The letter reviews some of the legal precedents for Mr. Bonner's gloom, and then it ends with more noninformation about DNA:

My prior clerk never completely ran down to the end of the DNA testing business. I am asking my new clerk to see what she can learn. I expect I will have something back from her in a few weeks. I also expect that the major problems are going to be the preservation of the evidence and the costs. I would like to hold on to your transcript at least until then.

The page ends with his signature, but curiously there are two other pages – another entire letter, in fact.

I hardly feel like reading the second letter. It is dated the day before my birthday, and birthdays are not happy occasions in prison. But I say a prayer, sigh deeply, and then begin reading.

7 July 1993

Dear Mr. Johnson,

Enclosed is a letter I wrote you toward the end of last May. I did not realize that I had never printed it off my portable computer and mailed it until I got your most recent letter. I am sorry my communications are so erratic. It is not because I take your situation lightly. It is because I take it seriously, because your conviction troubles me, and because any legal remedies I can conceive of are so slim and difficult. It is relatively easy to tell someone who is likely factually guilty that he has been validly convicted and that I cannot disturb his conviction. . . . It is quite another thing to have to give the same message to someone serving time under a dubious but lawful verdict.

First of all, I want to tell you that the only avenue which I think might possibly be open (establishing misidentification by DNA) is a new one to me and everyone else in my office. Pitches for innocence are not our stock in trade, for normally this sort of thing is not a basis for post-conviction relief. Relatively few lawyers . . . are familiar with DNA testing to exclude an identification, which is a fairly new and esoteric thing. After a final conviction, from a standpoint of litigation, the only use for it would be in an extraordinary motion for a new trial, which is essentially a discretionary thing with the trial judge, which is disfavored under the law, and which is, well, extraordinary. . . .

In any event, let me try to fill you in on the developments since my last letter. First of all, the physical evidence *is* necessary. The DNA tests which would have to be run cannot be run simply on the basis of the tests which might have been done in 1983. . . . They cannot be reconstructed from anything done in the past.

Secondly, although some D.A.'s offices have a policy of preserving all physical evidence in serious cases (at least as long as the defendant is confined), there is no statewide requirement. I spoke recently to an old student of mine who works in the Clayton D.A.'s office: he told me that they had no office policy in the matter and that he doubted the physical evidence from your trial (which he even recalled in some detail without me mentioning your name) had been preserved over this period. He checked but he could not be sure. He gave me the name of an investigator who could tell me for sure (not in when we talked). I tried to call him just this week, but he was out on a summer vacation. I will try again next week, and I will try to let you know promptly what I find out.

Regards,
James C. Bonner, Jr.
Attorney at Law

After eight months of silence, it is the first glimmer of hope. Even though he tries to discourage any expectation that we might be granted an extraordinary motion for a new trial, he does mention it as a possibility. So, like the coach of a losing team, I have to take that slim hope and use it to motivate. Before I actually call everyone, I practice my voice to make sure that it sounds fully confident against the obviously overwhelming odds. I pray that God makes me a good salesman.

When I first entered the prison system, we were allowed only five minutes of phone time a month. That included all the dialing and busy signals. The calls were monitored, and when five minutes was up, a voice on the line announced that the call would be instantly disconnected. After several years, the voice of the operator was automated and we'd get a two-minute warning before the computer cut-off. All of these restrictions led to unbearable frustration for men who were trying to contact their lawyers, wives, or children. Fortunately, the situation improved over the years, and eventually phones were installed in the dorms or hallways. The calls are still monitored, very expensive, restricted to certain hours, and must be made collect – but at least normal conversations can take place.

I call my dad, my sister, and even Mr. Bonner. I convince them all that the letter actually contains great news. I explain that my strategy has shifted to focus exclusively on DNA and that our goal is to submit an extraordinary motion for a new trial. I do this knowing full well that there is a vanishingly slim chance of success. James Bonner speaks earnestly to me about the odds. He is friendly, supportive, and honest.

Later that month I receive a letter from my sister. She has been working with Mr. Bonner, and serves as the coordinator of all our correspondence. The letter arrives just before a fellowship service, so I put it in my Bible and decide to read it just before lights out. Judith writes:

> Mr. Bonner has contacted Dr. Michael DeGuglielmo, the director of forensic analysis for Genetic Design in Greensboro, North Carolina. He runs the only company in the Southeast certified to do DNA fingerprinting. They might be able to produce DNA fingerprints from your old evidence.

I close my eyes thinking, "If only we had some evidence for them to test."

Two weeks later, I call James Bonner.

"Jim, what did they say at Genetic Design?"

"They are willing to try the tests—as soon as the evidence becomes available." His voice changes to a soft pessimism. "But, Calvin, we still have no idea if the evidence has been preserved—and even if it has, who knows what shape it's in."

"Well, let's just get it and test it," I say, as upbeat as I can.

"Calvin, unfortunately, it's not that simple," he says. He's an experienced lawyer and is professionally skeptical. "The evidence belongs to the court, and they can throw it out if they want. What I mean is, that even if they do find it, they are under no compulsion to allow the tests. If the district attorney fights us, we will have a hard time forcing transfer of the samples to the laboratory. I've done a little checking around, and a lot of courts are not allowing DNA testing on old evidence. Georgia courts tend to be very conservative on these types of motions, and I don't like our chances if the D.A. resists."

"You can do it," I reassure him. "Just don't give up. You'll find the box, and we'll get it tested."

"I hope so. I'm just afraid that all of this might take years." He pauses, and I hear some papers shuffle. "Calvin, I've been doing some thinking, and I'd like to propose an unusual strategy to you. In order to speed things up a bit, I'd like to try something very unorthodox—we'd be breaking new legal ground. I want to file an 'extraordinary motion for a new trial based on new evidence'—as soon as possible."

"You mean when we get the evidence?"

"I mean now."

I laugh. "Without any evidence, you want to file a motion about new evidence?"

"We won't be granted a new trial right away, but I want to start this process so that everyone knows we're serious. It might help speed up the search for your evidence box."

"It sounds unusual, but if you think it will speed things up—I trust your judgment."

"I'm very troubled by your conviction, and while it may seem that I am moving slowly on this, I am anxious to see you freed."

Without really understanding his strategy, I am confident that God has brought him to me. "Do whatever it takes, Jim."

"There is a risk involved."

"What's the risk?"

"If the judge says no, we may never be allowed to enter DNA evidence later. We get one shot—so, it's your call."

"It's sounds to me like an all or nothing bet."

"It is," he says seriously.

"Well, that's easy. I've got nothing—so let's bet it all!"

I pray each night that the prosecutors will find the evidence box and agree to transfer it to the Genetic Design company. But there is no rush to answer my request at the D.A.'s office, and the law does not compel its own officers to expediency in such cases. It seems as if the harder I work, the slower the wheels of justice grind.

In late August 1993, I receive a copy of Mr. Bonner's letter to Genetic Design. He mentions that we have still not located the evidence from the trial, but that we hope the slides from the rape kit have been properly preserved. He also mentions that my sister Judith will send the initial eight hundred dollars. That fee will cover one evidence sample and a reference sample of my blood.

"Oh, no, they need my blood," I think. I shudder at the realization; I have been in prison long enough to know that my blood is not my own and that it will require a court order to obtain a sample for testing. This means months of paperwork and new delays. I immediately write to my lawyer and ask that he file the forms for my blood as soon as possible.

The next twenty-four months are a roller-coaster ride of hope and disappointment. In the midst of my fight for innocence, the nation is gripped by the O. J. Simpson murder trial. The proceedings have a huge following in the prison, and suddenly the letters "DNA" are on everyone's lips. As a result of the case, I grow increasingly anxious about getting my samples processed correctly, especially since mishandling seems to negate DNA's effectiveness in the Simpson trial.

Even I get a little caught up in the O.J. excitement, and I compose long letters to two of his lawyers, Johnnie Cochran and Robert Shapiro, explaining the salient facts of my case. A few months later I receive short, courteous responses from both of them to add to my collection from lawyers, congressmen, and organizations across the country. They are all very similar: sorry we cannot be of help; good luck, etc., etc.

As time goes on, I believe more and more that DNA will set me free, but every month we are beset with delays that come with the regularity of a curse. I've had to apply several times for permission to have my blood drawn, and since it is not a common request, no one wants to deal with it.

When I get word that our extraordinary motion has been filed, I call James Bonner and ask him about our next step.

"If the judge doesn't like the motion, he doesn't even have to consider it," he tells me. "In that case, we'll withdraw it voluntarily – there is no appeal."

"I guess it's my only shot."

"We're lucky that he even agreed to take a look at it. In the state of Georgia, the law says that a motion for a new trial must be filed within thirty days of the judgment, 'except in extraordinary cases.' Since your conviction is more than a decade old, it would set a new precedent for the state – which might be something that the court is reluctant to do."

"How do you expect him to rule?" I ask, trying to assess our chances.

"There really is no precedent. In the brief, I had to acknowledge that we are asking for something very unusual. I wrote that we realize such motions are disfavored, and properly arise only from extremely unusual circumstances. The way the courts word it, 'circumstances that do not ordinarily occur in the transaction of human affairs.'"

"You mean, a miracle."

"I guess so."

"I believe in miracles," I say with heartfelt conviction.

Because my original trial judge has retired, the decision will be purely at the discretion of his successor, the Honorable Matt Simmons. Judge Simmons rises high on my prayer list.

Mr. Keller, who prosecuted my case, is still the district attorney in Clayton County. He cooperates with our request to search for my evidence, but there are others in his office who seem reluctant – even hostile. They are the keepers of the evidence, and without their help, I am helpless. I pray that God will protect the fragile proof from mishandling, and that the D.A.'s office finds it soon. The case is now eleven years old, and rape kits are usually thrown out long before that. Without specifying my need, I ask the brothers in the prison fellowship to pray for my miracle. It soon arrives.

James Bonner cannot contain his joy on the phone: "They found it! Calvin, they found the box!"

"Is it intact?"

"It's a miracle! I've got to tell you the story. The district attorney says that when Judge Boswell retired, his court reporter went with him. So the D.A.'s staff went through the courthouse with shopping carts and threw out all the old evidence boxes and rape kits. Your box was loaded onto one of those carts and was actually thrown in the trashcan with dozens of others. Then for some reason – no one can explain why – someone from the D.A.'s office pulled it out of the trash and put it on a storage shelf. It's the only one from Judge Boswell's court that was rescued – and it's safe!"

"Praise God! PRAISE GOD! – I told you to expect a miracle."

He laughs joyously. "I called the judge, so at least he knows that we have some evidence now."

"Are you sure the box is intact?"

"No, I haven't seen it yet, but I'm hoping for the best. It has to remain in the D.A.'s custody until they hand-deliver it to Genetic Design."

"How long might that be?"

"Weeks or maybe a month – but the important thing is that we have the rape kit."

"Praise God!"

I have a hard time calming down after the phone call, but I decide not to tell anyone the full story yet. When I close my eyes to pray, I imagine the hands of angels protecting that box. If you have never had your fate sealed in a dusty container on someone else's shelf, it is impossible to imagine my relief. If that box had been lost or compromised, my reputation, my freedom, and my hope would have vanished. Two cotton swabs, some pubic hairs, a sheet, and a stained pair of panties, all sealed in a plastic container that has remained unopened since my day in court. That box contains my only hope of freedom.

I still don't know if there is any DNA on the few items in the box. At the time of my arrest in 1983, no one thought about preserving molecular evidence. The technology needed to amplify small amounts of nucleic acid had not even been invented back then, so the nurses and technicians who collected the evidence were certainly not trained to isolate DNA. No one can estimate the chance of finding useful material in that box, but it is my only chance, and I pray that the miracle of the evidence will continue. I am reminded of a scripture from the book of Hebrews: "Now faith is the substance of things hoped for, the evidence of things unseen."

At first, everything appears to go smoothly. The district attorney agrees to send the evidence bag to Genetic Design, and an officer hand-delivers the sealed contents to scientists in North Carolina. However, since DNA analysis is so new, Mr. Bonner warns me that most of the companies performing the tests are young and problematic. How right he is.

It is months before we get even an initial response from Genetic Design. When we finally do hear from them, it is because they are concerned that some of the items in the bag are not labeled, and others have been compromised for various reasons. This is obviously troubling, but fortunately they report that several biological samples are still intact and can be tested.

The technician sends us a long letter with many questions concerning how the samples had been obtained, what tests had been performed, and what storage conditions the box had been subjected to. I can't answer any of the questions, and it is left to my sister Judith to read through every line of my transcript, the medical reports, and the evidence forms just to get some rudimentary answers. She sends as complete a list of responses as she can, three weeks before Christmas 1995. It is clear that I will pass the holidays in prison for at least another year.

The next set of letters from the lab asks for even more details on the tests performed by the state thirteen years before. The chief geneticist, Dr. DeGuglielmo, actually wants copies of the original lab reports. He also has questions about some of the evidence items that he received, including, "Ten clear plastic bags (no indication of what is in the bags)." I have no idea how we are going to identify unlabelled items in an out-of-state laboratory.

Once the inventory process is completed, I get a list of the samples for possible analysis: a bedsheet and pillowcase, a broken glass vial, bedclothes and other articles of clothing, vaginal swabs, and pubic hairs. I am most interested in items that might contain DNA left by the perpetrator. Sperm is an excellent source of DNA, and sperm cells can be easily separated from the victim's cells in a stain or swab. What we really need is a semen stain or an intact vaginal sample. The stained underwear and two vaginal swabs offer the best hope for DNA, but the lab will not proceed without complete answers about the evidence history. My sister supplies all the available information, but it seems they always want more.

It takes almost a year to get my blood sample drawn, and the certified tube doesn't arrive in Greensboro until late 1996. Once I get word that the lab has received my blood, I finally begin to relax a bit. But then my sister calls with horrible news.

"C.C., I don't know what to do. The company that has your evidence has *reorganized*—Dr. DeGuglielmo is gone!" She is distraught and exhausted.

"What do you mean reorganized, where's he *gone*?"

"I can't find anyone who knows where he went."

"Did you call the company headquarters?" I ask, a little louder than necessary.

"No one at Genetic Design has any idea about the doctor, the status of the tests, or what's going on. They told me that the lab is shut down—temporarily."

I remind myself that ultimately God is in charge, and I modulate my voice. "Judy, please keep trying. We can't lose track of that evidence."

Several months later we talk again, and she sounds worse. "Not only is Dr. DeGuglielmo at a new company, but Genetic Design has now disappeared completely."

"What!"

"They are no longer in business. I'll try to find out where the evidence is, and I'll contact you as soon as I learn anything."

Through prayer, I avoid panic. I know that what I really need is some high-powered legal help, experts in DNA. *There must be another way to get help.*

I pray more earnestly, thanking God for all he has done and asking for someone to help me. I remind myself that Jesus is my advocate and counselor; he will never leave me nor forsake me. I am calmed by His presence. However, I am unprepared for the next shock.

A letter arrives from James Bonner that sounds like the death knell for my cause. He writes, with deep regret, that the Prisoner Legal Counseling Project has lost its funding and will be shut down. Mr. Bonner's generous help will be cut off.

I take inventory of my situation. My evidence is lost, my legal support has been pulled out, and my family is exhausted. I don't even have a parole hearing scheduled for several years. I need another miracle.

Before lights out, I study the scriptures. The God of the Bible is not stingy with his miracles. Just because I have experienced a few along the way doesn't mean that I am no longer eligible. At this low point in my struggle for freedom, I meditate on Joseph languishing in Pharaoh's jail for a rape that he did not commit. The same God who loved Joseph loves me. He restored him to a position of honor and rewarded him for his faithfulness.

I think of Joseph being thrown into a pit by his brothers—how dark it must have been there. *It is always darkest before the dawn.* Surely the Lord will bring me some light soon. I close my eyes and quote the psalm, "Weeping may endure for a night, but joy cometh in the morning."

The Innocence Project

A new man in the dorm is depressed, because he misses his
children. He cries each night knowing that he will not see
them for at least five hundred days. A few years ago I would
have berated him for crying about fifteen lousy months, but
now God moves me to comfort him. We look at pictures of
his kids, and I ask if he would like to pray with me about
their school day. He smiles as he prays for each of them, but
his voice breaks up at the mention of his wife's name, so I
help him finish. When we are done, he is visibly relieved,
and we commit to pray together like this each day. I feel
no need to mention my struggle for freedom, nor my five
thousand days behind bars. God knows my needs, and I
am truly grateful to serve my Lord wherever he leads me.

Four hundred miles away in Cincinnati, my mother's
best friend, Marti, is volunteering at her church. She is
serving in the Mission Pantry, a ministry that gives food
and clothing to the poor. Marti is a generous woman who

gives freely of her time, but she doesn't suffer fools lightly. When a healthy young man comes through the line full of energy and strength, she asks to see his I.D., a requirement of the charity. She also asks him why such a strong young man needs church support. The poor fellow is taken aback by her directness but answers her politely. "Ma'am, I just got out of prison, and I don't have anything, not even an I.D."

"Well, I hope you learned your lesson, young man," she responds curtly.

"It's not like that, ma'am," he continues apologetically. "I was innocent, and a prison ministry got me out with DNA evidence."

She immediately thinks of me and strikes an unusual bargain with the stunned ex-con. "I will not only give you what you need from the pantry," she says in a surprise turnabout, "but I'll also get you a trunk full of my son's clothes—provided you do something for me."

"What is it you want, ma'am?"

"Go home to wherever you're staying and get that ministry's address and phone number. I know someone who needs that information."

The young man returns the next day with a small scrap of paper, which Marti trades for the promised wardrobe. She immediately gives the information to Kim, who calls the ministry directly. Unfortunately, it turns out they only serve clients in the North, but it is the first time we hear of a legal foundation that specializes in freeing innocent convicts, and that alone is a big encouragement.

A few months later Kim sends my 1996 Advent countdown package. It contains a series of envelopes, each dated with a note saying, "Open this one on December ___." She sends me these countdown letters at all the major holidays, including Valentine's Day. But in this particular bunch, she also encloses an article from *Jet* magazine about some lawyers who are helping prisoners get DNA tests. The article refers to Centurion Ministries, another group that works up north, in New Jersey and Chicago. Kim's letter says that she called the ministry and explained my situation. The receptionist told her that, unfortunately, they have not yet expanded to Georgia. Kim thanked her and was about to hang up when the woman suddenly remembered something.

"I don't know if they can help, but there is a group in New York that works on cases from all over the country. It's run by Barry Scheck and Peter Neufeld. They call it the Innocence Project."

She called them right away, and a student volunteer explained the screening process for new cases. Kim's letter ends with the plea, "C.C., call me so I can tell you about the Innocence Project."

As soon as I'm able to use the phone I call her, eager to hear what she's learned.

"C.C., you remember the lawyer Barry Scheck from the O.J. trial?"

"Sure, the DNA guy."

"Well, he teaches at Yeshiva University in New York, and he and Peter Neufeld started the Innocence Project—do you have a pen?"

"Yeah, go ahead."

"Okay, it's the Cordozo School of Law, Yeshiva University—and they're gonna send you a letter with an eleven-page questionnaire about your case."

"Scheck is going to send *me* a letter?"

"Yes, I called him—well, I spoke to his student. He has volunteers, just like the ones at the University of Georgia who worked for your other lawyer, what was his—"

"Kim."

"Yeah?"

"You are wonderful."

"C.C., we all just want you home."

An envelope from Barry Scheck and Peter Neufeld arrives a week later. They are two of the most famous lawyers in the world, and I rejoice just to see their names in the return address. There is no way that I can afford their help, but I figure that if God has brought me this far, he will provide everything I need. I open the large envelope carefully. The top page looks like a form letter, but it is hand-signed by Barry Scheck. Behind it are several sheets of technical questions about the trial. The letter is carefully worded to prevent false hope, and it explains that DNA tests typically cost from two thousand to five thousand dollars.

It states clearly that this is just a preliminary screen, and there is no assurance that they will take my case. But I know that God has answered my prayers. I am going home soon.

I fill in the form as best I can, and then compose a letter to the Innocence Project. I am careful not to be too forceful in my declaration of innocence, because I want the facts to speak for themselves. "Don't believe a word I say, just read the transcript that my sister is sending." I am confident that they will see the obvious travesty.

Within a month Mr. Scheck's assistant speaks to both my sister and my dad by phone. He requests additional documents, including lab reports, appellate briefs, the prosecutor's summation, and any expert testimony that might have been left out of the trial record. He explains that we should not call the Project directly but wait for their response. When my sister tells me all this, I tell her to call them as soon as she sends the material. She repeats what Mr. Scheck's assistant said, and I repeat that she should call them as soon as she sends the material. There is a silence at the other end of the phone that seems to last a long time. Then she says, "C.C., why don't you call them?"

"Good idea – we'll both call them."

Once again my family rallies to help me, but their abilities and resources are severely taxed. Mom's health problems and my legal troubles have severely affected the family's finances. Judy has already sent the money for the first DNA tests, but I know that she can't afford another five thousand dollars. I call Dad and tell him that if they don't have the money, I understand; we could just store the evidence until a later time.

My mother, too sick to do any of the legwork for me, overhears my father on the phone talking about money. I hear her in the background, "Of course we'll pay. We'll do whatever we have to do to get C.C. home." Without blinking, she pledges to cash in her retirement fund to pay for an obscure test that she doesn't understand. When I hear that, I ask to speak to her.

"Mom, I promise that I will pay back every penny as soon as I get home."

"Just come home, Calvin."

With Mom's money – and Judy's pledge to pay whatever else is needed – I am able to tell the Innocence Project that we are ready to proceed.

Christmas 1996 fills me with a terrible longing. I miss my family, and my mother's health has worsened. I find the prospect of freedom to be almost unbearably tantalizing. The Innocence Project is still reviewing my case, and there is no promise that they will take it; but their help is the only wish on my Christmas list.

A few days after the holiday I receive the happiest Christmas card of my life. Barry Scheck writes, "Based upon the information you have provided us, we are prepared to work with you in your efforts to prove your innocence." The letter is personal and encouraging. I can't help but tell some of my close friends in the prison fellowship, "I'm going home soon."

"Did that company find your evidence box?"

"No, not yet, but I've got some help."

The next day, just before New Years Eve 1997, I call my dad to share the good news. "Dad, forget everything else – don't waste your time with lawyers or the parole board. The Innocence Project is going to get me out." With those words I consolidate the efforts of my family behind a single strategy. God has given me a couple of million-dollar lawyers who are working for me pro bono. "Pops, just help Judy find the evidence box."

After months of detective work, my sister finally unravels the package trail. Apparently, Genetic Design had been bought by another DNA start-up, LabCorp. Supposedly, all the samples from the old company were placed in safe storage and will eventually be forwarded to the new corporate office. In March 1997, I call Judy in order to get an update.

"It's maddening, C.C. That package was escorted to Genetic Design in October of 1995 – eighteen months, and they still haven't started testing." She is angry enough for the both of us.

Waiting for important test results is never easy, but in this case every day of delay is another day that I get older in prison, and my mother gets sicker. It is a testimony to the power of God in my life that throughout these trials I have peace in my heart.

While I wait for the lab results, I prepare for my first parole hearing in several years. Each time I have a hearing, they increase the time between our meetings. This is not the usual pattern for a man they expect to parole.

Instead of meeting with the full board, this time they send just one representative. He is quite friendly and seems interested in my responses. He listens carefully as I answer his questions about my prison record, my work history, and my family's phenomenal support. But then he brings up the rape, and we basically replay my earlier hearings. As soon as he asks if the victim was white, I realize that the suite of questions will be almost identical. He rehearses some of the details about the crime. When he pauses to encourage remorse, I again explain that I was not actually at the crime scene, and so I can't supply him with any more details than are in the record. I try to tell him about my fight for innocence, but he politely discourages that. Finally, I tell him that I will never lie, that I have decided to be honest – even if it makes me look like a liar. I will not join the Sex Offenders Program, because it requires an admission of sex crimes – and I have none to offer.

He smiles warmly, and tells me that I will be informed of the board's decision in writing after their deliberations.

A few days later, the letter arrives. The reasons for my denial are more strongly worded than before: "circumstances and nature of the offense, multiple offenses, and history of violence." They again recommend that I volunteer for the Sex Offenders Program and remind me that "failure to participate in such a program will be looked upon with considerable disfavor by the board." But the board does not stop there; they add insult to injury. Even though I have already served fourteen years, they put off my next parole hearing for six years, to March 2003.

Back when I was sentenced to "life" it usually meant eight to ten years if you were white, and fourteen to sixteen if you were black (now it's a lot longer). The racial discrepancy isn't codified, but all the guys know what to expect. Of course, these "life expectancies" are like those that doctors give to the terminally ill: they are statistical averages based on the observation and experience. The date of my next hearing means that the parole board is making sure that I will exceed my life expectancy. Even if they do grant parole at my next hearing, I will have served two decades. Obviously, I haven't told them what they want to hear, and my honesty is being measured in years.

The evidence package finally arrives at LabCorp, and we wait to receive the test results. After another six months of waiting, Judith calls and asks to speak to the person responsible for testing. When she finally gets to the man in charge of the lab, he says that he never received the box. So, Judy spends another four weeks making calls, and then finally learns that the box had never been forwarded from LabCorp's "storage facility" to its "analytical unit." When she tells me this, I am disheartened. *Why would God allow so many mishaps?*

I decide to share some of the story with a man from my fellowship group, and he suggests an explanation for my bad luck. "Maybe the science just isn't good enough yet. It has to be right before God lets them use up your evidence – He is watching out for you, Calvin, he's gonna take care of you."

Spiritual Growth

By 1997 our Bible study is meeting twice a week, usually
late in the evening just before bed. Most of the time we
gather around a small table in the dorm, but sometimes we
squeeze into one of the smaller rooms. At Hancock Prison
the dormitories include some two-man bedrooms, and while
we aren't supposed to have more than two in a room, the
guards often allow our group an exception. It is clear to
them that our mission is peaceful, and we have had a positive
impact on the other convicts' morale. The guards know
that we sequester ourselves only because we don't want to
disturb the other men. By letting us meet, they promote a
more manageable atmosphere, and even those who are not
Christian respect the value of prayer.

We see ourselves as soldiers for Christ. This prison is our
training ground, preparing us to proclaim freedom in Jesus.
Freedom from sin, anger, hatred, worry, and even death.
As our ministry grows, we try to have a "church meeting"

once a week, to let the men preach and lead in worship. Sometimes the guards unlock a utility closet so that we can crowd in and speak without disturbing anyone. On those occasions, we turn over a garbage can to improvise a pulpit; our pews are large milk cartons or room trashcans. It is here that I learn to preach: in a closet, locked within a prison. This is the only seminary available, and it is a great education. I promise myself never to forget this setting. In comparison, no church will ever seem small or unattractive. I will be happy to worship anywhere, because I am happy to worship in this closet.

Kairos Prison Ministry becomes an integral part of our fellowship. They visit once a month, allowing the prisoners to plan the meetings, and provide half of the speakers. Because of my radio training, I am often asked to be the emcee. I remember what my mentor Douglass Whatworth Steele taught me, "Whenever you announce, remember the ringmaster."

So I don't just introduce a speaker, I promote him: "And now, gentlemen, may I have your attention for our next speaker. He resides in metropolitan Atlanta with his wife and three children. He is a baritone soloist at Grace Baptist Church and has been a Christian for twenty-seven years, Bill Golden!!!!"

In the fall of 1997 I attend the Kairos Walk at Hancock prison. The walk is a rigorous three-day event filled with teaching, prayer, music, and fellowship. Men come in from the free world and share with us about how to thrive in Christ. Each day we meet from morning until supper, and at the end of the walk there is a sort of graduation ceremony. For the closing talk the leadership chooses a commencement speaker from among the prisoners who have been on earlier walks. The single qualification for the speaker is a life that demonstrates Christian love and commitment. It is a great honor to be selected as an example of such behavior, especially by men who spend every second in your presence.

A year after my walk, I am chosen to give the closing talk. The man who introduces me says that I am often seen sharing my faith, or walking about the courtyard reading my Bible. It sounds strange to hear public praise for my religion, but it is true. I have come full circle, and my faith is strong.

In 1998 I receive my ordination while in prison, and I continue to serve the Lord with a glad heart. I am a minister of the Gospel, and not just prisoner EF140280.

Even after years in prison I still enjoyed the rigors of physical exercise. However, in the 1990s, Georgia prisons went through a massive overhaul. Two "tough on crime" governors, and their even tougher prison directors, decided that life behind bars was far too appealing. As a result, they took away my favorite recreation – the weights. Instead of lifting, we had "mandatory exercise" each day: a monotonous stroll around and around the courtyard. The entire prison population would be corralled onto the dirt track, and then told to circle like oxen grinding corn. It probably benefited some of the more sedentary men, but it made many of the weight lifters bored and angry. Necessity, however, is truly the mother of invention, and prison is the mother of necessity. So, when they took away our weights, we lifted plastic milk jugs in the kitchen, did pushups with a man sitting on our shoulders, curled the floor buffers, lifted the beds, and even pressed each other. I managed to stay in shape, not because of our evening promenades but because of my determination to control at least the flexing of my arms and legs.

While the removal of weights dampened our spirits, the prison continued occasionally to offer courses designed to improve morale and reform the men. I enroll in one called Positive Mental Attitude: The Science of Success, based on the teachings of the motivational speaker Napoleon Hill. When the teacher learns of my background, he asks me to assist with the audiovisual equipment, and I become the de facto teaching assistant.

On the first day of class the instructor is obviously unprepared, so I scramble to keep the course running smoothly. For the next two meetings he shows movies and brings in a couple of articles – but mostly he just reads from the textbook. At the fourth weekly meeting, he tries to get a discussion going about how failure can be used to spur success.

"Can you give me some examples of failures in your life that have turned into successes?" he asks.

The room is silent.

For most prisoners examples of the opposite come to mind more easily. Many of these men were successful until they messed up and landed in prison.

The teacher continues to prod by repeating the question in similar terms. "What failures have you had, that turned into successes?"

More silent stares.

In order to end the stalemate I offer some stories about prisoners who have used their time to become more educated. By breaking the ice and removing the word "failure" from the discussion, I get the class to open up. Our teacher is so impressed by the students' responses, that he asks me to prepare a short introduction for the following week's class.

Unfortunately, the following week the teacher is late. As soon as the men take their seats in the classroom, I begin my ten-minute presentation. This is followed by twenty minutes of active discussion (while I wait for the teacher to show up), which is then followed by thirty minutes of improvisation on the next chapter topic (because he never shows up at all). Fortunately, I always read ahead, and the class goes very well. As the students file out, I receive a number of compliments: everyone seems to think that I was a scheduled guest lecturer.

The next week I come prepared with inspiring newspaper clippings and magazine articles, just in case the same thing happens, but the instructor arrives on time and teaches the whole class. When he sees my materials, he asks me to bring them in to share the following week. I take his advice, and the following week I teach until he arrives—just as class is ending. He offers no apology, but again praises my ability to "assist" him with the class.

By the end of the twelve-week course, I have taught about half the lectures. My reward is a certificate of completion: just like the other men receive. The teacher doesn't even bother to write a note for my file.

Later in the year, I am approached by a female counselor who has heard of my teaching abilities. "Mr. Johnson, I've been asked to teach the Napoleon Hill curriculum, and Mr. Allen told me what a fine job you did in assisting him."

"Thank you, ma'am."

"I was wondering if – now that you have completed the course – you might be willing to assist me," she smiles warmly.

"I would love to help you out," I answer.

Once again, I soon become the lead teacher – covering most of the twelve sessions for our twenty-five students. And once again I receive a certificate for my wall, but nothing to help me with the parole board.

The next year yet another counselor asks me to "assist." He is full of praise about my PMA (positive mental attitude), but I politely turn him down.

It is important to stay busy in prison, and after my teaching experiences, I look for other opportunities to help my neighbors. Perhaps because I am ordained, the guards ask me to be an assistant on the lockdown ward. I accept the job, and in that lonely place I discover the height and depths of humanity.

On my first day, one of the trustees, Lucky Strike, explains what to expect. "There are strict rules in the lockdown ward," he begins. "Anytime a cell is opened, the prisoners have to be cuffed and chained – and two officers are required to be present. There is always a guard in the booth over there," he says, pointing, "and sometimes it's a woman." He looks at me with a wry grin. "I mention the sex of the guard, because it occasionally leads to the Bankhead Bounce."

"The what?" I ask.

"See that cell with the high window?"

I look over at the small glass plate near the top of the door.

"Sometimes those boys in solitary get bored, and they jump up for a glimpse of the woman – and sometimes they're doing more than just looking as they bounce. That's the Bankhead Bounce."

He takes me further down the hall and points to the last cell on the ward. "That's Mr. Clean's room. Mr. Clean is a frequent boarder who has some *peculiar* habits."

"Like what?" I ask.

"He keeps his toilet clean. He likes to empty it when we deliver the food – just work fast, Johnson."

The next day I arrive on the ward and immediately smell smoke. Somehow an inmate in lockdown has lit a fire and is burning his clothes and blanket. The windowless area fills with a dark cloud, and the duty guard panics. He rushes into the cell with a fire extinguisher and forgets about protocol. It is especially easy (and dangerous) to ignore protocol in an emergency. Obviously, this inmate is deranged and needs extra precautions, not fewer, but the guard reacts to the fire first, ignoring the inmate. He puts out the flame but soon finds himself under a very angry man who is cursing and throwing wild punches.

I do not see it as my duty to get directly involved, and instead I watch as several guards subdue the prisoner and manage to extract their colleague from a tangle of wet, smoldering sheets. No one is hurt too badly, but it does make me a bit wary.

"Don't worry about him," Lucky Strike says. "They'll bring him back as soon as we clean up in there."

"Won't he do it again?" I ask.

"No. This time there won't be a mattress, or pillow, or blanket, or even clothes. He'll just get a small plastic sheet. It usually calms them down."

As soon as we finish clearing out the fire damage, we hear shouting from one of the two-man cells. This time the guards use proper precautions: one man is removed from the cell in cuffs, and the other remains, shouting in a corner, "He is hitting me, he is hitting me," all the while smacking his own head as hard as he can.

Lucky finishes his shift, and I am left to complete the day on my own. As I deliver the meals, I approach each door, praying and considering what Jesus would do. I remember his words: "I was hungry, and you fed me. I was thirsty, and you gave me drink. I was a stranger, and you took me in. Naked, and you clothed me. I was sick, and you visited me. I was in prison, and you came to me. . . . As much as you have done these things for the least of these my brothers, you have done them for me."

The last door that I visit is Mr. Clean's. When I get to the door, I pause for extra prayer. I decide not to follow Lucky's advice. Instead of quietly and quickly delivering the tray, I say, "Good day, sir. I have your meal for you." I know that he has not heard a human voice in more than a week.

The response sounds like muffled cries. While crying is not unusual in that ward, his anguish is disturbing.

I kneel down beside the slot and ask, "Would you like to pray?"

There is no answer, but the crying stops.

I then do what no one with good sense should ever do—I stick my hand in the slot. I keep it there and start to pray, "Father God, we thank you for this day, a day in which we are alive and well. I pray that you would give my friend encouragement and peace—"

"—and a Bible," the man whispers.

I smile. "Yes, Lord, and a Bible."

The next day I slip a small New Testament in with the food tray: it is contraband. As I look down at the metal slit, I see a weathered hand reach toward the opening.

"Shall we pray?" I whisper.

"*Please,*" he whispers back, and his hand comes out of the slot.

We pray together like that each day until he gets out of solitary, and then I lose track of him. As I walk past his empty cell, I have no idea that one day, when we are both out of prison, he will write to me and thank me for saving his mind and his soul.

The Last Judgment

The DNA tests are finally performed at LabCorp, and the
results are reported to Peter Neufeld and Barry Scheck. The
student volunteer assigned to me, Gennifer Binder, calls my
sister Judy just as she is leaving for the airport to pick up my
mother.

"I'm sorry, but the lab test on your brother's evidence
samples were inconclusive."

"What does that mean, exactly?"

"Well, the DNA didn't amplify properly. There probably
just isn't enough there."

"What should we do next?"

"We are no longer going to work on the case – we only
deal with DNA cases, so there is really nothing else that we
can – "

"But what do *we* do next?"

"There is very little evidence left and – "

"What does Barry Scheck say that we should do next?"

"Hold on, let me ask him — I'll call you right back."

Barry calls five minutes later. "Judy, I'm sorry about the lab report. We were really hoping for a clear answer."

"What should we do next, that's all I want to know. My brother is innocent, and he needs to come home."

"Well, there are other labs, one in California, but it's much more expensive."

"Can they get a definitive answer?"

"It's hard to tell, and the problem is that most of the evidence is gone. Calvin will really have to decide what to do with the rest."

I receive the following explanation from Ms. Binder by letter:

> There are two slides with sperm — one slide was tested but unfortunately the results were inconclusive. There is one remaining slide to test. If the slide is tested, all the evidence will be consumed. Mr. Scheck and Mr. Neufeld are deciding whether to go ahead with further testing, or perhaps wait until new testing procedures are developed. We would appreciate your thoughts and opinions as to whether or not to test the last of the evidence.

I am numb at the prospect of losing the last sample. It is irreplaceable, and the test is destructive. I write to Gennifer, and ask her four questions that I want answered before I decide the fate of that last slide:

> What do they mean by "the results were inconclusive"?
> What are the chances that a test of the final slide will yield better results?
> How long will it take for better technology to be available?
> Is the laboratory that we are using the very best in the world?

She responds with a three-page letter. The tests were inconclusive because although my DNA was not present, there weren't enough visible bands on the DNA fingerprint to definitely exclude me. Apparently, they could not extract enough sperm from the panty stains or microscope slide. Either the samples did not contain much sperm, or the scientists were losing the material during processing. On the second and third questions, she could not promise me anything about the retest, and said the consensus opinion was that no extraordinary improvements in technology were on the horizon. But it was my final question that generated the most intense discussion at the Innocence Project. I called them to make sure that they understood me.

"I want the best DNA fingerprinter in the world," I told Gennifer, "the rest is up to that scientist and to God."

When Peter Neufeld calls, I ask him if there is a Michael Jordan of DNA. He answers without hesitation, "Dr. Edward Blake. He pioneered the amplification of minute traces of DNA. He has an established reputation for thoroughness, and forensic scientists all over the world consider his work the gold standard. But I have to tell you, he's not cheap. It could be another three to five thousand dollars."

"I'm not looking for a bargain," I respond. "I just want the very best."

"He's the man – no question."

Once again my family is asked to provide the money before we start the process. My mother cashes in the remainder of her retirement plan, and Judy transfers the funds to Dr. Blake. Peter then arranges for the evidence to be shipped to the California laboratory. The waiting game begins anew, but Dr. Blake gives the evidence his personal attention, and the tests are performed right away. On November 20, 1998, he reports his results. It has been six years since I first sought legal help concerning DNA, and four years since the evidence box was rediscovered; but now I stand in awe of God's amazing ability. The best legal and scientific minds in the world are working on my freedom.

In a letter about his progress Dr. Blake explains that he first looked for DNA on all the textiles: the bedsheets, the towel, the underwear, etc. However, LabCorp had extracted all of the useful stains, so the cloth evidence had to be abandoned. Next, he examined the two slides prepared from the vagina of the victim. The scientists at LabCorp had wiped one slide clean, but the other one still had half its material intact. That was all he had to work with, and yet he was able to isolate and purify more sperm than his predecessors had from all the other evidence combined. He even found a few sperm cells on two errant fibers from a cotton swab.

When I get word that the results are in, I immediately call Peter Neufeld in New York.

"It's great news, Calvin." He picks up the report and begins summarizing the findings. "Dr. Blake characterized six different genes in the sperm cells isolated from the victim; he then compared those DNA fingerprints to the genes in your reference sample. He concludes that the attacker was an African American whose DNA profile fits only one in eleven thousand black men. Your genotype is not a match. You are completely excluded as a possible donor of the sperm."

"Hallelujah! Now they have to believe that I'm innocent."

"Let's hope so."

"You don't think they'll challenge it, do you?"

"No, but there aren't any guarantees. The next move is up to Keller."

The report is sent to District Attorney Keller, who consults with Dr. George Herrin, head of the DNA unit of the Georgia Bureau of Investigation. Everyone at the G.B.I. crime lab is familiar with Dr. Blake's work, and Mr. Keller is told that whatever Blake says should be believed.

I know that the district attorney has several options to choose from. Some prosecutors, when confronted with evidence of innocence, simply dismiss it, or challenge it based on a number of potential problems. Other prosecutors faced with the same type of science move quickly to free the wrongly imprisoned. In the end Keller chooses a middle-of-the-road approach, and that means more time.

The delays multiply faster than the days pass. However, I am content ministering to the men in prison, and I avoid getting too anxious. Actually, I'm rather joyful—but I would like to see my mom soon.

At first the prosecutors say that they are looking for the victim in order to obtain a reference DNA sample from her. Then they submit a number of questions for Dr. Blake to answer. For example, was it possible that the victim had consensual sex with someone, and that the semen on the vaginal slide belonged to that man? Peter responds by explaining that this was unlikely since the DNA clearly indicated an African American, and the victim testified that she never even had a black man in her apartment, let alone as a consensual sexual partner. The district attorney still wants to try to find her former boyfriend for testing. (Barry Scheck refers to this as "the unindicted coinseminator theory.")

One of the silliest delays concerns my transcript. The district attorney's office apparently lost their original copy, and they didn't bother to get a photocopy from the state archives. This, they claim, prevents them from completing their investigation. My own photocopy, which Dad made at the archives, was sent to the Innocence Project in New York. I complain to Peter that surely someone from the D.A.'s office could make a copy at the archives downtown.

He understands my frustration and decides to photocopy his transcript for the prosecutors. He mails it with the following note:

> As per our discussion last week, enclosed please find a copy of the transcript. It has been three months since we forwarded to Mr. Keller the DNA results excluding Mr. Johnson as the donor of the semen in the rape of Ms. Mitchell. I re-reviewed the transcript last night before photocopying it, and I was reminded that this case not only involved an eyewitness who picked out someone else other than Mr. Johnson at a lineup; it's a case in which a Negroid pubic hair recovered from Ms. Stewart's sheet also excluded Mr. Johnson.
>
> I appreciate the enormous difficulty in locating files and transcripts seventeen years old, and I am grateful for your efforts. But given the reality that a factually innocent man has spent sixteen years of his life languishing in prison for something he didn't do, it is imperative that your office immediately locate Ms. Mitchell, secure the necessary biological material, and take whatever steps are necessary to resolve this tragedy.
>
> I look forward to hearing from you shortly and, again, we all appreciate your efforts.
>
> Very truly yours,
>
> Peter J. Neufeld

Once the transcript is mailed, I figure that I am home free – but then the district attorney comes up with a new reason for delay. He decides that he will be convinced of my innocence only if sperm recovered from the victim matches DNA from the pubic hair that was found in her sheets. It is ludicrous. During my trial the state's fiber expert had testified that the hair belonged to an African American and that it was not mine. At the time Keller dismissed the hair as insignificant. But now, the pubic hair, which Keller proposed had come from a public laundry facility, has to match the rapist's sperm or else I won't be freed. After all I have been through, and with my mother's health failing, this is absurd. Because of this test, I will spend another Christmas behind bars.

To further complicate matters the state decides that it wants the test to be done in North Carolina, back at LabCorp. When Dr. Blake, in California, receives the request for the pubic hair to be sent to LabCorp, he is puzzled. The request is for the single pubic hair removed from the victim's bedsheet, but the only slide in the evidence box has three hairs—all of which appear to be African American pubic hairs. So, Dr. Blake calls Peter to ask if the request had the wrong number of hairs. Peter is dumbfounded.

At my trial the prosecutor told us about only one African American pubic hair found at the crime scene. That hair didn't match mine, and the prosecutor claimed that the hair taken from the sheet must have come from the laundromat. But if there were indeed three Negroid pubic hairs, it would have been much harder for the prosecution to dismiss them as accidental.

Peter writes to the district attorney's office, barely concealing his anger.

> That there are three hairs instead of one raises two serious concerns. If, in fact, only one hair had been recovered from the bedding (as described in the transcript), then what is the source of these two other hairs? Do they belong to Mr. Johnson, and were they all mounted on the same slide for the purposes of comparison? Or, were all three Negroid pubic hairs recovered from Ms. Mitchell's bedding? If so, the presence of three Negroid pubic hairs makes it all the more improbable that they could have been casually deposited at a laundry or by a previous tenant in the apartment, two years before the rape.

Before sending the evidence back across the country, Dr. Blake examines the hairs carefully. He finds that only one hair actually has enough of a root to allow possible DNA testing. It is the hair that the fiber expert had testified did not match mine. Peter calls the district attorney's office and argues that since they had already agreed at trial that this hair was not mine, it is just a waste of time to test it for DNA. But Keller stands firm: he wants it independently tested. So, the hair makes its cross-country flight back to LabCorp to be tested at the state's expense. Once again, my freedom turns on a very small thing, the single root of a stranger's pubic hair.

Easter 1999 arrives with me still behind bars. The fellowship celebrates the death and resurrection of our Lord, with a keen understanding of his suffering and new life. I know that it is just a matter of time before I am released from my bondage, and soon I too will begin a new life. But no one can say how soon it will be. I pray against further delays. When we gather for our circle on Easter morning, we celebrate with praise and songs. At prayer time we thank God for one brother's impending release, and we pray for another who was denied parole.

"Kairos," he says with a deep sigh, "in God's time."

We pray for our families, and especially for my mother. "She's hospitalized with a stroke," I tell the men. "Please pray that God will preserve her life to end in happier days."

As the weather turns to spring, the judge finally announces my hearing date. On June 15, 1999, he will consider our motion for a new trial. I will travel from Hancock Prison to the Clayton County jail on June 11 – and I hope that I will never return. Peter tries to persuade the district attorney to support my release before the hearing, but Mr. Keller still wants to see the results from the single hair. So, Peter writes to him in late May and pleads for expediency. "It is imperative that whatever testing you wish to pursue be accomplished quickly since, as I mentioned to you, Mr. Johnson's mother has been hospitalized since January and her prognosis is not very good. My goal is to secure Mr. Johnson's freedom by the June 15 hearing, to enable him to be with his mother before she dies. Surely, it should not take more than a week to test the single crime scene hair with root."

On my last day in the penitentiary I call Peter to check on the progress of the motion.

"There's good news and bad," he says. "The bad news is that you aren't going home immediately."

"What's the good news, Peter?"

"The very good news is that LabCorp has finished their tests. Yesterday, they determined that the same African American rapist left the sperm and the pubic hair. It was a perfect DNA match," he says and takes in a sharp breath.

"So now that they have sperm and hair from the guy, they ought to be able to find him."

"They had good evidence all along," he says with sad irony. "Their fiber expert had it right from the start. Keller's laundromat theory has been exposed for what it was—utter nonsense."

"Will he support my release at the hearing?"

"He hasn't promised anything. They could delay, or try to persuade the judge that the evidence was mishandled, but after this last test, it would be a real stretch."

"Thank you, Peter. I look forward to finally meeting you." Peter Neufeld has become more than my primary advocate, he is my trusted friend.

After I hang up the phone I feel as if a great weight has come off my shoulders. I sit alone in the middle of the concrete floor and try to grasp the reality of my situation. It is like waking from a disturbed sleep. The nightmare is fading, and soon I will be with my family.

I have been transferred to the Clayton County jail for the hearing. It is Friday, and the court date is the following Tuesday. After they remove the cuffs I meet my new roommates. Some of them have just been convicted and are about to begin the journey that I am soon to complete. Others are awaiting trial, in the strange purgatory between arrest and judgment. Those who have been here the longest share the two-man rooms; the rest of us crowd into the dormitory. My bed is a small mattress on the floor that I have to put up against the wall during the day.

Some of the established men have organized an evening Bible study. I attend and listen without speaking. I haven't told the men why I am here, but after the meeting I ask them to pray about my hearing. I don't want to stir their curiosity, but they seem especially attentive to my comments, and they watch me carefully. I do not mention that I have been ordained or that I hope to be released through a series of miracles.

Peter has advised me not to discuss my case at all. Even my friends in the fellowship are kept in the dark about the details. There is enough pressure on the D.A. and the court without attracting undue attention. I am happy to settle the matter quietly. I'm not demanding a public apology or compensation: I simply want my freedom back.

On Friday, the intercom squawks and we all turn unconsciously toward it.

"Johnson, your lawyer, Peter Neufeld in New York, wants you to call him."

One of the established prisoners says, "Man, I ain't never heard anything like that — *your lawyer in New York?*"

Another man mumbles, "Neufeld? *Hey, isn't that O. J.'s lawyer?*"

I smile and realize how God has blessed me with competent counsel. As I dial the number the entire room is staring at me like I'm the CEO of Wal-Mart.

"Calvin, I've got good news and bad," Peter says, his usual opening. "The bad news is that you'll have to tough it out in jail until the hearing on Tuesday." He pauses to allow a response.

"No problem, I've toughed it out for sixteen years."

"The good news is it appears that Keller is not going to fight it."

"Does that mean I'm going home?" I ask for the last time.

"Yeah, you're going home." There are a few seconds of silence. He says, "I'll be there Tuesday morning."

I put the receiver down, and the room is silent. My heart has paused, and at first I can't really feel anything. The void of sixteen years seems to swirl about in my spirit, and then leap out of me.

"What'd he say, man?"

I remain frozen.

"Johnson, what'd he say?"

"I'll . . . be here till Tuesday," I stammer.

"And then what?"

"Then. . . ." I take a deep breath. "Then, Praise God! — I'm going home!"

The brothers from the Bible study all gather round, and we rejoice together. Some of them will never see another free day in their lives, but everyone is smiling and happy for me.

We form a circle and hold hands. The study leader begins to pray.

"Father, we just thank you for Brother Calvin's release, and pray that your hand would be upon him all the days of his life. We pray that he will go out and share the good news about God's faithfulness in dark days and bright. You are with every one of us—always—both in celebrations and in the cold and lonely times. You have never left us nor forsaken us. Be with us evermore—and thank you, Lord Jesus, for your faithfulness."

The four days pass at a snail's pace. I attend a church service on Sunday and the Bible studies each night. I keep busy by ministering to the discouraged men, of which there is never a shortage in jail. But I don't join in on the card games or watch television, so there is a lot of waiting time.

They won't allow me to receive street clothes, even though it appears that the district attorney will let me walk out of the courtroom a free man. I am told that even if I am released, I will have to come back to the jail and check out. Only then will I be allowed to don street clothes (hopefully there won't be a photographer from the local paper at the hearing). I call my dad and ask him to bring pants and a shirt for me to wear home. I suppose that he will have to buy them, because I am sure that all my old clothes are long gone.

On the day of the hearing I am shackled, cuffed, and transferred to the old jail beside the courthouse. I am now in the very same room where I sat sixteen years ago. I was shackled then—in the same way that I am now—and strangely, I remember that I was just as confident back then that the truth would soon come out. I was wrong—the truth remained hidden for a long time. It is an eerie feeling.

Just before the hearing I am told that I have visitors. Two men approach the cell. I guess that the tall, blond man with curly hair is Peter. The other man is dark-haired and has the shoulders of a linebacker.

"Hello, Calvin, I'm Peter," the taller man says, "and this is Jim Dwyer, a writer with the *Daily News* in New York."

I am honored to finally meet the man who has secured my release, and I thank him for all he has done. For a few minutes he and I talk like old friends. Then Jim explains why he has come down for the hearing.

"We're writing a book with Barry Scheck about some of the Innocence Project cases. We might put in a few lines about you."

Jim's comment is the first hint of any media interest in my story, though I can't imagine why anyone cares. My case is sixteen years old, and I am the sixty-first person to be released on DNA evidence. From my experience in broadcasting I figure I'm old news.

"There might be some press in the courtroom," Peter warns me before he leaves.

"I wish I had something better to wear," I say. I look down at my old prison jumper, frustrated that they won't allow me to wear the clothes that my dad has brought to the courthouse.

Peter just shakes his head. "I'll see you in there."

A few minutes later, a guard comes to my cell and hands me a pressed shirt, slacks, and a tie. I marvel at Peter's ability to get things done. When I am dressed, the guard spares me the indignity of shackles and handcuffs. I walk into the courthouse with my head held high, expecting to see just my family and the officers of the court. But as soon as the door opens, I am blinded by flashing cameras and television lights. The room is mobbed with reporters, and I instantly realize that my life is about to change.

Free World

I can't believe how good it feels to be in free-world clothes.

The khaki pants and soft, blue cotton shirt are humanizing.
The colors, the belt, even the zipper-fly are contraband
inside prison. I have not worn pants with a zipper in
more than a decade, and God willing, I will never wear
a button-fly again.

Peter nods toward the reporters, then leans over to me
and says, "There will be even more press outside. Have you
thought about what you're going to say after the hearing?"

For the first time I feel like Calvin C. Johnson Jr.,
free man. "Don't worry, Peter," I say, smiling, "I won't
embarrass you."

Under these clothes I am a churning mix of unspeakable
joy and relief. I cannot suppress my smile, but at the same
time I feel like crying. Peter has assured me that I am going
home, but I know that nothing is certain in court. I have

worn free-world clothes before, only to be returned to prison. Until the judge says I'm free, I am still prisoner EF140280.

The courtroom is filled with an unusual mix of people. Over my shoulder, I see a familiar face—it's Tiffany Cochran, one of the pretty reporters we used to watch in prison. My sister and father are a few rows back—I smile at them. I can see by their faces that this has been a difficult ordeal for them, and they desperately need resolution. My seventy-year-old dad is obviously moved by the proceedings, but as usual, he refrains from tears.

District Attorney Keller looks sixteen years older, and I guess that I must look that way to him. He seems neither happy nor unhappy—just a politician doing what he knows is right. The judge doesn't look particularly pleased: the proceedings are cut-and-dry, and he has nothing to say about my suffering. The most exciting moment occurs as Keller describes how my evidence box had at one point been thrown out.

"Without going through all the facts and circumstances of the case, Your Honor, I would point out to the Court somewhat of a unique situation in how things work out. . . . The Honorable Stephen E. Boswell, who tried this case, left the bench, and when he left, his court reporter retired. Because of the age of this case and the circumstances, this evidence was going to be thrown away. In fact, the rape kit that Mr. Neufeld refers to was in the trashcan when members of the district attorney's office decided, 'Why don't we just keep this.' There was no reason for us to keep it at the time."

What the district attorney goes on to describe as a strange coincidence was actually a mighty act of God.

The judge concludes the brief hearing with an explanation of his decision. Our motion was only for a new trial based on new evidence, but the state has said that it will not reprosecute the case. In order to make this official, the district attorney files a motion called a "nol-pros." The Judge looks at me and says, "Mr. Johnson, a new trial being granted, . . . and the State having moved to nol-pros, I'm signing an order that you be released from custody immediately. . . . and you are free to go, Mr. Johnson."

The emotion is indescribable. Sixteen years—sixteen long years.

A deep sigh escapes my lips, and I realize that I have been holding my breath.

I hug my lawyer, my sister, and then my dad, who allows one tear to escape down his cheek. Then I see the district attorney moving toward our table. The corps of photographers wind their cameras — electronic shutters click and whirl like crickets in a campground. He approaches me, and it seems as though everyone in the room freezes. I get the feeling that the crowd expects a confrontation — maybe they think I'll jump up and choke him. Instead, I smile and shake his hand: the animosity and hatred was prayed away years ago. All I have now is what my Lord has given me, love and peace. We shake hands, he congratulates me, and the cameras flash like tornado lightning while reporters swirl around us. I look in his eyes and say, "Thank you, sir."

Outside the courthouse an impromptu press conference begins. It seems to me that all the questions are directed toward one objective: stirring up anger.

"Mr. Johnson, do you feel that your conviction was racially motivated?"

"Are you angry about the loss of sixteen years of your life?"

"Do you plan to sue the state or the prosecutor?"

They try to draw out any hint of animosity or bitterness, but I have none. I am a happy man, and I am not going to change. Complaining now would be an insult to the God who sustained me in my darkest hours.

"The past is the past," I answer. "You have to move on — there is no sense being angry." I smile so that all my teeth show. It is a joyous day.

"But don't you think that the people who did this to you ought to be punished?"

I turn to the reporter who shouted the question and reply, "You can't let bitterness eat at you, because in the end it will destroy you. I am just glad to be out. I have no hard feelings against anyone."

Peter and I walk down the courthouse steps together. "See, I told you I wouldn't embarrass you." He smiles back at me.

Our first stop after the courthouse is the hospital where my mom is recovering from a serious stroke. Peter holds the door for me as I enter, smiling.

When I walk in the room, I can see that she is heavily sedated: there are tubes in her nose and mouth. She looks as if she is almost asleep. My father warns me that she can't speak, but tears start flowing from her eyes, and her lips tremble as if she is trying to talk. I wipe her cheeks and cradle her head in my hands. "I know those are tears of joy, Mama," I say brightly. Then I whisper in her ear, "I'm free."

As I hold her close, I remember how hard she has fought for me. She's always cared as only a mother can. Now she is the one who needs care.

Dad and I arrive at my parents' apartment after sunset. I am exhausted, and as soon as I see the large mattress, I lie down to sleep.

The first reporter calls around midnight, and the phone does not stop ringing for the next twenty-four hours. Newspeople from around the country – and even overseas – call incessantly. I answer their questions politely, and even when I am very tired, I remember that I am an ambassador of Jesus Christ. I would have promised God anything to get home, but he set me free without any bargaining. I finally give up on sleep and just sit by the phone.

During a lull in the calls, I grab a soft towel and head for the shower. Within five minutes my dad is knocking on the door.

"Calvin, are you finished in there?"

"I'll be right out, Dad."

"There's a woman from the *Today Show* on the telephone; she wants to know if you can go on TV this morning."

"Pops, isn't that in New York?"

"Hold on, I'll ask. . . . She says that they have a studio in Atlanta – they can send a limo over right away."

"Well, okay."

The limo driver is a wonderful man who invites me to his church. I tell him that I'd love to join him some time, and we have a great conversation on the way to the studio. Once inside, I find a quiet place to pray, and then I meet the production staff. I can tell that some of them are a little uncomfortable with my faith, and when I say "Hallelujah," one of the producers actually looks worried.

On the air with Matt Lauer, I get to explain how God freed me from anger first and then from prison; I talk about joy and forgiveness. When he asks me what I'm going to do now, I put in a plug for a job: "Well, I'm a college graduate, and I really need work."

The interview goes very well, and Peter Neufeld, in the New York studio, seems pleased. After the show one of the producers gives me the name of a top agent that she knows. "He's one of the best in the country. He can fix you up with a writer and film producer. You really have a wonderful story to tell." I take her card but don't feel that God is leading me to those kinds of opportunities right away. When the time comes to tell the whole story, he will bring me the right people.

When I get home, my sister Judy is there, smiling uncomfortably, but my dad looks upset.

"What is it, Pops?"

He shows me the front page of the *Atlanta Journal-Constitution*. There is a picture of him and me walking away from the courthouse. "Son, they'll just chew you up and spit you out. Sure, you're on the front page today, but by next week no one will care about you. What the hell are you going to do then?"

"Hopefully, I'll have a job real soon, Dad."

He just shakes his head and lets loose with a great deal of profanity, so I leave the room.

Judy asks him to please watch his language, as it offends me.

"Offends him?" I hear, from the next room.

Somehow we all end up in the kitchen, and the air is charged for a fight.

"So my language offends you?"

"Dad, no one talks like that around me. My friends and even my peers in the prison won't talk that way around me."

"Sit down, boy, and let me tell you something to your face. I'm not your damn peer, and I'm not swearing at you. If I say that something you do is 'damn stupid,' that's not the same as calling *you* damn stupid—but don't you *ever* equate me with your damn peers again."

Judy steps in. "But Dad—"

"Judy, you shut your damn mouth, too."

Pops is still the king of his home.

Within ten days, I add MSNBC, the *CBS Morning Show*, Black Entertainment Television, three different Atlanta stations, and even *The Johnnie Cochran Show* to my television credits.

It turns out Pops is wrong. The media attention does not fade. In fact, it becomes more intense, with requests coming from farther and farther away. I'm on the *BBC London* one day, and *AP Television Worldwide* the next. But while the news agencies always pay for my transportation, I earn no money from my appearances, and the time really cuts into my job hunting. After more than two weeks of constant demands, I am exhausted, and feel bad that I have spent so little time with my mother. All I really want to do is start a normal life. So at the end of the third week, I decide that I won't do any more interviews. Surely, I've already said everything that I can say.

Once the word gets out that I'm turning down requests, things calm down at home, and I spend my first full day with my mom. Her speech improves, and I savor each slow word. I tell her how God has opened doors for my testimony, and how I embarrassed some folks at NBC when I praised Him aloud. She smiles, and slowly tells me that she watched the *Today Show* with some of the hospital staff. Throughout the day, nurses come by to meet me, and some of them want to pray with me about loved ones. They've all heard my story on television or in the newspaper, and they know about my faith. That's when it hits me – I am a witness. I have been a witness to a great miracle, and I am required to testify. Silence is perjury.

Getting a driver's license after sixteen years is no easy task, especially since my dad doesn't have a car. Since I need a license to be able to work, we rent a car and then proceed to the motor vehicle department. I've studied the manual, so the written portion is not a problem, but the road test is a different story. Dad has another appointment and can spare only fifteen minutes for me to practice in the parking lot – that is all the driving I have done in sixteen years.

Just as I get into the car for the test, the inspector says, "You can't get tested in a *rental car*."

"What? Why not?"

"I'm not even allowed to get into a rental car," she says, without sympathy.

I am reminded of the inflexible guards in prison and look around for a more sympathetic officer. I spot a test taker getting out of his car after passing the test. He looks happy—and perhaps generous—so I call out, "Hey, can I borrow your car?"

At first he is confused by the question, then he stares me dead in the eyes without saying a word. I repeat the question, "Can I borrow your car? I can't take the test in a rental car, so I need to borrow your car."

Again, there is a long silence as the man considers the risks of this unusual request. After about a minute of staring at me, kindness wins over common sense, and he hands me the keys.

I am now faced with a new problem. My knowledge of cars is many years out of date, and I have never even seen a Hyundai. I ask the inspector if I can have five minutes to play with the buttons, and she says, "All right, but no more than five minutes." As she walks away, one of the other inspectors who had overheard the whole exchange comes over to the window, laughing. "You better be careful, she's the toughest inspector in the state."

I try the blinkers and silently pray.

After precisely five minutes, she returns and sits beside me. We go for a ride, and she takes copious notes while watching every move I make. Even though I'm driving well, I am sure that she will cite me for something. Sometimes people in authority can be very particular, and she seems like one of them. When the test is complete, she turns to me and smiles. "Mr. Johnson, I have something to tell you." I steel myself, expecting the worst. "I have never," she looks down at her notes, "given a hundred points before—and you scored a perfect hundred." We both laugh out loud.

While looking for a job, I continue to accept interviews whenever I can. One invitation that I am glad to accept comes from an Atlanta radio station, V-103. It is a popular station with the prisoners, and I know that some of the guys will be listening. When I get to the studio, it is like homecoming, because I recognize several people from my previous work in radio and television. However, no one at the station wants to talk about working for Wayne Williams, even though several of them got their start on Wayne's little station, WRAZ.

The disc jockey starts the interview with a serious tone: "Calvin, you were in prison during a lot of technological and social changes. What surprised you the most upon your release?"

"Well, I went to Popeye's chicken, and they wanted five dollars for chicken—*five dollars! For chicken!* That surprised me."

After more small talk, he finally gives me a chance to vent my frustration. "On a more serious note, what do you think of the criminal justice system now?"

"Well, you've got to have laws," I say, without hesitation. He turns from his microphone, surprised. I continue, "The system isn't perfect, but it's better than other places. There are a few changes that would make a big difference. For example, in my second trial, having a mixed-race jury helped; and I think that lineups should be run by disinterested parties, and DNA evidence needs to be stored for appeals. But as long as there are criminals, we need a criminal justice system."

After the show, one of the female disc jockeys asks me about my debts from the DNA tests. She is very sympathetic and offers to take me to a function where she will be performing. "I'm playing the club tonight, doing my comedy thing. Why don't you come out, and I'll introduce you. We could take up a collection for you—I know the folks will be very generous."

I want to say yes right away—I certainly need the money, and I am anxious to stop living off my parents. I take her number and tell her that I will call in an hour. But when I pray about it at home, something just doesn't seem right. Even though her offer is very kind, a club just doesn't seem like the right place to be so soon after my release. So I call her up and say no. It is a tough call for me to make.

A few days later a stranger asks me to join her at New Birth Missionary Baptist Church, a large African American congregation in Atlanta. During the sermon Bishop Long mentions my story and then invites me onto the platform to pray with him. As he prays, someone is moved to bring some money to the stage, and then someone else—and soon money is being poured at our feet. It is a complete surprise.

"That's for you, Calvin," the bishop tells me.

The love offering helps me get on my feet and confirms that God will always take care of me, without any compromise in my values. I leave the church with a few thousand dollars in my pocket.

After the V-103 interview, I am invited to a completely different type of show: conservative talk radio.

Neal Boortz hosts a syndicated morning show from Atlanta and is well known as an irascible Libertarian. He calls himself "the Mighty Whitey." While I prepare for the interview, one of my black friends calls to warn me: "He's not exactly supportive of black folks – if I were you, I'd cancel."

I chuckle. "He's just a man. After all that God has brought me through, do you think that I'm afraid of what one man might say?"

As it turns out, Neal and I have a wonderful conversation. Although he tries – just like all the other reporters – to bring out some negativity from me, I get the feeling that we both really respect each other. In fact, it ends up being one of my favorite interviews.

The next Sunday, I am invited to church by the limo driver from the *Today Show*. The preaching is excellent, and the music moves my soul, but I am distracted by a pretty young lady sitting a few aisles to my left. I try to concentrate on the sermon, but something about her attracts my eyes, over and over again. I'm sure that she notices my glances, and I feel almost embarrassed by my curiosity. After the service, I work up the nerve to introduce myself.

She shakes my hand and says, "My name is Sabrina Middleton. I've seen you on television, and I heard you on the Neal Boortz show last week."

"I hope I didn't do too badly," I say.

"Not at all," she responds with a charming grin. "Will you be coming to church here next week?"

"Well, I really enjoyed the service, but actually I'm scheduled to speak at another church."

"Oh," she says, a bit disappointed. "Well, I have some friends in the media, so we just might run into each other again."

"I look forward to that," I say, as we part.

The next day I receive a phone call from a familiar voice – Neal Boortz.

"Listen, Calvin, you really need to call my cousin, Sabrina." The dubious family connection between the lily-white Boortz and the African American Sabrina makes me laugh, and I ask for her number.

"Thanks, Neal."

"She's a great lady, Calvin."

I call Sabrina and discover that she is a very down-to-earth and interesting woman. When she hears that I don't have a car, she offers to drive me wherever I need to go. I take her up on the offer often, and soon we are spending a great deal of time together in her car. She also begins attending the various talks that I am invited to give, and we discover that we have a lot in common.

Starting over in the working world is a great challenge. I find that I have to prove myself all over again. My first job at a rail yard lasts less than a week, because my boss gets nervous when a camera crew visits me on the job.

Fortunately, when I get home from my last day of work, there is a message on the answering machine. It's from a woman named Nancy Calhoun, who has a kind voice. "Calvin, I'd like to introduce you to Steve Foster. He's the owner of Tekrail, and if you're still looking for a job, he's hiring."

I learn that Tekrail makes railings for construction, and they have a large workshop for manufacturing. When I call the owner, he invites me down for an interview right away. Everyone in the front office is incredibly friendly, and Steve seems to understand my position in terms of the press.

"All I ask for is fair warning about reporters' calls or visits."

He offers me a job on the spot, and I accept. Unfortunately, the assembly site is far from my home, and since I don't have a car, transportation is an obvious problem. Steve notices my distress and offers to lend me a car until I can get one on my own.

The assembly work is hard, but the company is nurturing. Steve himself is a committed Christian, and after working for him a few weeks, I learn that he sponsors missionary projects overseas. One morning, he approaches me with an unusual offer.

"Calvin, I want you to pray about joining us on our next trip. I'll be going with two guitarists, John and David, and two preachers, Lester and Robert."

"Your next trip to where?" I ask.

"Uganda, Africa."

My jaw drops.

"Would you like to come – all expenses paid?"

"If I can get the time off," I laugh.

The press gets wind of my upcoming trip, and a camera crew comes out to the factory for an interview. Another television crew follows us to the airport, where the cameras roll as Sabrina gives me a good-bye hug. The city of Atlanta gets to watch us embrace before my flight to Entebbe.

I haven't been out of prison six months, and already I am in Africa. Students have packed the main auditorium of Makerire University, and Steve's musician friends are leading them in song. The audience sings and sways with a free-flowing African cadence. We are grateful that the electricity holds up, because brownouts are quite common.

Steve approaches me before the speakers take the podium. "Calvin, there's been a change in the program," he whispers. "We'd like you to give the main address. The students really want to hear from you."

I am hesitant to follow the two trained ministers who will speak first, but I take the leadership's recommendation and join the preachers on the dais.

When it's my turn to speak, I begin with the verdict that sent me away for sixteen years. The students are riveted, and I realize the universal appeal of my testimony: injustice, innocence, God's faithfulness, freedom. Freedom.

After my talk, the audience asks the same questions that American students do.

"How did you learn to forgive and not be angry?"

"Was it God's will for you to be in prison for so many years?"

I am amazed that people all over the world are looking for the same answers. Basically, they want to know if they can really take God seriously. Billions of people recite the Lord's prayer, but many wonder if they can really trust it. I know that they can.

Leaving the capital, we discover a world that has not changed much in a thousand years. The roads in the countryside are really just trails in the bush; without a four-wheel-drive truck we never could have made it outside the city. When we finally arrive in the first village, the only ones who amble out from among the straw huts are children. Their families live off the land, and the poverty is obvious. There is no electricity, no phone, and no way of announcing our visit. As I look around the small community, I can't see any meetinghouse or church.

"Where will we speak?" I ask Steve.

"That's what the bags of balls are for." He hands me a sack. "Go ahead, toss one out."

I follow his suggestion, and cannot believe the children's joy at receiving this simple gift. There are so many things we take for granted back home that are precious to these folks. The kids' laughter attracts the attention of the mothers, who soon join us in the village center. Once the women and children have gathered, any men who are not fishing also join us.

The crowd is animated, and the women are traditionally attired in beautiful wrap dresses. Each villager bows slightly as he or she greets us, and I am charmed by the ways of village life. The smile on my face comes straight from the heart.

We stand by the car, because custom does not encourage strangers to visit close to the homes. Unfortunately, we don't have an interpreter with us, but after a few minutes of sign language a man is brought forward who understands English. Steve encourages me to speak to the people, and I learn to break up my speech for the interpreter. The villagers stay with us and ask questions until it is dark, although dark is an understatement—the sky becomes black. The equatorial night is like spilled ink, covered with glitter. We wait until the moon rises to say good-bye, and then hop back into the truck.

The driver navigates the night roads with great care. I have already learned to respect the many dangers of this unstable land. Car-eating ruts, giant mammals, and bandits are not just the stuff of folklore. In contrast, the beautiful hills, silhouetted against the sky, suggest Eden, the land of the first humans. As I lean back in the truck, I revel in the starry sky — a view denied to me for so many years.

The university speeches are over, and we take two days to relax and pray before our final church appearances. Steve has arranged for a safari at Queen Elizabeth National Park. Driving to the park, we see salesmen by the side of the road. Several hold out fresh tilapia fish; others have goats with milk for sale. Finally, we enter the giant game preserve where we have been invited to spend the day. Just a few yards past the entry gate, we see herds of impala and waterbuck.

"This is no zoo," I say to Steve.

He points to what looks like a male lion resting in the distance. We keep a wary eye on his movements as we drive in our open truck.

At noon, we park beneath a large shade tree and watch gazelles drinking at the lake. Steve points out three zebras at the far shore, and someone else spots monkeys in the branches above our heads. I have never seen wildlife mixed together like this. It's as if the circus train fell off the tracks, and all the animals dispersed in small bands.

We enjoy the fauna so much that no one notices the baby elephant as it walks up to the parked truck. Suddenly, there is a pounding noise and a trumpet blow. The sound is frightening, and we all turn to see a full-grown mother elephant, staring at us. For a few moments, no one knows what to do. The mother trumpets again, threatening us. Then the baby looks at us as if to say, "Sorry, gotta go, Mom's calling," and trots off to join her. The two of them run toward a far grove of trees, and we all nervously laugh with relief. As we drive back to the gates, I glance at my watch and note that it's Saturday. Visiting day at the prison.

On Sunday, before church, one of our young hosts tries to explain more of his country's culture. "Tribal heritage is very important to us," he says. "For example, I am an Acholi, and your driver is Basoga. You see, each tribe has its own language, dances, and stories." He looks down as if to give me bad news: "We feel sad that our brothers in America are lost—you don't know your history. You don't even know what tribe you belong to?" He stares at me earnestly.

The term *tribe* is exotic to me. I realize that he is talking about something larger than family—more intimate than race, more personal than nationality—and he is right: I have no concept of my tribe. He continues to examine me, and then smiles and says, "I think you are Basoga—like the driver."

Three of us on this trip have lived through the transition in racial designation, from Negro to black to African American. Being in Africa, however, I learn that the term *African* is perhaps too broad. Tribal identity seems to be more important than even national identity here.

At the church, all of us are warmly welcomed, but special attention is given to the black members of our party, as if we are relatives who have finally come home. They add tribal designations to each of our names and introduce us to the elders of the group to which they have assigned our features. The service is passionate, and Christ is glorified in rich harmonies that rise and blend like the rainbow sunsets of the African plain. I am absorbed in their rhythm and join the happy chorus, which crescendos before the Gospel is read. Then, there is a time of prayer, and after that, the three African Americans are called forward.

Our hearts are warm from the exotic worship and the welcome that we have enjoyed, but we are unprepared for what is to come. The pastor is suddenly serious, and he looks at each of us with grave concern.

"My brothers, we have to apologize."

We hold still, before the now-silent congregation.

"Many years ago our chiefs committed a horrible sin: they sold some of their brothers." I feel a lump in my throat. "We are their children, we know who we are; but you, my brothers, are their children also. Children who were sold off for a herd of cattle or a box of guns. Our forefathers betrayed your fathers, and this shame wounds our hearts. But you must know, you must tell your children, you are our brothers."

We are engulfed by embraces from long-lost family members, who greet us with their names and tribes. For the first time I understand the loss that this continent has suffered. We accept their apology, and their love, with tears of joy.

When I get back to the states, I return to my assembly job at Tekrail and begin work on a book about my ordeal. But when I hear about a management opportunity at the Metropolitan Atlanta Rapid Transit Authority, I jump at the chance. I've always loved working with people, and the position of station manager seems tailor-made for me.

The interview at MARTA consists of a series of tests and live discussions. They ask extensively about my work experience, and I describe the prison jobs that I have held over the years. My interviewer stresses that "a station manager has to deal with all kinds of people, some of whom are trying to beat the system."

I laugh, because that's something I have had a lot of experience with.

They hire me the next day, and the skills that I developed in prison serve me well. While some station managers are quick to call the police at the first sign of trouble, I've found that oftentimes people just need to be reminded of civil behavior. Sometimes it's as simple as insisting that squabbling passengers get on separate trains, heading in opposite directions.

As the manager, I have a lot of conversations with my customers and coworkers. I am careful not to force my views on them, but some of them bear their hearts to me, looking for answers. My first week, one bus driver was so depressed that I spent my entire break with him on the bus. We ended our time together by praying, and he later told me that he had been suicidal until then. There are needy people everywhere.

Often it is the passengers traveling late at night who require the most assistance. One night, a man came through the turnstile and seemed disoriented. He was sober but explained to me that he had lost his wife to cancer the week before and could hardly summon the strength to walk. He was without purpose and didn't know which train he wanted. As we talked, it was clear that his most pressing problem was loneliness. He loved his wife dearly and had spent every waking moment caring for her over the last twelve months. My dad's loyal care of my mother helped me to understand this nice old man. We spoke for only a few minutes, but he smiled when we were done, and gently squeezed my hand. "You have lifted my spirits," he said, and then he made his way with strong steps to the right platform.

One Friday night, near the end of my shift, I saw another old man waiting alone for the bus. It was my job to inform him that he had missed the last one. There is a special van that comes around for those who arrive late, but it goes all over the city and can make a normally brief trip last for hours. The man was weak and had trouble communicating: when I spoke, he waved his hands as if he could not hear. I tried writing on my clipboard in order to converse with him.

You missed the last bus?

As I explained the van procedure, his face got sadder with every word I wrote. Then I changed my mind and scribbled *I'm leaving soon, I could drive you home.*

He smiled like a baby and wrote down his address. I took him home, although it was quite out of my way, because part of freedom is the freedom to do good. Sometimes it seems there isn't enough time to be kind, but freedom—just like prison—is all about how you spend your time.

I have not been allowed back into the prisons where I was incarcerated, but I do visit other prisons about once a month. I love meeting with the men, because they know that I understand their situation, their temptations and frustrations. In ministry, there is nothing like a peer. I am praying that God will open the doors of my former prisons to me. He did it once to let me out, and he can do it again to get me in.

To some convicts, I'm a symbol of hope. Not the hope of release from prison, but the hope of forgiveness and a new life. Most of the men I visit are guilty of their crimes, but they all want a second chance. When they see me, they are encouraged, because they know that I was punished just like them, felt the same pain, was subjected to the same treatment; and yet I believe in the goodness of God. Prison ministries are so very important, because most of the men will eventually get out, and the statistics say that many of them will return to crime. We would all rather see these men committing their lives to Christ than committing new crimes.

I know that God can change a man's heart.

Epilogue

In prison, you have plenty of time to invent fantasy women,
and I have probably conjured up a few, but Sabrina
Middleton is the real thing, and a true surprise. I had not
expected to fall in love. I was certainly not looking for love,
but God brought us together; and when God makes a match,
it's best to pay attention. After a month of more practical
outings, like shopping, speeches, and job interviews, I finally
ask Sabrina out on a real date, to watch the Fourth of July
fireworks. It is on the way home, in the train seat beside
her, that I realize I am completely in love. When we say
good-bye at her porch, we are no longer just friends, and I
kiss her. In April of 2000 I take her out to the best restaurant
in town and ask for a window seat overlooking Stone
Mountain. There, on one knee, I propose to her.

A few days later my coauthor and I fly to New York to visit
the Innocence Project's headquarters. We take a cab to

Greenwich Village and walk up to the small meeting room at the Yeshiva Law School. I am wearing a new tailored suit. Sitting around a large wooden conference table are twelve law students who have come to the Innocence Project from all over the world. Each of them has been assigned ten cases, representing ten men who languish in prison, proclaiming their innocence. The prisoners send transcripts and court records, usually two or three feet thick. The student interns must carefully read every page, and then begin the endless phone calls to prosecutors and judges—many of whom are reluctant to investigate their own mistakes.

Barry Scheck, introduces me to the students. I look around the room and see that they are eager to hear from me. I am the first one they've met: a man freed by the Innocence Project. Barry and Peter Neufeld, who started the project in 1992, have become my good friends. Peter and I were on *Court TV* earlier in the day, and tomorrow Barry and I will appear before the nation's science writers at the Gene Media Forum. The forum includes many of the top writers in the country, and I will be introduced by a vice president of NBC. The media events are very prestigious, but speaking to these students is the real honor, because they are giving up their summer to help the helpless.

I begin, "I came here to thank you. . . ."

After the talk, we all shake hands, and the students ask me questions. When Barry suggests that we have supper together, I cancel a dinner with relatives in order to extend my time with the volunteers. At the restaurant their curiosity does not abate, and I talk so much that I begin to lose my voice. But I won't leave them, because I know that they need to know a real freed man: someone who spent years in jail, falsely accused. I represent the stacks of men, back at the law school, who plead in crudely written letters, begging for someone to take up their cause. I remember writing such letters, then waiting for months, wondering if they were actually read. I cannot forget that when I first started fighting for my own release, no one would help me. Each letter I sent took me days to compose but was usually answered with a terse form letter. I had faith that God would somehow clear my name, but for years it was faith alone that encouraged me. These students are heroes.

Finally, the coffee cups are cleared away, and I say good-bye to the volunteers. Barry hails a cab, because he is late for another television appearance.

"I'm doing one of the reactionary shows," he says, dismissively. "They want someone to talk about the guy down in Texas." He looks down and shakes his head as if talking about a close friend's bad prognosis. "Unless he gets a reprieve, he'll be executed on Thursday."

For a long time we just stand there and watch for cabs. Then Barry asks about my schedule. I tell him that I had to say no to *The Geraldo Rivera Show,* and that I sent a letter to the Congressional Committee instead of testifying. "I need to stay home in Atlanta for a while," I explain. "I've got a job, and Mom's still sick."

"Good luck with the media forum tomorrow," he says as his cab pulls up, "and thank you for visiting my students."

All of the attention seems almost routine now; a lot of people want to hear my story, but I remember that it wasn't always so. I remember writing the letters that no one read.

Compensation for wrongful imprisonment is a tough issue. DNA testing is exonerating an unprecedented number of falsely convicted men, and the states are facing a difficult problem. We have to have laws, and there are going to be mistakes; but what should we do for people who have been wrongly convicted by an imperfect system? The folks at the Innocence Project said that they had "seen it all," in terms of remuneration. There were several awards in the millions of dollars, and many other cases in which a bus ticket home was the only compensation.

Unfortunately, Georgia grants the criminal justice system total immunity from lawsuits for wrongful conviction. So when I was released, I was told that no help would be forthcoming, because I had been legally convicted by a jury of my peers. After a few months, however, some people in the government begin to take a different view. State Senator Frank Bailey is the first.

From the moment I enter his office, I recognize that he will do what is right. I share my story with him and tell him how I have experienced the power of forgiveness through Jesus Christ. He listens carefully and then says that while he can't guarantee anything, he will look into the issue of compensation.

A few weeks after our meeting, Senator Bailey tells me that any compensation would require an extraordinary act of the Georgia legislature—a special law just for me. He promises to see it introduced.

For several months I hear nothing from my local attorney about the state house's deliberations. In May, I am invited to speak on Black Entertainment Television (BET) and fly out to Los Angeles. The network puts me up in a wonderful hotel, and I have a great interview. When I return to my room, there is a message from my dad.

"The newspaper says that your compensation was cut by 80 percent, because you had been rightly convicted of some recidivist charges, and would have spent eight years in prison anyway." Pops is steaming mad. "I think the district attorney has released those old mistaken files again—the ones that say you were convicted of rape before. You better call your lawyer."

I immediately call the firm that is supposed to be working with the state on my behalf. "What's going on with the compensation bill?" I ask.

"What do you mean?"

"The newspaper says my compensation was cut by 80 percent because I should have served time for crimes that *I did not commit*—haven't you been following the bill in committee?"

"I'm sorry, this is the first I've heard of it."

"Well, make some calls and find out what's going on—I'm in L.A., and *I* found out." I am more upset that my reputation is being smeared again than I am about the money. No amount of cash can compensate for my lost years—but I insist that the truth to be known.

After a few months, the questions are all answered, and the record is finally cleared up. I am told that next year five hundred thousand dollars will be appropriated for my debts and compensation.

Our wedding day is a wonderful reunion of family and friends. My old pals from college are here, and even my childhood neighbors from Cincinnati. Pastor Hazel Horne, who used to minister to me when I was locked up, is here to perform the ceremony. Since my release Hazel and I have visited several prisons together, and every time I look at her today, she smiles to the point of tears. Senator Bailey, who worked so hard on my behalf, congratulates me and tells one of my friends that he has become a dedicated Christian since our last conversation. Just before the music starts, a prison chaplain gives me a hug and passes on good wishes from friends behind bars.

Some old cameramen buddies have decided to professionally film the day as their gift to us, and one of the men from Kairos carries a small camera to shoot stills. He will take the photos to Hancock prison, my last home in the penitentiary system. While I am still forbidden to go there, perhaps through his pictures my brothers in the fellowship will see that I really did make it. God has restored my life, and like Job, the end is more blessed than the beginning.

Just before we say "I do," I look down and see my mom smiling from her wheelchair. She is able to attend just a few minutes of our vows before returning to the hospital, but I am grateful. God has answered my prayer: my mother has lived to see happier days.

Twenty days after my wedding I get an emergency call from the hospital. It is late at night, and I fear the worst. Dad says only, "It's time to come."

In the car I have a few moments to prepare, to consider my mother's last few years. I remember her voice on the phone from inside prison, her hand on visiting days, the silence of her time in the coma or after the strokes. Love has nothing to do with how much is said. Love is proof of itself.

When I arrive, my father is beside her bed, as he has so often been. The room is dark and quiet; there are flowers picked from the small hospital garden that Dad planted to make Mama feel more comfortable during her occasional strolls outside. He looks up at me with a look I will not try to describe. Mom is hardly breathing, and her eyes are closed. I reach out to hold her one last time, and pray. She responds to my touch by moving a few fingers. That is how we say good-bye. She had waited for me to arrive.

Sabrina and Calvin C. Johnson Jr. live in the Atlanta area and are the proud parents of a beautiful little girl. Calvin serves as a founding board member of the Georgia Innocence Project. He works as a manager for the Metropolitan Atlanta Rapid Transit Authority and is a frequent speaker on college campuses and in prisons, churches, and schools.

Afterword

Barry Scheck

As <u>Exit to Freedom</u> goes to press there are 130 unique and
complex human beings who were wrongfully convicted and
subsequently exonerated through postconviction DNA testing.[1]
The mechanism that leads to their liberation – DNA tests on crucial
pieces of biological evidence (bloodstains, hairs, saliva, or semen
stains) – is a marvel, but one a daily press corps without much time,
energy, or resources perceives, after a while, to be repetitive, even
boring, and not especially newsworthy. Media coverage of these
exonerations devolves into unimaginative, formulaic patterns:
What does it feel like to be free after all these years? Are you bitter?
What will you have for your first meal? What has changed the most
since you were locked up, cell phones? The extraordinary, rich,
and varied stories of the underlying cases, both the causes of these
wrongful convictions and the struggles waged by an impressive cast
of characters against impossible odds, are routinely ignored.

For each new exonerated prisoner, the scene at the courthouse
or outside the prison walls is a celebration. Surrounded by family

and friends, whether they supported him or not during incarceration, he has his fifteen minutes of fame, a measure of reassurance that in America we admit our mistakes and try to correct them. The cameras record the jubilant homecoming and that first meal. The survivor who has just been liberated, on that day, declares little bitterness, and observes that bitterness and hatred consume you, and he learned long ago to move on. Some even declare that they have achieved a measure of serenity. I have been privileged to attend these remarkable occasions many times, and I react to the forbearing sentiments of the newly released with great admiration and little true comprehension – if this had happened to me I'd be infuriated, consumed with rage, unforgiving. I can tell that these men are not faking it; they mean it. I just don't understand how, upon their release, they can manage to get beyond the anger. Indeed, I don't understand how they kept their sanity.

Then everyone leaves.

And the loneliness closes in fast. Night sweats and nightmares of violence seen and experienced in prison come back again and again, disrupting sleep and haunting the waking hours. Everything has changed. Friends and families have grown up and moved on, and the true measure of years lost sinks in with sickening and frustrating clarity.

And, of course, the full story, the real story, the intricate, painful tale of survival, the nightmare of being convicted as an innocent and imprisoned, is rarely told. Instead, the lucky ones can move beyond it – push it away somewhere, for decent intervals at least, and function. The unlucky ones are condemned to reexperience it all the time, frequently with debilitating effects. Everyone is trying to escape the nightmare and create a new life.

Calvin Johnson stands out among a remarkable brotherhood of the wrongly convicted. He is astonishingly articulate, intact, and self-possessed. He speaks with authority and moral gravity. He has true serenity. He has moved on most impressively – marriage, employment, compensation from the state, close family and friends all seamlessly gathered into his loving orbit. He genuinely eschews the bitter pill of anger. His smile lights up a room and he smiles all the time. I have seen Calvin inspire and move audiences large and small. He's such a polished communicator, so easygoing, and so secure in his faith that one cannot imagine he was ever any different.

That's why *Exit to Freedom* is such a revelation and service. The miraculously together Calvin Johnson was not always that way at all. With the estimable help of Greg Hampikian, Calvin has managed to share with us the untold tale of wrongful conviction and imprisonment with great clarity and detail. His portraits of Mount Vernon and River State Prison rebut the myth that America's state prisons have become country clubs. It's not the surreal atmosphere of gangs and constant violence conveyed on the television show *Oz*, but a deadening, regimented, oppressive existence. He offers a realistic but not altogether surprising picture of imprisonment.

What stands out, what's so important, is Calvin's meditation on what it feels like to be imprisoned and innocent; he makes this experience more comprehensible than any description I've read. Just consider these two paragraphs that describe how Calvin felt after being denied parole because he would not admit guilt and show remorse:

> Anger is not a trait I was born with. It began in prison, and it grows each day. After ten years my anger has started to assert itself. For most of my life I took pride in being easygoing, slow to react, and naturally calm. But I have changed. I have become unsociable and quick to argue—but who wouldn't? I wake up each morning to prison bars, in the company of men I would not choose as friends. My time—and my life—are totally controlled and hopeless. As soon as I open my eyes, I am mad. The gnawing in my stomach now accompanies the dawn of each new day.
>
> I am so angry that complete madness cannot be far away. Bitterness is a drug, an addictive substance—it haunts me each minute, whispering its catechism of complaints. As much as I try, I cannot calm the increasing volume of these voices. I cannot reason my way out, because my anger is so reasonably constructed—I am innocent, I have been railroaded, and no one will help me. I have followed all the rules, been patient in my appeals for help—and nothing. Nothing! My case for hatred is airtight, and the facts arrange themselves in my mind without effort. It is consuming me, and I am losing myself. Up until now I have contained the rage beneath a thin shell of control, but now the surface has cracked.

He has no tolerance for the complaints of inmates with sentences shorter than five years; he describes those who weep looking at pictures of their families on the outside as "insufferable moaners—crybabies." This is a most unchristian, un-Calvin-like sentiment! He sends home all his photos, his trial transcripts, anything associated with hope. Accepting the fact that he is hopeless and vengeful, he becomes the hardest of hardened inmates. "Religion has become my enemy, because faith is the purest form of hope, and hope disgusts me more than anything else."

This is Calvin's low point, of course, and his telling observation that the loss of hope ultimately leads a prisoner to shut out all tender sentiments and become unfeeling and violent applies equally to the guilty and the innocent. It is reminiscent of a process recounted in Hurricane Carter's autobiography (and depicted in Denzel Washington's unforgettable performance in *The Hurricane*), when Carter decided to shut all loved ones out of his life because he believed he would never be released.

Calvin's way out, his exit to spiritual freedom before anyone thought of performing a DNA test, was not a sudden beatitude, a single epiphany of religious conversion:

> There is no instant miracle; the anger and looming threat of madness do not vanish right away. But God does give me a hunger to read the Bible, and in those pages I begin to find my answers. Day by day, verse by verse, it shows me the way to a sound mind: to freedom from bitterness, anger, envy, and hate. The way is prayer. Not just the usual repenting or pleading; my prescription is to pray for my enemies, for those who despitefully used me, for those whom the devil has convinced to convict me.

One does not have to believe in God or any particular religious order to appreciate what saved Calvin. It is a very powerful idea: Through enormous self-discipline, force yourself to forgive your enemy, your tormentor, or your oppressor, but never obscure or fail to recall precisely what happened. Hate hurts the vessel; love can heal it. It is an idea that Ghandi, Martin Luther King Jr., and Nelson Mandela used to change history. This ethical imperative to love your enemy does not mean to forget the history of an injustice or who inflicted it. Calvin says, "I finally understand that I don't need to forget, I need to remember those who keep me behind bars. I need to pray for every aspect of their lives. That is what Christ taught about forgiveness. It is not passive, and it is not easy."

The Holocaust survivor Elie Wiesel teaches the same lesson: the need to forgive but not forget. When protesting President Reagan's 1985 visit to Bitburg, a cemetery in Germany where members of the SS were buried, Wiesel explained to Reagan why survivors, who "have tried to teach their contemporaries how to build on ruins, how to invent hope in a world that offers none, how to proclaim faith to a generation that has seen it shamed and mutilated, . . . believe . . . that memory is the answer—perhaps the only answer."[2]

Calvin Johnson is an important leader in a new civil rights movement that challenges the causes of wrongful convictions in America. One cannot help but recognize after reading his story that racism, mistaken eyewitness identification, and inadequate defense counsel must inexorably lead to the conviction of other innocents like Calvin. There are remedies for these and other problems that plague our system of justice. At the Innocence Project web site there are studies, and links to studies, that lay out the remedies in ample detail.

But no study can compete with the impact of a personal narrative that forgives but forgets not one compelling detail, that inspires without being phony, and that demonstrates the power of love and faith without being sectarian or preachy. Calvin Johnson has given us a narrative with those marvelous qualities because that's how he lives his life. He makes it look easy and natural, but he has pulled back the curtain to show us, with honesty and passion, how hard it was and is. We are in his debt.

NOTES

1. For an updated list and a detailed summary of every postconviction DNA exoneration case, go to the web site of the Innocence Project, www.innocenceproject.org.
2. "Remarks on Presenting the Congressional Gold Medal to Elie Wiesel and on Signing the Jewish Heritage Week Proclamation," April 19, 1985, www.pbs.org/eliewiesel/resources/reagan.html (accessed June 5, 2003).

DNA and the Science of Justice

Greg Hampikian

What is DNA?

It is fortunate for forensic scientists that DNA is a stable organic molecule. Pieces of it have been isolated from carpets, eyeglasses, bites of leftover food, hairbrushes, clothing, and even urine in the snow—all of which have been used in court. DNA is so hearty that it can be isolated from insects frozen in amber for a hundred million years (as Michael Crichton pointed out in *Jurassic Park*). In forensic cases DNA is usually obtained from a suspect through a blood sample (United States) or a cotton swab of the mouth (Britain).

DNA is made from only four nucleotide bases, abbreviated A, G, C, and T. Every cell in the body contains a copy of the entire genome: all three billion bases that spell out an individual's genetic makeup. The DNA is stored on twenty-three pairs of chromosomes; one member of each pair is inherited from each parent. It is estimated that only 1 percent of the genome actually codes for traits; the rest of it has no known purpose and is slowly accumulating mutations through evolution. Some writers refer to this noncoding DNA as "junk DNA." Much of that genetic "junk" is still highly conserved between individuals, but over time some areas have become noticeably different. Since 99.7 percent of our DNA is identical across the species, an individual's DNA fingerprint is obtained from those segments of DNA that are known to vary. These areas are aptly named: hypervariable regions. Many of the hypervariable regions are found in junk DNA.

There are several types of hypervariable regions, but forensic science is primarily concerned with those that cause noticeable changes in the length of DNA. These differences in length occur because the regions include short sequences that are repeated various numbers of times. For example, there is a region on human chromosome 5 that contains a variable number of the repeat "TAGA." Most people have between fourteen and thirty-two copies of that repeat sequence (TAGATAGATAGATAGA . . .) at this location or "locus." Since we inherit one chromosome 5 from our mother and one from our father, we each have two forms of this locus. The unique sizes of each form are called alleles. So, for example, I may have one chromosome 5 with sixteen repeats of TAGA and another chromosome 5 with twenty-two repeats. That particular combination is not likely to be the same as yours, but it is not unique. In order to get a unique DNA fingerprint it is necessary to identify the alleles at several different chromosomal loci. The F.B.I. uses thirteen such loci to complete a DNA fingerprint. By multiplying the probabilities of the alleles from those thirteen loci, they can usually match a DNA profile to a single person. The chance of a random person producing the same print is usually less than one in a hundred trillion.

How are the lengths of hypervariable regions measured?

In order to determine the length of each repeat unit, forensic scientists use a technique called polymerase chain reaction, or PCR. This technique is capable of copying specific segments of DNA based on their sequence. It is done by using primers, short pieces of DNA that bind to the ends of the region of interest (figure 1). The enzyme DNA polymerase is then added, and the genetic sequence between the primers is copied; this results in a doubling of the sequence. Repeating this doubling reaction thirty times produces up to one billion copies of the sequence of interest. After amplification the sequence of interest is so abundant that it can be seen and measured. In order to produce a complete DNA fingerprint, the F.B.I. uses thirteen pairs of primers (one pair for each locus) and a special pair to determine sex. This results in up to twenty-eight DNA fragments, or "peaks," which can be separated by size. The separation of the peaks is achieved by passing them through a thin capillary tube in a process called capillary electrophoresis. Figures 1 and 2 depict results using a single pair of primers.

How are the statistics figured?

The F.B.I. and other groups have done large population studies to estimate the frequency of different alleles in various human subpopulations. For example, the chromosome 21 locus contains a four-base sequence that is repeated twenty-four to thirty-eight times (Fregeau et al.). We know from dozens of racial and ethnic studies that 25 percent of the chromosomes in African populations have twenty-eight copies of the repeat linked in a row; this same twenty-eight-copy allele is rare in the Chinese population of Singapore (found in less than 4 percent of that subpopulation). Therefore, finding a twenty-eight-copy allele at a murder site in Singapore could be more informational than finding it at a crime scene in Africa. But in neither case does it point clearly to a particular suspect or even to a racial group. It is like finding an envelope with only a few letters of the addressee's name. Such information allows investigators to exclude some people but not to identify the specific individual.

Once a sample has been processed and the allele sizes for all thirteen loci have been determined, it is important to know how often we can expect to find an identical match in the population. Since the frequency of each allele type varies among ethnic groups, we must calculate how often we expect to find a match within a suspect's racial grouping. This information is important in order to properly determine the odds of a coincidental match. For this reason the F.B.I. database contains information about the allele frequencies found in different racial populations.

The astronomical odds generated by using thirteen separate loci are often enough to convince a jury that a match is significant and a nonmatch is exclusionary. Technically, DNA can only exclude a suspect: a match is just a probability. But an expert can often say that a suspect matches an evidence sample to "a reasonable degree of scientific certainty." The odds of a random match in the population are often less than one in a hundred trillion. Because there are only six billion people on the planet (and very few are suspects in any one case), juries and experts alike consider a match to be very solid evidence.

What can go wrong with DNA evidence?

Like all evidence, DNA evidence can be lost, mislabeled, planted, or contaminated. Most defense lawyers rely on these factors to fight against DNA evidence. Take, for example, the celebrated case of O. J. Simpson: the defense agreed that Simpson's blood was found at the crime scene and other places;

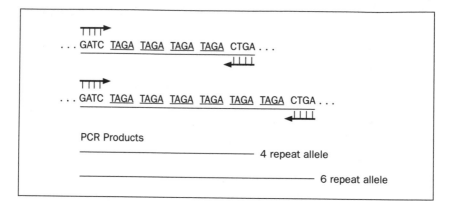

FIGURE 1 **PCR amplification of the chromosome 5 pair from Suspect 1**

A portion of the chromosome 5 pair is depicted as a series of DNA bases. The arrows indicate where the PCR primers will bind to the sequences. The suspect depicted here has two different alleles. On one chromosome 5 he has four of the TAGA repeats; on the other he has six TAGA repeats. The amplified products from each chromosome are illustrated below. The PCR reaction amplifies, or copies, only the region between the primers. This results in two PCR products, one with the primers plus sixteen bases, and the other with the primers plus twenty-four bases. These amplified products can be separated by capillary electrophoresis. The products are then measured by a computer and appear as peaks (figure 2).

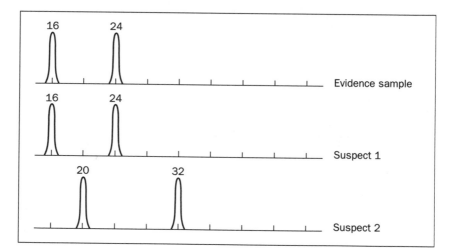

FIGURE 2 **DNA profile of chromosome 5 alleles**

Results are shown for the primer pair shown in figure 1. Suspect 2 is excluded as the donor of the evidence sample. Suspect 1's profile is consistent with being the donor; however, these peaks represent results from only a single DNA locus. A typical DNA fingerprint includes thirteen loci. The number above each peak indicates the bases of DNA between the primers.

however in each case, they contended that it had been planted, mishandled, or left there by innocent means.

In addition to malicious events and accidental errors, there are also scientific limits to consider when examining DNA evidence. It must be remembered that DNA fingerprints are not unique: twins, triplets, quads, and clones will all have identical DNA. While these exceptions are popular plot devices for novels, there have been actual crimes in which multiple births are were an issue. The most interesting case was a sexual assault in Florida in which the suspect refused to give a DNA sample. When police discovered that he had a twin, they requested DNA from the twin, but he also refused to cooperate. Eventually, the detectives removed items from the suspect's garbage at the curb and developed a DNA profile (see Tisch). So far, no judge has compelled a suspect's twin to submit DNA, but this case does show the potential forensic importance of samples derived from relatives—especially twins.

The statistics explained above demonstrate that a chance match is highly improbable. But in the early days of the British system, a clear mistake was made. In 1999 the protocol for British DNA analysis was to examine only six loci from DNA evidence. In a well-known case (reviewed by Moenssens) DNA recovered from the scene of a burglary was processed and submitted to the DNA database, where a single match was found. The suspect identified by DNA fingerprint, however, suffered from advanced Parkinson's disease, lived two hundred miles from the crime scene, had alibi witnesses, and was in the database because he had been arrested (but later released) for hitting his daughter in a domestic dispute. He claimed that he could not have committed the burglary and just happened to have the same alleles as the perpetrator; he was arrested nonetheless. Theoretically, a random match in those six loci should occur only once in thirty-seven million profiles, and at that time there were just seven hundred thousand profiles in the database. When the evidence and suspect were retested using a ten-allele test, the man was excluded. This demonstrates the importance of determining the odds of a database match—two people in the database with the same profile. To do so we simply divide the number of people in the database by the odds of a random match. In the above example we get seven hundred thousand divided by thirty seven million, or $1/53$. That is, with six alleles, the odds of finding a coincidental pair of identical profiles in the database are fifty-three to one against. Those are not astronomical odds, and the larger the database, the more likely a database match. British authorities now use ten-loci analysis, assuming less than a one in a billion chance of a random match. U.S. authorities employ a thirteen-loci analysis and assume less than a one in a trillion chance of a random match.

As astronomical as those odds appear, the more DNA profiles are logged into the system, the greater the chance of a database match. With or without DNA evidence, good detective work is the key to solving crimes.

While Calvin Johnson's story demonstrates how the use of DNA evidence can improve the criminal justice system, it is important to remember that criminals can also use DNA to their advantage. There are several cases of suspects planting anonymous DNA evidence, sending DNA samples from prison to be left at crime scenes, and trying to convert their own profiles through injection (for blood tests) or lozenges (oral swab tests). One case involved a rapist who evaded detection for a long time. The break in the case occurred when a sharp detective discovered that several years before the crime, the suspect had had a bone marrow transplant. Because of this, he no longer made his own blood cells, but rather made blood from the donor's tissue. The result was that the suspect assumed the donor's DNA fingerprint and blood type in blood cells but retained his own profile in sperm and other body tissues left at the crime scene. Once this suspect's medical records came to light, he was arrested. Forensic scientists must keep up with changes in the medical field, as new treatments have the potential to perturb established methods of analysis. From reproductive science comes the example of an in-vitro fertilization baby with two different DNA profiles in different tissues. This resulted from the accidental fusion of two implanted embryos in the mother's womb. That is, the baby was a melding of two different (male and female) early embryos. Some of this patient's tissues present the DNA profile of a boy, and other tissues appear to come from his sister. As with any siblings, the different samples have only 50 percent of their genes in common. How often such "chimeras" are produced in nature is not known, but several cases have been reported (reviewed in Pearson). This type of person produces different DNA profiles depending on the tissues sampled.

The rapid rise in the use of DNA evidence has also unintentionally revealed some interesting facets of human behavior. For example, in missing children cases DNA is often taken from the parents to match against unidentified remains. In such cases we would expect one set of the child's chromosomes to come from each parent. In some cases, however, the mother's DNA is a match, but the father is found to be unrelated to the remains. In the one case with which I am most familiar, the laboratory personnel did not feel it was their business to inform the family of the doubtful paternity; forensically, it was enough to say that the remains were unquestionably related to the mother. Estimates of the frequency of doubtful paternity are hard to come by, but the widespread use of paternity testing in child support cases (and even on television talk shows) indicates that it is not rare. In fact, several fascinating cases of doubtful paternity involving twins have proven that it is possible for women to give birth to fraternal twins who have different fathers.

Who committed the rapes for which Calvin Johnson spent sixteen years in prison?

As a result of the exoneration proceedings that Calvin initiated, the district attorney now has a partial DNA fingerprint and several hairs from the man who raped two Georgia women. When I asked District Attorney Keller about his intentions to pursue the case, or at least to pursue the DNA fingerprint, his response was that he could not find the victim. In fact, before Calvin's final hearing, the D.A. asked for court permission to run a credit search on the Clayton County victim in an attempt to locate her. That search failed. The D.A. has more pressing needs than to reinvestigate a sixteen-year-old case, especially without an available victim; meanwhile, someone has gotten away with rape.

WORKS CITED

Fregeau, C. J., W. F. Tan-Siew, K. H. Yap, G. Carmody, S. Chow, and R. M. Fourney. "Population Genetic Characteristics of the STR Lodi D21S11 and FGA in Eight Diverse Human Populations." *Human Biology* 70, no. 5 (1998): 813–44.

Moenssens, Andre A. "A Mistaken DNA Identification? What Does It Mean?" October 2000. http://www.forensic-evidence.com/site/EVID/EL_DNAerror.html (accessed March 3, 2003).

Pearson, Helen. "Two Become One." *Nature* News Feature (Sept. 20, 2001), 413, 244–46.

Tisch, Chris. *St. Petersburg Times,* April 19, 2001.

Coauthor's Notes and Acknowledgments

Greg Hampikian

I first heard of Calvin C. Johnson Jr. the same way that most
people did. On June 16, 1999, the front page of the *Atlanta
Journal-Constitution* featured an incredible story. "Innocent man
released after sixteen years in jail . . . DNA evidence . . . positive
attitude . . . holds no grudges." I read the article several times,
tacked it up in my office, and said out loud, "I would love to
write this man's story."

A month or so later as I was driving into work I heard a
fragment of an interview on a radio station—it was the same
Calvin C. Johnson Jr., and his comments were just as upbeat as
the quotes in the newspaper. When the interviewer asked him,
"What do you think of the criminal justice system now?", he
answered in a bright voice, "Well, you've got to have laws." I
just shook my head with surprise and admiration. I had to talk
to this man.

As soon as I arrived at the university, I contacted the new

chairperson of our Lyceum committee, Deborah Greer, and begged her to invite Mr. Johnson to campus.

So it was that Calvin Johnson and I met in October 1999, and after his two inspiring talks to our students, I invited him to my office for a chat. He had already received a tremendous amount of publicity and was just about to leave on a speaking trip to Africa. I mentioned my interest in writing a book about his story and asked him to think about working together. We got along well, and he agreed to the project.

Thereafter, we met weekly to get the story on audiotape, but the writing required more attention than I could give it while teaching genetics at Clayton College and State University. So, I took a complete leave of teaching and research for the summer, and focused solely on writing.

Once the initial interviews were done, Calvin and I tried to meet every couple of weeks and were in frequent contact by phone. The interviews were informal events that took place at my home or office. I would ask some questions to get Calvin talking, and then turn on the tape recorder. Each taped session lasted about an hour. Afterward, I would transcribe the tape, then shape the content into a chapter (or insert various pieces into appropriate earlier chapters). Once the material was roughed out, I would check facts and fill in the gaps by cross-checking with the source material supplied by Calvin and his family—more than a thousand pages of trial transcripts, correspondence, and prison records; videotapes of television appearances and speeches; family photos; and journals. Later, I interviewed others involved in the story: family members, attorneys, friends, inmates, and law enforcement officers, including District Attorney Robert Keller. Finally, I prepared a rough draft of each chapter for Calvin's review.

Both Calvin and I were involved in the editing process. At first, he had to be encouraged to cut sections, but soon he was happily placing an X over pages of the manuscript that he found uninteresting. His most frequent comment was, "This is boring, I don't think we need it."

After doing some fact checking and conducting background interviews, I was pleasantly surprised by the accuracy of the stories that Calvin told extemporaneously. When he couldn't remember something precisely, he would say, "I'm not sure; check with so-and-so." But the written record and testimony of others always backed him up.

The characters in the book are all real people, but some of the dialogue had to be crafted from fragments that Calvin remembered. I have endeavored to represent the conversations as accurately as possible. The excerpts from transcripts, letters, and all official documents are practically verbatim, though I have edited a bit for clarity without changing meaning.

My greatest thanks go to Calvin C. Johnson Jr., for his life, his example, his story, and his friendship. Calvin's family, please forgive any oversights. Yours was the harder task. Thank you for providing very candid interviews, personal correspondence, access to family photos, and answers to innumerable questions.

My wife, Janet, has been unceasing in her encouragement of this project, even when her anxious, sleepless husband got ornery. Thank you for being a partner in this work and encouraging me to trade income for calling and chores for duty. I am also grateful to our children for their enthusiastic interest.

There would be no story without Peter Neufeld and Barry Scheck. Their boundless energy and warm support of this project made it much easier to complete. The students and directors of the Innocence Project are a true inspiration, and I am grateful for the opportunity to observe them for several days. I especially wish to thank the volunteers who were assigned to Calvin's case for their work and correspondence: Spencer Schneider, who worked on the case until the end of spring semester, 1997; Kristina Ross (until the end of summer 1997); Gennifer Binder (until spring 1998); and Kristen Skog (September 1998 until Calvin's release).

Calvin and I are indebted to Nancy Grayson and the University of Georgia Press for putting the manuscript on the fast track for publication and suggesting many useful changes. This book would not have become a reality without the excellent work of the Press staff, especially David DesJardines, John McLeod, Jennifer Reichlin, and Allison Reid. Our manuscript editor, Kelly Caudle, is a writer's best friend who made more than four thousand suggested changes to the text, a few of which I took.

Jim Dwyer was the first to comment on the early manuscript, and his endorsement was critical to our success. Beth Karas contributed valuable legal and editorial insights and several bouts of apoplectic laughter. Perry Ellis contributed important comments on Georgia law. Dr. Henry Lee gave us insight and inspiration. And I am grateful for the comments and tour offered by my friends at the Connecticut forensic scientist laboratory; special thanks to Drs. Mike Burke and Carol Scherzinger. Dr. Carll Ladd provided invaluable help with DNA evidence.

District Attorney Robert Keller gave me complete access to all records pertaining to Calvin's case and personally answered many of my questions.

The staff of his office was very helpful and made me feel quite welcome. I am grateful for access to and permission to use correspondence from Barry Scheck, Peter Neufeld, James Bonner, and Kim Robinson.

There are special people who supplied wonderful meals and a quiet place for me to write: my mother in Paris, George Whitman at Shakespeare and Company in Paris, and my late father, Dr. Aram Hampikian, in Connecticut. In addition, Tim and Tamara Albrecht supplied a car for me to use (and encouragement) during my summer writing. I am grateful to the good people of Kairos prison ministry, who were always ready to answer my questions and meet with me.

Marlene, Dave, Gina, and Susan at Tall Tales Books in Decatur: I don't think that my hours in the shop qualify as pure research, but thank you for lending me books from your private collections when I could not afford to purchase them.

Thanks to the staff of the Clayton State Library and the Westport Public Library in Connecticut for your assistance in research; and a special thanks to my student assistant, Tiffany Monroe, who makes order from chaos. The staff of Coffee Plantation and Caribou Coffee in Decatur supplied electricity, free refills, and a place to proofread aloud. Finally, thanks be to God.